OXFORD WORLD'S CLASSICS

THE BODHICARYĀVATĀRA

ŚĀNTIDEVA was an Indian Buddhist monk, a scholar, philosopher, and talented Sanskrit poet. He may have lived sometime between 685 and 763 CE. Apart from that we have no reliable information concerning his life story. As he had written so movingly of the spiritual path, however, and perhaps also through hazy memories of a person of real spirituality, legends of his life developed in the centuries after his death. According to these, he was born a crown prince. He fled royal consecration to adopt the religious life, meditating particularly on the Buddhist 'patron saint' of wisdom, Mañjuśrī. Having received visions and teachings from Mañjuśrī in person, Śāntideva became an effective minister to a king, showing by a miracle that behind his ordinary appearance he was really a powerful spiritual figure. He subsequently became a fully-ordained monk at the great monastic university of Nālandā, and while there, although he appeared to be thoroughly lazy, really he reached a very high level of the spiritual path. After delivering his *Bodhicaryāvatāra* before the monastic assembly, Śāntideva disappeared into the sky. He is sometimes said to have reappeared elsewhere in India and to have lived as a hermit and wanderer, doing good, defeating religious rivals in debate, and performing miracles. Always, it is said, he worked to fulfil his spiritual vows to act for the benefit of others in every possible way. Of his death nothing is known. Śāntideva fades out of legend, but many Buddhists are sure he is still present in some appropriate form, continuing to labour for others as he vowed to do 'as long as space abides and as long as the world abides'.

KATE CROSBY studied Buddhism, Sanskrit, and other South Asian languages at the University of Oxford, Hamburg, and Kälaniya. She recently held a lectureship in Sanskrit at the University of Edinburgh. Currently she teaches at Oxford where she is completing her doctoral dissertation on Tantric Theravāda Buddhism in Sri Lanka.

ANDREW SKILTON has taught in Buddhist teaching centres, at the Universities of Bristol and Oxford, and at Bath College of Higher Education. He is currently a Junior Research Fellow at Wolfson College, Oxford, where he wrote his doctoral dissertation on the Sanskrit text of the Samādhirājasūtra, a major Mahayana Buddhist scripture. His publications include *A Concise History of Buddhism* (1994).

PAUL WILLIAMS is Reader in Indo-Tibetan Studies and Co-director of the Centre for Buddhist Studies at the University of Bristol. He has been a Buddhist within the Tibetan tradition for many years, and is a trustee of the Lam Rim Buddhist Centre on the Welsh borders. Among Dr Williams's many publications is *Mahāyāna Buddhism: The Doctrinal Foundations* (London, 1989), a book widely used in university teaching.

OXFORD WORLD'S CLASSICS

For almost 100 years Oxford World's Classics have brought readers closer to the world's great literature. Now with over 700 titles—from the 4,000-year-old myths of Mesopotamia to the twentieth century's greatest novels—the series makes available lesser-known as well as celebrated writing.

The pocket-sized hardbacks of the early years contained introductions by Virginia Woolf, T. S. Eliot, Graham Greene, and other literary figures which enriched the experience of reading. Today the series is recognized for its fine scholarship and reliability in texts that span world literature, drama and poetry, religion, philosophy and politics. Each edition includes perceptive commentary and essential background information to meet the changing needs of readers.

OXFORD WORLD'S CLASSICS

ŚĀNTIDEVA

The Bodhicaryāvatāra

Translated with an Introduction and Notes by
KATE CROSBY *and* ANDREW SKILTON

With a General Introduction by
PAUL WILLIAMS

OXFORD
UNIVERSITY PRESS

OXFORD
UNIVERSITY PRESS

Great Clarendon Street, Oxford OX2 6DP

Oxford University Press is a department of the University of Oxford.
It furthers the University's objective of excellence in research, scholarship,
and education by publishing worldwide in

Oxford New York

Athens Auckland Bangkok Bogotá Buenos Aires Calcutta
Cape Town Chennai Dar es Salaam Delhi Florence Hong Kong Istanbul
Karachi Kuala Lumpur Madrid Melbourne Mexico City Mumbai
Nairobi Paris São Paulo Singapore Taipei Tokyo Toronto Warsaw

with associated companies in Berlin Ibadan

Oxford is a registered trade mark of Oxford University Press
in the UK and in certain other countries

Published in the United States
by Oxford University Press Inc., New York

First published as a World's Classics paperback 1995
Reissued as an Oxford World's Classics paperback 1998

British Library Cataloguing in Publication Data

Data available

Library of Congress Cataloging in Publication Data

Śāntideva, 7th cent.
[Bodhicaryāvatāra. English]
The Bodhicaryāvatāra / Śāntideva; translated with introduction
and notes by Kate Crosby and Andrew Skilton.
Includes bibliographical references.
1. Mahāyāna Buddhism—Doctrines—Early works to 1800. I. Crosby,
Kate. II. Skilton, Andrew. III. Series.
BQ3142.E5C76 1995 294.3'85—dc20 95–5654

ISBN 0–19–283720–6

3 5 7 9 10 8 6 4

Printed in Great Britain by
Cox & Wyman Ltd.
Reading, Berkshire

CONTENTS

GENERAL INTRODUCTION: ŚĀNTIDEVA AND HIS WORLD

The author

IT is natural to want to know a little about the author of a great work of literature, and a work of spirituality perhaps more than most others stimulates curiosity about what the author was really like, and the inner struggles which led to his or her profundity. We want to know of the author as an individual, and in this post-Freudian world perhaps we hope to see behind the wisdom to a tortured soul. Traditionally in India—and Tibet too, where Indian Buddhist ideals were and still are so important—this search for the individual apart from the profundity, this fascination for the psychological truth, the real spiritual agony, is rather alien, and psychological truth is thought to be a matter between the pupil and his or her spiritual master, not of concern to the public. Indian and Tibetan commentators sometimes recognize an interest in the life of an author, but his life story (the author is almost always male) is told in order to show his greatness, his almost superhuman miracles and spiritual attainments, to prove that his work and teaching can be trusted to lead to spiritual depths, and, of course, to justify the commentary. Thus we learn almost nothing about the author as a psychological individual, a real person. He is a type, an example of attainment, and his life a story of prediction, visions, triumphs, and magic. Learning, for such great examples, is straightforward and easy. There are no psychological torments, for most of the learning had been completed in previous lives and the torments, if there were any, overcome aeons ago. A recurrent theme in these life stories is how the author was taken by others to be a mere ordinary person before circumstances showed that actually, usually from a very early age if not from birth, he was a Great Being of wondrous attainment.

So it is with the traditional story of Śāntideva. Even the earliest version we possess is hundreds of years later than the life of its subject, and is already a completely legendary hagiography.[1] It is quite possible that the story involves an amalgamation of two different persons, and even the claim that Śāntideva was a prince from North India who fled royal consecration for fear of implication in the evils of kingship repeats a traditional Buddhist theme and has no independent corroboration. Śāntideva is generally thought to have flourished some time between 685 and 763 CE, although the reasoning behind this dating is by no means conclusive. It is as certain as it can be, however, that Śāntideva was a Buddhist monk, who followed the Mahāyāna form of Buddhism, and it is possible if we can follow the *Bodhicaryāvatāra* itself that Śāntideva was particularly devoted to Mañjuśrī (or Mañjughoṣa), a 'celestial' figure who in Mahāyāna Buddhism plays a role rather like a god—or patron saint—of wisdom.[2] Śāntideva is associated with the great Buddhist monastery of Nālandā, the impressive ruins of which can still be seen in the state of Bihar in North India and bear fitting testimony to an enormous monastic university which was the pride of the Buddhist world, visited by scholar-monks and pilgrims from as far away as China. We know that Śāntideva was extremely learned. His other great work, the *Śikṣā Samuccaya*, consists in the main of quotations from nearly a hundred Mahāyāna Buddhist scriptures (*sūtras*). Śāntideva must have had access to a large library—and used it. The ninth chapter of the *Bodhicaryāvatāra*, the difficult chapter on Wisdom, is one of the principal sources for Mahāyāna philosophy, written in the form of a complex debate which must echo the debates which took place in the refined scholastic context of Nālandā university.

We know so little of Śāntideva, and yet the depth and spiritual profundity of the *Bodhicaryāvatāra*—for sentiment, intention, and direct practical meditation one of the greatest works of world spirituality—indicate a person of rich compassion, honesty, humility, and wisdom, surely the qualities which make a

[1] For a modern retelling, based on the standard Tibetan sources, see Lobsang N. Tsonawa (trans.), *Indian Buddhist Pandits from 'The Jewel Garland of Buddhist History'* (Dharamsala, 1985), 60–4.

[2] Although it should be noted that there is a problem as to how much of the present text of the *Bodhicaryāvatāra* was contained in the original. The second, ninth, and tenth chapters have all had their detractors, and all the versions of Śāntideva's life mention disagreements as to the length of the work.

saint. It is the *Bodhicaryāvatāra* which supplies the ideals and practice of His Holiness the Dalai Lama, who so frequently cites as his highest inspiration *Bodhicaryāvatāra* 10.55:

> As long as space abides and as long as the world abides, so long may I abide, destroying the sufferings of the world.

There can perhaps be no higher human sentiment. Anyway, this is the aspiration of Mahāyāna Buddhism, and it is also the aspiration of Śāntideva, as a Buddhist monk trying to live the Mahāyāna vision, and of those many since him—famous and ordinary—who have seen in his words the most beautiful expression of their noblest ideals and intentions.

It would be pointless to try and demythologize the traditional Life of Śāntideva in order to find some historical core. Yet throughout the story of his life there is a recurrent theme in which he appears to be quite ordinary, quite mundane, although actually a figure of immense spiritual development. One such story relates to the origins of the *Bodhicaryāvatāra* itself. In the version known to Tibetans and their followers who still practise the religion of the *Bodhicaryāvatāra* (this is itself a corrupted version of our earliest legendary account), the story goes that Śāntideva—although he was an advanced practitioner who had visions of Mañjuśrī and received direct teachings from him—seemed to the other monks simply to laze around doing nothing, as Tibetans like to put it, with one of their infectious laughs, 'just eating, sleeping, and defecating'. The other monks decided to humiliate him by showing his lack of learning, and asked him to give a recitation before the monastery from the scriptures. Śāntideva initially refused, but assented when they insisted and agreed to erect a teaching-seat for him to sit on. The first stage of the humiliation was to erect the seat so high that he could not reach it. One can imagine the monks whispering and giggling as he approached, but it is said that with one hand—plus the magical powers which seem to descend on saints—he lowered the seat, sat on it, and asked what they wanted him to recite, something old or something new. At the request for something new he began to recite the *Bodhicaryāvatāra*. When he reached Chapter 9 (perhaps it was verse 34) it is said that he ascended into the air and disappeared, although his voice could still be heard. Śāntideva then refused to return to a monastery which had not understood that spiritual depth may not always be obvious, and that we can never tell who may or may not be saints working in their own way for the benefit of others.

Appearing to be ordinary when actually one is a saint, extraordinary—this admittedly is a common theme in Buddhist hagiographies. Yet perhaps we can combine it with the message of the *Bodhicaryāvatāra* itself in order to glimpse through the mists of devotion the real Śāntideva, a Śāntideva who for all his learning appeared to be an ordinary monk and yet in his humility, wisdom, and compassionate warmth to those who knew him showed an inner development which maybe some guessed but few really understood.[3] We need not believe that Śāntideva disappeared into the sky, although he may well have had visions of Mañjuśrī; nor that the *Bodhicaryāvatāra* was delivered spontaneously on a throne before the assembled monks of Nālandā, assembled to humiliate him. We can believe, however, that while he did not appear to be anything special to his fellow monks, in trying with all honesty to practise genuinely the teachings of Mahāyāna Buddhism that he found in the scriptures cited in his earlier *Śikṣā Samuccaya* he became something very special, and the record of that practice—his aspirations, intentions, and meditations—is the *Bodhicaryāvatāra* itself, a testimony to its author's greatness not only as a poet, not only in spiritual sentiment, but in making these teachings real.[4]

Buddhism and Mahāyāna

Śāntideva was a monk, and a Mahāyāna Buddhist. As a monk he was expected to live a simple life which, in the reduction of

[3] According to our traditional Tibetan story, Śāntideva's *Śikṣā Samuccaya* was among works found on a shelf in his room after he had left. It was no doubt compiled for the use of himself, plus perhaps a few like-minded friends. That same humility, I suspect, surrounded the *Bodhicaryāvatāra*.

[4] Although it is the traditional view, there is no compelling evidence that the *Śikṣā Samuccaya* was written before the *Bodhicaryāvatāra*. Nevertheless those early writers who considered it was had their reasons and we have no reasons for thinking that it was not. I prefer it on aesthetic grounds. I like to think of Śāntideva composing his *Bodhicaryāvatāra* while trying to practise the life he found in the scriptures through constructing his *Śikṣā Samuccaya*.

distractions, left space for following the spiritual path. He probably wore an orange or faded yellow patched robe, and had no hair. It is doubtful, if he came from the well-endowed monastery of Nālandā, that Śāntideva needed to go to local villages on the alms-round, but if he had he would have kept his eyes down and spoken little. When he did speak he would have weighed his words carefully in order to make sure that they were suitable to the occasion and beneficial for the person to whom they were addressed (see *Bodhicaryāvatāra* 5.79). He would have kept his simple, sparsely furnished room tidy and clean, seeing the cleaning as part of his spiritual practice, a metaphor for cleaning the mind of taints. In one corner we can imagine a shrine, with a statue of the Buddha, and for Śāntideva perhaps a statue or representation of Mañjuśrī. Possibly, as is common with Tibetan statues, Mañjuśrī is portrayed seated cross-legged on a lotus throne with the right hand holding aloft a flaming sword, the Sword of Gnosis, while the left hand holds the stem of a lotus which curls round to the left side of his body and contains, resting on the flower, a book—the *Eight-Thousand Verse Perfection of Wisdom* scripture.[5] Śāntideva would sleep little, eat but one meal a day, and as a serious practitioner devote many hours to study, teaching, perhaps debate, but certainly devotional practices—making offerings before the Buddhas and figures like Mañjuśrī and visualizing the assembly of Buddhas, holy beings, and saints, praising them as a means of recollecting their great qualities and aspiring to attain the same qualities—and meditation, stabilizing the mind, contemplating the teachings, regret and purification of previous transgressions, all the time increasing his insight into the way things really are, and his aspiration to help all other suffering sentient beings.

The Mahāyāna Buddhism which Śāntideva practised was the result of a gradual evolution, a maturation of reflection on the message and example of Śākyamuni Buddha, the so-called 'historical Buddha' who lived and died sometime between the sixth and fourth centuries BCE. Modern critical scholarship has shown that it is not possible to know very much in detail about the

[5] Although as far as I know no such representation of Mañjuśrī has yet been found in India from as early as the supposed lifetime of Śāntideva.

actual words of Śākyamuni, although we can be reasonably clear about the sort of spiritual perspective and path the Buddha advocated.[6] In social terms Śākyamuni was a renunciant, one of those who can still be seen in India today who have chosen to renounce their families, social status, and ties in order to live a wandering life seeking for a higher truth than that of social place and function. This truth is commonly portrayed as the truth which leads to freedom from all sorts of suffering and, in the Indian context, from the round of repeated rebirth into still further repeated unhappiness—as Buddhists put it, the endlessly repeated anguish of old age, sickness, and death, the state of unenlightenment (*saṃsāra*). As far as we can tell, Śākyamuni's message in its simplest expression was that of a very deep sort of 'letting go'. He seems to have discerned that most—he would say all—of our unhappiness and frustration comes from holding on, reifying, when actually things are always changing. Seeking for a raft in the sea of change, we particularly grasp at some sort of self-identity for ourselves. To hold onto all such unchanging self-identities is a fundamental misapprehension which ends in tears. Ourselves and others, animate and inanimate, are composite collections which come together and part again bringing life and death, purpose and apparent uselessness. That is the nature of things, against which we fortify ourselves through the misapprehension of grasping an unchanging identity which is at variance with the way things really are and thus invariably produces suffering. The principal dimension of this misapprehension is reifying ourselves into Selves, the feeling that somehow I must have an unchanging core which is the 'Real Me'. Thus, unlike other spiritual teachers in India, the Buddha did not teach the search for the True Self behind the changing world, but rather the opposite: he taught that there is no True Self either in or behind the changing world, and grasping at such Selves is the cause of suffering. The permanent truth is that there is no such thing. To seek to dissolve away apparent unities into their constituent flow of parts is a hallmark of the Buddhist approach. Thus, as far as we can tell, the Buddha seems to have taught that what we call ourselves is actually a construct super-

[6] For an excellent short study see Michael Carrithers, *The Buddha* (Oxford, 1983).

imposed upon an ever-changing flow of physical matter, sensations, conceptions, further mental contents such as volitions and so on, and consciousness. That is all there is. There is no unchanging Me, my Self. To understand this deeply in a way which truly leads to the cessation of grasping after all fixed identities is to destroy completely the very forces which lead to continued embodiment, rebirth into suffering. That is enlightenment, *nirvāṇa*.

The practice of the Buddha and those specially adept monks and nuns who followed him in the centuries after his death was 'insight', seeing through deep thought—meditation—beyond the way things appear to the way they really are. This seeing the way things really are (a common epithet of *nirvāṇa*) carries with it a change of behaviour, a letting go, an 'existential relaxation', a cessation of grasping. This relaxation and cessation of grasping can when cultivated in a particularly sensitive way lead to great compassion, a compassion which no longer has any egoistic involvement. Such great compassion for those who still suffer was thought to be a quality of the Buddha himself, who did not sit alone in a forest meditating and 'letting go' but rather felt a need to help others, touring North India, teaching in forests, certainly, but also in market-places and palaces.

Reflection on the compassion of the Buddha was surely one (but only one) of the factors which led some centuries after his death to the emergence of scriptural texts claiming to represent a 'Great Way (or Vehicle) to Enlightenment' (Mahāyāna), eventually to be contrasted with an identified 'Inferior Way' (Hīnayāna). These scriptural texts purported to be the words of Śākyamuni Buddha himself. The origins of the Mahāyāna, and even its exact nature, are obscure in the extreme. Mahāyāna could not be called a 'sect' of Buddhism, nor, we now know, was it the result of a schism. There might be monks holding to Mahāyāna ideas and others holding non-Mahāyāna views living together, as far as we can tell, quite harmoniously in the same monastery.[7] Rather, Mahāyāna concerns a vision of what the ultimate intention of the Buddhist practitioner should be. In

[7] There is no space to deal here with the fascinating and hotly-debated issues surrounding the historical origins of the Mahāyāna. For an extensive discussion see my *Mahāyāna Buddhism: The Doctrinal Foundations* (London, 1989), ch. 1.

Mahāyāna this ultimate intention is said to be to attain not just enlightenment, as some Buddhists might think—one's own freedom from suffering and rebirth—but perfect Buddhahood for the benefit of all sentient beings. One who has through great compassion for others taken a vow to attain this Buddhahood no matter what it may cost, no matter how many times one must be reborn on this long and difficult path, is called a *bodhisattva*.[8] Mahāyāna advocates the path of the bodhisattva as the highest and final path for all or most sentient beings—all (or most) will eventually become fully-enlightened Buddhas, and the reason for this is the benefit of all.

Perhaps the best way to understand the nature of Mahāyāna Buddhism is through its own self-definition reflected in a work from three centuries after Śāntideva, the *Bodhipathapradīpa* (*Lamp on the Path to Enlightenment*) by the great missionary to Tibet, Atiśa (982–1054). Atiśa speaks of three 'scopes', three aspirations which one might have when engaging in spiritual practice. The first and lowest aspiration is that of a person whose goal is purely within the realm of unenlightenment—religion for wealth, fame, or even a favourable future rebirth. This aspiration—if they were honest the aspiration of so many people—is not particularly Buddhist, although at least in its higher concern with future rebirths it is somewhat better than having no spiritual aspiration whatsoever. In some of the earlier sections of the *Bodhicaryāvatāra* Śāntideva seeks to generate in himself (and his readers if they are interested) this aspiration, reflecting for example on death and impermanence, which leads to a concern with future lives (Chapter 4) governed by the morality of actions and a need to purify misdeeds already committed (Chapter 2, verses 28 ff.). According to Atiśa the second and middling aspiration is that of one who turns his or her back on all concern with future pleasures and future rebirths (with their invariable attendant sufferings) and aims for freedom. The

[8] An expression perhaps meaning an 'enlightenment being' or, with the Tibetan, an 'enlightenment mind hero'. The name of Śāntideva's great work, the *Bodhicaryāvatāra*, means 'An Introduction (*avatāra*) to the Conduct (*caryā*) which leads to Enlightenment (*bodhi*)'. There is some reason to think that the original title may have been *Bodhisattvacaryāvatāra*, 'An Introduction to the Conduct of the Bodhisattva'.

hallmark of this aspiration is renunciation, and the goal is enlightenment, understood as freedom from suffering and rebirth. The many verses in which Śāntideva tries to inculcate in his mind a spirit of renunciation belong to this scope. It is a stage of a progressive path which involves an accurate assessment of the practitioner's level of spiritual development, and transformation into that which is higher through meditations, which are taken as medicines appropriate to the particular spiritual illness. Thus Śāntideva's many verses on the foulness of the female body (Chapter 8), a foulness which he also perceives in his own body, should not be read as a strange form of misogyny or bodily hatred. They express a specific meditation practice appropriate to a specific stage on a clearly-discerned spiritual path. It is misleading in reading Buddhist writings—or indeed any writings on the spiritual path—to take what is intended as counselling, meditation instructions embedded in a particular context, as abstract statements about the universal way things actually are.

In following this second middling scope the practitioner can attain freedom from rebirth, enlightenment. Such a person is called an *arhat*, a Worthy One. The goal is held to be a difficult one requiring intensive practice and great insight which will fuel the letting go, the deep renunciation which leads to freedom. Perhaps this was the main concern of serious Buddhist practitioners in the immediate centuries after the death of the Buddha. Yet from the Mahāyāna perspective, no matter how many of their fellows follow it, this is not the highest goal and its aspiration is not the supreme aspiration. There is something higher than simply attaining enlightenment, the state of an arhat, and that is the state of a Buddha himself. What characterizes a Buddha, the Mahāyāna urges, is not just great insight, supreme wisdom, but his (or sometimes her) immense compassion as well. Compassion for others is missing in the description of the second scope which leads to the enlightenment of the arhat. Atiśa adds that those of the third and highest scope wish in every way—even by means of their own sufferings—for the complete destruction of all the sufferings of others.[9] In fact, so

[9] For a translation of Atiśa's *Bodhipathapradīpa*, with a commentary attributed to Atiśa himself, see Richard Sherburne, SJ, *Atīśa: A Lamp for the Path and Commentary* (London, 1983).

long as someone else is suffering the Mahāyāna practitioner cannot attain peace. Superior to the arhat is the bodhisattva, one who vows to attain perfect Buddhahood, the perfection of insight and compassion, for the benefit of all. The great poem of the bodhisattva, embedded within a progressive path which will lead to the cultivation of that supreme aspiration, is the *Bodhicaryāvatāra*, in which Śāntideva the bodhisattva vows (3.7):

I am medicine for the sick. May I be both the doctor and their nurse, until the sickness does not recur.

Those Buddhists who follow the path to their own personal enlightenment—sometimes called the Hearers (*śrāvakas*) and Solitary Buddhas (*pratyekabuddhas*)—are termed by the Mahāyāna followers of an Inferior Vehicle (Hīnayāna). In the last analysis Śāntideva's concern is to help himself and others pass through (but without ignoring) this conception of the spiritual life towards what he sees as the great integration of insight, wisdom, and compassion which is found in the bodhisattva and eventually flowers in full Buddhahood. In aiming for Buddhahood the bodhisattva turns away from his or her own personal peace, the *nirvāṇa* of an arhat.[10] Indeed from a Buddhist point of view time is infinite, and from a Mahāyāna perspective compassion is so strong that surely there must also be many, infinitely many, Buddhas still present in the infinite cosmos, and many advanced bodhisattvas of great power, all acting for the benefit of others. For the follower of Mahāyāna a being such as a Buddha would not really have abandoned us at the age of eighty, as Śākyamuni Buddha is supposed to have done. The death of a Buddha is mere appearance. Really Buddhas remain, benefiting sentient beings (not just human beings) in innumerable appropriate ways. Thus some Mahāyāna texts speak of a Buddha having three types of body: his (or her) actual body as a Buddha which remains in what is called a 'Pure Land', a realm where a Buddha sits in glory helping sentient beings; his emanated bodies—one of which was the Śākyamuni Buddha who appeared

[10] Let me stress here very strongly that it seems clear to me the bodhisattva does not, as books often have it, *postpone* nirvāṇa. A little thought would show that this is incoherent. See Williams, 1989, 52–4.

to die at the age of eighty; and the 'Dharma-body', another name for the ultimate truth itself as perfectly understood by a Buddha (see 1.1).[11] It is therefore felt to be possible to enter into a relationship of devotion and prayer with these Buddhas, and also with advanced bodhisattvas. One such advanced bodhisattva who may well have been particularly important to Śāntideva is Mañjuśrī, the bodhisattva of wisdom.[12] But—and this is important—in terms of the Mahāyāna spiritual path the real purpose of such prayer and devotion (found, for example, in *Bodhicaryāvatāra* 2.1–27) is the transformation of the mind of the devotee towards greater wisdom and compassion. It is helpful for us in reading Buddhist texts, in meeting their strangeness, to be constantly sensitive to the practical context: 'How does this perspective, or this practice, transform the mind of the practitioner in a way which Buddhists would see as beneficial—the cultivation of wisdom and compassion?'

The bodhisattva

Thus in terms of Mahāyāna self-understanding, to follow the Mahāyāna is not a matter of robes, philosophies, or sectarian traditions and differences. It concerns the deep motivation for leading a spiritual life. One who follows the Mahāyāna is a bodhisattva, or truly aspires to be a bodhisattva. Śāntideva has a clear idea of what a bodhisattva is, and of those meditation practices which can lead to the development of that supreme aspiration. A bodhisattva is one who has generated the 'Awakening Mind' (*bodhicitta*), that astonishingly rare but totally transformative intention to work solely for the benefit of others right up to Buddhahood, the full development of one's own potential.[13] Śāntideva's hymn to the power and significance of this supremely altruistic intention opens the *Bodhicaryāvatāra*, and its implications are contained in the vow of 10.55 quoted

[11] On the bodies of the Buddha see ibid., ch. 8.

[12] For the names of others see in particular *Bodhicaryāvatāra*, Chs. 2 and 10. Alongside Mañjuśrī the most important is Avalokiteśvara, the bodhisattva held in particular to personify compassion.

[13] The emphasis and praise given to the Awakening Mind remind one sometimes of the conversion experience in certain forms of Protestant Christianity.

above—always on the Dalai Lama's lips—with which Śāntideva ends his great poem. With a characteristically Buddhist love of classification, Śāntideva refers in general to two types of Awakening Mind (1.15–16). The one, termed 'the Mind resolved on Awakening', is like someone really wishing to go on a journey, really wishing from the depths of one's heart to follow the path of a bodhisattva. The 'Mind proceeding towards Awakening' is actually embarking on the long and difficult path of insight and altruism, the Mahāyāna journey. Thus one who truly wishes to be an active and altruistic bodhisattva can also be said to have the Awakening Mind—to *be* a bodhisattva—albeit in a derived and lesser sense.

Tibetan writers have developed a number of meditations intended to generate this supreme aspiration, and one of these meditations is particularly associated with the eighth chapter of the *Bodhicaryāvatāra*, the chapter in which Śāntideva gives specific instruction on meditation practices said to lead to the 'perfection of meditative absorption'. This meditation is called 'exchanging self and others'.[14] Śāntideva makes it clear that such meditations presuppose that the practitioner lives in solitary, undistracted retreat, and he offers reflections intended to enhance the necessary spirit of renunciation (8.1–89). After that, he urges that we meditate on the essential equality of ourselves and others in that we all have one fundamental quality in common: we all wish for happiness and the avoidance of suffering. In this fundamental respect we are all equal, and feelings of favouritism or repulsion are, it is argued, the result of relatively unimportant adventitious factors—a particular person was nice to me, another harmed me, and so on. To reflect that others, no matter how much I may dislike them, are just like me, and in their confused manner like me simply want to be happy, is an interesting way to cut through the complexities of life and their many barriers and boundaries. It is, Śāntideva argues, the identification of certain sufferings as 'mine' which causes me such problems. This sense of 'I' brings about a perception of inequal-

[14] See here also the handy commentary by His Holiness the XIVth Dalai Lama, *Āryaśūra's Aspiration and A Meditation on Compassion* (Dharamsala, 1979), 122–43.

ity between self and others which actually causes a great deal of unhappiness. In reality:

All those who suffer in the world do so because of their desire for their own happiness. All those happy in the world are so because of their desire for the happiness of others. (8.129)

Śāntideva holds anyway that there is in reality no enduring entity to which the term 'I' corresponds: it is simply an imposition upon an ever-changing flow of psycho-physical elements (8.101–2; cf. also Chapter 9). The notion that certain pleasures or sufferings are somehow more important because they are *mine* has no grounds in reality and is beneficial neither for myself nor others (8.92 ff.).

Having generated a sense of equality between oneself and others, the next stage in this meditation is to reflect that while I am one, others are infinite. In terms of the previous meditation, since I am no more important than others, in aggregate others are infinitely more important than I am. The rational person who has abandoned prejudices of egoism will thus exchange self and others, that is, will always place others before oneself. Śāntideva states (8.105):

If the suffering of one ends the suffering of many, then one who has compassion for others and himself must cause that suffering to arise.

Thus through deeply meditating in this way the practitioners can begin to replace their own strong self-concern, which is actually the cause of unhappiness, with a pure altruism which turns out—in an unintended way—to be the fulfilment of their own aspirations as well. Thereby the meditator generates the Awakening Mind. In aiming for full Buddhahood as the perfection of wisdom and compassion, the supreme state most completely suitable for benefiting others, the bodhisattva also finds his or her own (unintended) fulfilment. The very being of the bodhisattva is the welfare of others. That, it is argued, is the only source of true happiness. The Dalai Lama has summarized the essence of the whole *Bodhicaryāvatāra* and indeed all of Mahāyāna Buddhism when he states: '"The only purpose of my existence is to be used by others and to serve others". This idea, this attitude, this determination must arise from the depths of one's heart, from the very depths of one's mind.'[15] And elsewhere:

We should have this [compassion] from the depths of our heart, as if it were nailed there. Such compassion is not merely concerned with a few sentient beings such as friends and relatives, but extends up to the limits of the cosmos, in all directions and towards all beings throughout space.[16]

Wisdom

There is no denying that *Bodhicaryāvatāra* Chapter 9 presents a problem. It is not properly understandable (if at all) without a commentary and a great deal of thought and study.[17] Scholars keenly debate verses and even half-verses of the text. For those lacking the perverse intellectual masochism of scholars and monks the details are scarcely crucial or helpful. Chapter 9 concerns insight or wisdom (*prajñā*), and wisdom in this context refers to an understanding of the way things really are, the ultimate truth. For Śāntideva and Indian Buddhists like him who follow what is known as the Madhyamaka ('Middling') school or approach to Buddhist philosophy, understanding that liberating ultimate truth is not a matter of waiting for some sort of mystical influx or sudden overwhelming vision. The ultimate truth is seen as what

[15] *Āryaśūra's Aspiration*, 140. [16] Ibid. 111.

[17] There are a number of commentaries reasonably easily available in English. Most reflect the influence of the dGe lugs (pronounced Geluk) school of Tibetan Buddhism, and are based on the Tibetan version. (i) The translation of Ch. 9 with onrunning excerpts from a classical Tibetan commentary: Shantideva, *A Guide to the Bodhisattva's Way of Life*, trans. Stephen Batchelor (Dharamsala, 1979). Also contains the verses of the other chapters, from the Tibetan. (ii) Geshe Kelsang Gyatso, *Meaningful to Behold*, trans. Tenzin Norbu (London, 1986). This is a commentary to the whole of the *Bodhicaryāvatāra*. (iii) H.H. the Dalai Lama, *Transcendent Wisdom*, trans. B. Alan Wallace (Ithaca, NY, 1988). Based on an oral commentary given to Ch. 9 alone. There is also a short oral commentary by the Dalai Lama to the whole text: *A Flash of Lightning in the Dark of Night*, trans. Padmakara Translation Group (Boston, 1994). Another oral commentary by the Dalai Lama to Ch. 9 is forthcoming, translated by the Padmakara Translation Group. (iv) Two commentaries by Khenchen Kunzang Palden and Minyak Kunzang Sönam, *Wisdom: Two Buddhist Commentaries*, trans. by the Padmakara Translation Group (Peyzac-le-Moustier, 1993). For a background commentary see Williams, 1989, chs. 2–4.

is ultimately true about things, and it can only be understand through investigating things in order to find out what is the case. Thus although he is a poet of great spiritual sensitivity, Śāntideva does not see the poetic and intuitive, spiritual faculty as in some way opposed to sharp, incisive analytic thought. Since the Buddhahood which the bodhisattva strives for is the perfection of wisdom and compassion, it must employ to the full and stretch to their limit both the nurturing warmth which expresses compassion and a deep understanding which results from the sharp critical investigation that leads to insight. In the bodhisattva not only must both compassion and insight be developed fully, but they must be integrated into one spiritual being who acts most effectively for the benefit of all sentient beings.

In Western thought the idea that the rational and analytic is diametrically opposed to the spiritual and intuitive goes back many hundreds of years and is often accepted uncritically in contemporary writing (particularly writing associated with the so-called 'New Age'). This perhaps explains the shock many people feel when, lulled by happy sentiments of compassion, they reach the ninth chapter of the *Bodhicaryāvatāra* and are required to engage their brains in philosophical analysis. Yet Śāntideva states that all that has gone before served as a preliminary to this analysis and the integration of the results of analysis into one's being (9.1). We have already seen that implicit in the very origins of the Buddhist perspective was a distinction between the way things appear to be (things appear to have an enduring permanent or quasi-permanent identity, a 'self'), and the way they really are. Things are not the way they appear to be. Actually—as a little reflective thought will show—things are changing all the time. In particular I, a sentient being, am not really the same as I was ten years ago, last year, yesterday, or even a minute ago. I can investigate my own nature and discover, it is claimed, that I am no more than an ever-changing flow of physical matter, sensations, conceptions, further mental contents such as volitions and so on, and consciousness ('the aggregates'). I come to know this through investigation, not through simply believing it is so because I have been told, or waiting for it to dawn upon me out of my psychological depths.

The more I become familiar in a very deep way through meditation with the difference between the way things appear and the way they are discovered actually to be, the more deeply that actuality affects my behaviour. I begin to 'let go', to relax, to put things in perspective. Out of insight I become wise. This distinction between the way things appear to be and the way they really are is behind the distinction made by Śāntideva in *Bodhicaryāvatāra* 9.2 concerning the ultimate and conventional truth. The ultimate truth is what is discovered at some stage, through sharp analysis, to be finally, ultimately the case concerning things. There is some debate among later Tibetan commentators concerning what exactly is the conventional truth, but in general we can think of it as the things themselves. Thus the ultimate truth is what is ultimately true about the conventional truth. Or, to use a concrete example, the ultimate truth of a chair is what is ultimately true about the chair. Since conventional objects are plural, we can thus speak more accurately of conventional *truths*, and since ultimate truth is about conventional truths we can also speak in the plural about ultimate *truths*.

But what, for Śāntideva, is an ultimate truth? The answer is that it is called an 'emptiness' (*śūnyatā*), and only emptinesses are ultimate truths. An emptiness for Śāntideva and his Madhyamaka tradition is a very specific sort of negation. Things appear to exist in a particular sort of way. It is claimed that things appear to us unenlightened beings to exist as if they have independent, fixed, inherent existence—the sort of existence things would have if their existence were completely contained within themselves, if they existed not as the result of some sort of combination of components or some other causal operation. We must think that things exist this way, Śāntideva wants to say, because we think of things as *inherently* satisfying or *inherently* repulsive, and fail to see the role of our mental constructions in the way things appear to be. But things are not so inherently, they exist in dependence upon our mental projections and inevitably change and decay. The gap between our perceptions of the inherent status of things and their actuality is the source of stupidity and suffering.

Sharp critical investigation shows that things do not have the inherent status we project upon them. They are *empty* of that inherent existence. The very quality of being empty of inherent existence is an emptiness, a negation of inherent existence. Thus the chair, which is the result of a construction with a very practical purpose, does not have inherent existence, unchanging self-contained existence. It is empty of inherent existence. The chair is a conventional truth (if it did have inherent existence it would itself be an unchanging ultimate truth), and its emptiness of inherent existence is the ultimate truth concerning that chair.

We discover the absence of inherent existence through investigating a subject to see whether it has inherent existence or not. This analysis which discovers the ultimate truth is very much a mental and conceptual activity. However, in more advanced stages of meditation it is thought to be possible to enter a state where the mind is held absorbed unwaveringly on the ultimate itself, in other words the negation of inherent existence which is emptiness. This state, when fully developed, is said to be experienced beyond the normal dualistic mind, 'like water entering water'. This, according to certain Tibetan commentators, is why Śāntideva speaks of the ultimate truth in *Bodhicaryāvatāra* 9.2 as 'beyond the scope of intellection'. Obviously he could not mean that it is not an object of mental activity in all senses, otherwise one could not discern the ultimate truth and become enlightened. The meaning of this verse was much debated in Tibet, and serves as an example of the difficulties involved in interpreting Buddhist philosophy.

The claim of Madhyamaka Buddhism, of which Śāntideva is one of the most famous Indian exponents, is that absolutely nothing, no matter how rarefied, will be found under analysis to have inherent existence. This includes the Buddha, *nirvāṇa*, and even emptiness itself. In other words if we think of ultimate reality as an Absolute, the really inherently Real, the Madhyamaka claim is that there is no such thing. *There is no Absolute*. Finally we need to let go of that grasping as well. Madhyamaka thinkers do not put forward the inherent existence of anything, but take claims by other thinkers that something inherently exists and investigate to see if that makes sense. Other thinkers all maintain the inherent existence of something: God, matter, atoms, the Self, causality, and so on. The Madhyamaka considers it has good arguments against these inherent existences. In particular

Śāntideva devotes considerable space to a complex refutation of rival Mahāyāna co-religionists who follow a tradition known as Yogācāra and teach that while the inherent existence of most things can be negated, we cannot deny the inherent existence of the flow of consciousness itself. Understood properly, according to this teaching, consciousness is non-dual (subjects and external objects are erroneous constructions) and is characterized by its reflexivity, which is to say that it is a unique quality of consciousness that it is not only aware of things but also aware of itself at the same time. It is the truly existing substratum to all illusion and unenlightenment, as well as enlightenment itself. This tradition is thus sometimes known as Cittamātra, since it teaches mind or consciousness (*citta*) only (*mātra*). For Śāntideva in the last analysis the Yogācāra tradition, for all its spiritual subtlety, represents an attempt to grasp at something instead of the complete letting go which he feels is necessary for the bodhisattva in order to develop perfectly both insight and, most of all, effective compassion for others.

Thus the main purpose of Chapter 9 is to refute claims by rival traditions, mainly Buddhist but also non-Buddhist, that something has been found which really inherently exists, and also to defend the Madhyamaka claim to show that all things exist only conventionally 'like illusions'. Later Tibetan commentators make it quite clear that such a claim, that something does not inherently exist, is not a rather obscure way of saying that it does not exist at all. Rather, it lacks the sort of existence called 'inherent existence', which is a sort of existence we tend to project upon things. This projection of inherent existence causes us considerable problems. But if things did have inherent existence that existence could be found when analysed. The fact that analysis shows something to be incoherent means that it does not have *inherent* existence. For example, if I investigate a chair to find out if it inherently exists, as something existing independently of my mental operations and the functions to which the bits of wood are put, I will discover that such an inherently existing chair cannot be found. Actually there is just a collection of bits which I employ in a particular way (and for Śāntideva the bits themselves could, of course, be further analysed *ad infinitum*). This does not mean that there is no chair. The chair does exist as a conventional truth, but not in the way I thought it did. The chair *as I thought it existed* is what does not exist at all. It is in this respect that Madhyamaka writers say all things are like illusions. There is a strong contention among many Tibetan commentators that this should not be taken to mean that things are literally illusions. That would be incoherent, although it is sometimes said for dramatic impact. Rather, things are not true but are *like* illusions in that they appear one way and actually exist in another. Thus the Madhyamaka is 'Middling' in that it avoids the two cardinal errors of under-negation (something exists inherently) and over-negation (nothing exists at all, in any sense). Of these two errors the second, an understandable misunderstanding, is by far the worst, for it was thought to have serious repercussions in a moral nihilism which could scarcely be Buddhist. Madhyamaka writers urge accordingly that emptiness should be taught in an appropriate way and only at the right time.

One of the principal difficulties of *Bodhicaryāvatāra* Chapter 9 is that it presupposes a considerably sophisticated knowledge of the details of rival schools' tenets, and does not seem to be easily applicable to our current situation. It is debatable whether modern attempts to grasp at inherent existences can be fitted into the template offered by ancient Indian 'errors'. It would, I think, be unwise for most readers to try and wrestle with the detailed complexities of this chapter. What is of enduring value and contemporary significance here is the critical enterprise itself, the employment of the analytic investigative mind in the spiritual path in a way which refuses to be taken in by new and often subtle forms of grasping attachment but sees relentless critical probing as a means of letting go, creating a more balanced perspective which will aid in the project of effectively helping others. The spiritual path is not one of comfortable feelings and acceptance. It is deeply uncomfortable, and one cause of that necessary uncomfortableness is the persistent search for truth through employing rather than denying our critical faculties.

This integration of the analytic into a spiritual path based on altruism and compassion is but one aspect of the *Bodhicaryāvatāra* which is of enduring relevance and significance. Though it was composed in India over a thousand years ago by a Buddhist monk for himself and a few like-minded friends, even allowing for the verses concerned with a Buddhist monastic environment, the *Bodhicaryāvatāra* nevertheless presents us with a series of brilliant meditations directly relevant to our own present lives. We are still sentient beings living with others, squabbling and loving, laughing and dying. We all need compassion, altruism, insight, and wisdom, and these qualities have not changed so very much over the years. Nor, I suspect, have the means of bringing them about.

I should dispel the suffering of others because it is suffering like my own suffering. I should help others too because of their nature as beings, which is like my own being. (8.94)

To heed so many of Śāntideva's wonderful verses does not require an acceptance of Buddhism or a denial of any other faith. All that is necessary is that one is human, living an ordinary human life. On the other hand the *Bodhicaryāvatāra* is not a work to be devoured in our normal greedy way, nor is it a book to be skimmed through. That changes nothing. This is a meditation manual (however you do your meditation), a work for the proverbial desert island, a work to be slowly contemplated. And when our desert island dweller is rescued he or she will have perceptibly changed and will henceforth, to use a Zen saying, 'move among us with bliss-bestowing hands'.

PAUL WILLIAMS

Centre for Buddhist Studies,
University of Bristol
July 1994

TRANSLATORS' INTRODUCTION

ŚĀNTIDEVA'S *Bodhicaryāvatāra* has a remarkable appeal and impact. It is felt in this century as strongly as it has been in others. Doubtless this is because he addresses spiritual issues which are as relevant now as they were for him and his audience over twelve centuries ago. Yet a text composed in a mediaeval Indian monastic university cannot be presented to a general readership without some introduction and commentary. It is our hope that this present translation is clear, and, where possible, self-explanatory. Even so, there is much that will only be comprehensible to the specialist reader and cannot be passed over in silence by a responsible translator. We have attempted, so far as space and our own understanding allow, to give some explanation of such matters. We introduce each chapter with a discussion of its structure, along with other relevant issues. Annotations to individual verses are provided at the back of the book. We hope the reader will appreciate that all of this material is offered by way of explanation for the general reader, rather than as the exegesis of scripture for the purposes of religious practice. Our attempt has been to translate the work as accurately as we can, in the belief that Śāntideva is thereby enabled to speak for himself. Some who read this translation and our explanatory material will be Buddhists already familiar with one or another tradition of exegesis of the *Bodhicaryāvatāra*. If our explanations vary from any of these received traditions, it need not be taken amiss, but rather as evidence of the richness of the Buddhist tradition in general and of Śāntideva's work in particular. We have sought to give nothing more than the simplest explanation of often complex matters, from a non-partisan point of view.

We have been surprised by how much explanatory material has seemed appropriate. In large part this is because Śāntideva practised within a religious tradition which had seen, by his day, a millennium of uninterrupted growth and development on Indian soil. Particularly pertinent to Śāntideva's work was the development of the monastic university at Nālandā, where it is said that he lived as a monk during the period at which he composed the *Bodhicaryāvatāra*. By this time, the early eighth century, Nālandā was the pre-eminent educational institution of medieval India. Tradition has it that it was first established by King Śaurāditya, otherwise known as Kumāragupta I (*c*.415–55 CE). Although the work begun by Śaurāditya was interrupted, building continued at that site on a number of different monasteries and temples under the patronage of a succession of later Gupta kings, the entire complex eventually being enclosed as a single establishment by a high wall with one main entrance. By the time of the Chinese monk I-tsing, who resided at Nālandā for a number of years in the second half of the seventh century, its prestige as a centre of learning and its wealth had grown to vast proportions. According to I-tsing, it received the revenues of lands containing more than 200 villages bestowed by kings of successive generations. There were around 3,000 students, both monk and lay, all of whom came to Nālandā to further their education, and had to pass an exacting entrance examination, conducted orally. Many were said to come for this education as a stepping-stone to a prestigious political career. In addition to these resident scholars, others came for short visits. Patronage came not only from local royalty, but even from abroad. For example, in the early ninth century King Devapāla of Sumatra donated the revenue of five villages to the maintenance of monks for the copying of manuscripts.

The Gupta kings were not Buddhists, but Brahmanical Hindus, and were responsible for a revival of Brahmanical Hindu culture in their empire. It would seem, therefore, that their patronage was of learning and of general religiosity, and seen by them as a part of their duty as righteous kings, rather than as the expression of a personal interest in Buddhism. Not all students at Nālandā were Buddhists. While Mahāyāna Buddhist philosophy was reputedly a compulsory subject, the curriculum also included other Buddhist literature, both Mahāyāna and Hīnayāna, as well as the Vedas (the scriptural authority of Brahmanical Hinduism), logic, grammar, medicine, magic, Sāṃkhya philosophy, and a number of other subsidiary subjects, such as art. According to Tibetan sources, there were vast manuscript libraries at Nālandā, but these were burnt down. Fortunately there do survive from Nepal a few examples of the manuscripts that were copied there, since they were regularly taken away by visiting monks to their homelands in Nepal, Tibet, China, and South-East Asia.

The entire Nālandā complex was sacked in 1197 by Moslem invaders. However, modern archaeology has uncovered the foundations of eleven monasteries and a number of other features, along with a mass of figures of Buddhist and Hindu deities, which substantiate the descriptions of its glory in Chinese and Tibetan accounts. No remains have been found of its famous towers, which were described as 'cloud-licking' in an eighth-century inscription from the site.

The Nālandā community followed a daily programme, marked by the striking of a bell. This included morning and evening rituals, themselves reflected in the present work (see Introduction to Chapter 2). Studies were conducted one to one, in group discussion or debate, and through discourses or lectures. No mention of nuns appears to be made by the Chinese visitors, and so we are probably justified in assuming that Nālandā was a largely male institution—a suggestion circumstantially confirmed by the *Bodhicaryāvatāra*, which assumes a male audience throughout. This is not to say that there were no women at all on the premises; I-tsing mentions a female orchestra accompanying the morning worship! He also describes how a woman visitor would only be allowed to speak to monks and students in the corridor of a monastery, after which she would have to leave.

We should not assume that the *Bodhicaryāvatāra* was unique. As one might imagine, in the milieu just described numerous accounts of the Path were written, even if few survive in their original language. As a single example, interesting comparison can be made between the *Bodhicaryāvatāra* and the *Pāramitā-samāsa*, or 'Compendium of Perfections', written by Āryaśūra, a near contemporary of Śāntideva (see Meadows 1986). The subject of that work is the same, and yet its author, similarly an erudite man with considerable understanding of his subject, deals with each perfection (excepting that of forbearance) on a different basis from that employed by Śāntideva.

The Structure of the Bodhicaryāvatāra

The theme of the *Bodhicaryāvatāra* is the cultivating of the Awakening Mind or *bodhicitta*. Śāntideva indicates this in the title, an ambiguous compound term which can be unpacked in different ways. Of the three separate terms compounded here, the first, *bodhi*, means 'Awakening', while the second, *caryā*, means 'the way to go or to act', with metaphorical usages deriving from the sense of the 'proper way', such as 'path', 'good conduct', 'way of life', or 'training'. The final element, *avatāra*, means literally '(bringing about) a descent into' something, but with the metaphorical usage of 'entrance into', 'introduction to', or 'undertaking'. This richness of connotation allows several interpretations, but we have adopted here the translation 'Undertaking the Way to Awakening', in the hope that this captures some at least of the ambiguity of the Sanskrit. Before we examine the structure of Śāntideva's account of 'Undertaking the Way to Awakening', however, we have to address a significant question.

Every translator of a traditional text must at some point consider whether or not the text they are translating is the original, the faithful record of the ideas and words of the author. Often such a question is unanswerable, or at best an answer will only be able to draw upon judgements of such criteria as style and content. In the case of the *Bodhicaryāvatāra* one is left with an uneasy sense of an occasional lack of coherence or continuity in a number of chapters, while the famous ninth chapter on Understanding is fraught with interpretational problems.

The suspicion that the text as we now have it is either a compilation, or an edited version of an originally coherent composition, is confirmed by the recent identification of three manuscripts of a hitherto unknown Tibetan translation of Śāntideva's classic work. These were amongst the hoard of manuscripts, hidden away *c.*1000 CE, in the library at Tun-huang recovered by Sir Aurel Stein during his expedition to Central Asia in 1906–8. Work has only recently begun on the comparison of this early translation with the present state of the Sanskrit text, but the work of Prof. Akira Saito, of Mie University, Japan, allows us to draw the following conclusions:

1. The Tun-huang manuscripts record another recension of the *Bodhicaryāvatāra*. Saito (1993) points out that at least two recensions of the *Bodhicaryāvatāra* were known to medieval

Tibetan historians, and that in all likelihood they corresponded to the two versions that we now have. The Tibetan tradition judged that the longer recension, represented by our present Sanskrit text translated in this volume, was the authentic version, and incorporated it into their canon. For this reason we will refer to it in this discussion as the canonical recension. The Tun-huang recension was translated into Tibetan in the early ninth century, whereas the canonical recension was translated twice, in the eleventh and twelfth centuries respectively.

2. This Tun-huang recension is considerably shorter than the present version, by some 210½ verses (701½ as against 912). Furthermore, a number of the verses appearing in the Tun-huang recension are not in the canonical recension. The bulk of the internal differences between the two recensions appears from Chapter 5 onwards.

3. The Tun-huang recension is divided into only nine chapters, one less than the canonical recension.

4. The title recorded in these manuscripts, and possibly the original title of the work, is *Bodhisattvacaryāvatāra*, 'Undertaking the Way of the Bodhisattva'. This is also the title transmitted by the canonical Tibetan translation.

5. The author is named as Akṣayamati, rather than Śāntideva, although Saito concludes that this name is used as an epithet of the latter.

6. On the basis of internal consistency, the Tun-huang recension can be provisionally identified as being closer to the original composition than the present Sanskrit text, which is now known to have been edited and added to by a later hand or hands (see Saito 1993 and 1994, and the introductions to Chapters 5 and 9 below), although there remains the unlikely possibility that the second recension was a revision from the hand of the author himself.

Leaving aside for the moment this Tun-huang recension, there is also a second measure against which we can test the authenticity of the text of the present version of the *Bodhicaryāvatāra*, and that is the other major work of the putative author to have survived in Sanskrit, the *Śikṣā Samuccaya*. This work, identified by its title as a 'compendium of the training', consists of a more discursive account of the Bodhisattva's training, based upon a set of twenty-seven core verses written by Śāntideva, but elaborated by him with prose explanations, and illustrated extensively by often lengthy quotations from Mahāyāna *sūtras*, or scriptures. These quotations are of great interest in their own right, since they are often the only record of the original wording of scriptures now lost in their language of composition.

It is still not clear which of these two works Śāntideva composed first. This is despite the evidence of *Bodhicaryāvatāra* 5.105, which recommends the study of the *Śikṣā Samuccaya* (implying that the latter existed prior to the *Bodhicaryāvatāra*), since this verse does not occur in the Tun-huang version and was presumably added by a later hand. Comparison shows that some of Śāntideva's core verses from the *Śikṣā Samuccaya*, as well as single verses and even entire passages from these quoted scriptures, occur without acknowledgement in the canonical Sanskrit text of the *Bodhicaryāvatāra* (see, for example, 6.120–34 and 8.96 *et seq.*). Whether these were inserted by the hand of a later editor or by the author himself is not clear, although further work upon the Tun-huang manuscripts may well shed some light on the matter. In the separate introductions to each chapter, we note which verses are shared in this way with the *Śikṣā Samuccaya*, drawing largely upon the observations of De la Vallée Poussin and Bendall.

Neither the text nor a translation of the Tun-huang *Bodhisattvacaryāvatāra* has yet been published. A detailed analysis of the early text surviving in Tun-huang is not yet available, other than for Chapters 5 (Tun-huang ch. 4) and 9 (Tun-huang ch. 8) (see introductions to these chapters below), and so it is not possible to determine whether all or even much of the additional material in the present Sanskrit text has been taken from the *Śikṣā Samuccaya*. For the mean time, we infer that this is the likely source of much of the extra material in the canonical recension, since Saito reports that it is from Chapter 5 of the canonical recension onwards that the greatest differences begin to appear between the two recensions, and it is also from this chapter onwards that the greatest amount of material is shared between the *Bodhicaryāvatāra* and the *Śikṣā Samuccaya*. It is possible that a later editor decided to integrate appropriate material from the *Śikṣā Samuccaya* into the text of the *Bodhicaryāvatāra*. In the mean time we can now look at the present Sanskrit text with the understanding that its original structure may well have been obscured by later editorial activity. That previous attempts to analyse the structure of the canonical *Bodhicaryāvatāra* seem unconvincing and strained can be put down to this cause. Exegesis of the *Bodhicaryāvatāra* appears to have been dominated by the commentary written in Sanskrit by Prajñākaramati towards the end of the tenth century, which is also based upon this longer text, and which appears to have superseded any pre-existing commentaries. Surviving Tibetan exegetical traditions appear to have favoured the translation, made by Blo-ldan-shes-rab (1059–1109), which was based upon the present Sanskrit text.

In the light of these comments we can now look at the *Bodhicaryāvatāra* and see what structure is visible. The most striking feature is that the present text is divided into ten chapters. Some scholars have doubted the authenticity of at least two of these: Chapter 2 on stylistic grounds, and Chapter 10 because it has no commentary by Prajñākaramati, suggesting that it was not a part of the text in his day. The Tun-huang manuscripts help allay these doubts, since they include materials which constitute these two chapters. However, they also show that the present arrangement of chapters is a later feature, since the present Chapters 2 and 3 form one single chapter in these manuscripts. As will be discussed below, this makes a more coherent plan for the work, and it may be that this subsequent division of the original chapter two reflects a fashion for decades of chapters.

Chapter titles of the Tun-huang recension

1. untitled (= present Ch. 1, 'Praise of the Awakening Mind')
2. *bodhicitta-parigraha*, 'Adopting the Awakening Mind' (= present Chs. 2 and 3, 'Confession of Evil' and 'Adopting the Awakening Mind' respectively)
3. *nairātmya*, 'Selflessness' (= present Ch. 4, 'Vigilance Regarding the Awakening Mind')
4. *samprajanya-rakṣaṇā*, 'Guarding of Awareness' (= present Ch. 5)

5. *kṣānti*, 'Forbearance' (= present Ch. 6)
6. *vīrya*, 'Vigour' (= present Ch. 7)
7. *dhyāna*, 'Meditative Absorption' (= present Ch. 8)
8. *prajñā*, 'Understanding' (= present Ch. 9)
9. *pariṇāmanā*, 'Dedication' (= present Ch. 10)

What of the arrangement of the chapters? For a large part of the *Bodhicaryāvatāra* this has always seemed relatively easy to understand, since if the theme of the work is the cultivation of the Awakening Mind, then Śāntideva's purpose is to outline the training of the Bodhisattva. From an early period this has been described in terms of the practice of six 'perfections', *pāramitās*: generosity, morality, forbearance, vigour, meditative absorption, and understanding. Of these, the last four have each a separate chapter, beginning with Chapter 6 on forbearance, in due order up to Chapter 9 on understanding. The first two perfections are not neglected, however, but are dealt with together in the fifth chapter. Even so, this asymmetry raises a doubt. If the perfections had been the original basis of the structure one would expect a chapter on each, as, for example, is the case in the *Pāramitāsamāsa* of Āryaśūra (Meadows 1986). Even this structure, then, may be the result of the superimposition of a different scheme on the original.

Now that we know that the present Chapters 2 and 3 were originally one, we can see that the first three chapters constitute an extended *anuttarapūjā*, or 'Supreme Worship', a ritual usually composed of seven parts, and associated by Śāntideva with the generation of merit and the Awakening Mind. (These sections will be discussed in the introductions to these chapters.) The fourth chapter is an extensive exhortation to uphold one's resolve, as the necessary basis for the training. The final chapter consists of a lengthy series of vows, or *praṇidhāna*.

The overall plan of the *Bodhicaryāvatāra* is in any case a grand sweep of action, beginning with the praise of the subject, the Awakening Mind (Ch. 1), then generation of merit and adoption of the Awakening Mind through supreme worship (Chs. 2–3), and, via the strengthening of resolve (Ch. 4), to the training proper, i.e. the perfections (Chs. 5–9), and finishing with the proper undertaking of vows, made by all Bodhisattvas at the beginning of their active career (Ch. 10).

Concerning the Translation

Śāntideva was a medieval Indian Buddhist monk, who wrote for the benefit of his contemporaries and colleagues. To translate his work presents a number of challenges and problems to the modern translator. The intention of the present translators has been to produce a prose translation into standard British English, which will be accessible to the ordinary reader. Our emphasis has been upon accuracy and clarity, attempting to give, where possible, a literal representation of Śāntideva's text, so long as this is compatible with the canons of standard English usage. We have tried to eschew the clumsy and opaque hybrids which Sanskrit often generates in English, although the technical language of Indian Buddhism which the author employed has often stretched our determination. At the same time we are aware that there will be readers who will come to this translation with some knowledge of both Buddhism and the Sanskrit language. With these readers in mind we have occasionally noted the Sanskrit of some terms, if our translation of them is not standard. Needless to say, given the non-specialist audience for whom this translation is intended, these have been kept to a minimum.

One topical translation problem revolves around the issue of gender. Our policy has been to translate Śāntideva with the minimum of interpretation. It remains an unavoidable fact that he wrote the *Bodhicaryāvatāra* for a monastic audience which without doubt would have been predominantly male, if not exclusively so. Without statistical evidence to prove this assertion, it is all the same easily inferable from internal evidence in the poem itself. For example, sexual craving and attachment is understood entirely in terms of that of a man for a woman (e.g. 8.41 ff.). There could be little justification for translators to change this, unless they were offering an exegesis of the work for the benefit of practising Buddhists, whereby it would be very important to explain that such attachment is seen as a danger to both men and women, regardless of Śāntideva's specific audience or the traditional social status of women. More pertinently, we are confronted by the problem of the gender of the listener addressed throughout the poem. In Sanskrit the masculine gender is regarded as inclusive or universal. It may refer to males only or to males and females inclusively, whereas a feminine grammatical form refers only to females. Here, the author uses the masculine gender alone. Given this, and that men were probably in the majority in his audience, we have translated accordingly. However, whenever no gender is specified we have attempted to render the sentence into gender-neutral English, for we are both convinced that Śāntideva's message is, and should appear, as applicable to women as it is to men.

Some Sanskrit Buddhist terms could have been left untranslated, to be understood by a Buddhist audience according to their own received tradition, and explained to non-Buddhist readers in notes. There is, however, a school of thought which maintains that all terms should be translated, that not to do so is a failure of nerve. This argument is all the more convincing when the translation is intended for inclusion in a series such as the 'World's Classics'. In trying to meet this challenge of total translation we have been aware that some terms require introductory comment. Single instances of this in the text are dealt with in a note, but some terms appear so frequently and are so important as to warrant mention here in the introduction.

The most important case is our decision to translate the term *bodhicitta*, the subject of the entire work, as 'Awakening Mind'. This is a very literal translation, which we thought would best serve the range of uses to which the expression is put in the original language. Yet no English expression is perfect in this respect, and it remains to explain that the term *citta* has connotations which are not shared with the standard English translation, 'mind'. There is some sense of active mental process involved in this term, which under some circumstances would mean that *citta* would be better translated as 'thought, attitude' or even 'will', in the sense of 'the will to attain Awakening'. As it is, 'Awakening Mind' risks the possibility of reification by the unwary reader, and so we hope that readers will remember that the arising of the Awakening Mind involves the internal transformation of the individual rather than the evocation of an external entity. This latter is not to be confused with the sense in which Śāntideva talks of the Awakening Mind as a force which is active within the universe. In so doing he addresses it as the single, universal motivation shared by all who aspire to Buddhahood.

Another term appearing frequently throughout the

Bodhicaryāvatāra is 'defilement', *kleśa*. These are three in number: craving, *rāga*; hatred, *dveṣa*; and delusion, *moha*. They are frequently described as the three 'roots' of all the unskilful mental states which characterize the un-Awakened mind and bind the un-Enlightened person in the cycle of existence, and it is from these defilements that the Buddhist seeks liberation. In accordance with their treatment in scripture, Śāntideva conceives of them as an almost active force, which at times is not conveyed by the slightly passive sense of 'defilement'. Alternative translations might be 'torments' or 'afflictions'. With such important terms as Awakening Mind and defilement, we judged it best to maintain a single translation throughout, rather than vary it according to context, so as to give the greatest clarity to the referents in the text.

The state of liberation and illumination attained in Buddhahood is denoted by two terms in this work. Occasionally Śāntideva uses *nirvāṇa*, which we have translated as 'Enlightenment', but far more frequently he uses *bodhi*, or 'Awakening'. The realm of the un-Awakened, *saṃsāra*, we have given as 'cyclic existence', a not very literal translation, but one which at least suggests the view of the world as something repetitive, if not painful—a view of the world held throughout the Buddhist tradition. The term *prajñā* is commonly translated as 'insight' or 'wisdom' in a Buddhist context, giving emphasis to a transcendent connotation. However, it can also refer to the realization or understanding of any item of truth or knowledge, and we have usually translated it as 'understanding', emphasizing the sense of process. The exception to this practice is the now well established translation of the name *Prajñāpāramitā Sūtra* as 'Perfection of Wisdom Sūtra'. The term *dharma* has usually been translated according to context, i.e. variously as 'Teaching [of the Buddha]', and 'element', 'constituent', or 'phenomenon'. The Buddha or Buddhas are addressed by various epithets throughout the work, all of them traditional, and all translated, with the exception of Tathāgata and Sugata. Of these the former means literally 'one who has reached such a state', while the latter means 'one in a good state'—neither very euphonious or informative, and hence they have been left untranslated. Generally speaking, readers may assume that any positive epithet probably refers to the Buddha(s), and we have printed such epithets with the initial letter capitalized: Sage, Protector, Saviour, Teacher, Guide, Omniscient One, Compassionate One, Teacher of the Universe, Fortunate One. These epithets sometimes occur in a formula such as 'The Sage has said'. These, and the expression 'it is taught', should be understood to introduce a quotation from or reference to scripture. It has not always been possible to identify such scriptural sources, but where known they are explained in the notes.

Many writers on Śāntideva emphasize the beauty of his poetry, but some qualification to this statement is undoubtedly necessary, especially in so far as it determines the policy adopted in this translation. Śāntideva wrote his *Bodhicaryāvatāra* in verse, but what this means in a Sanskrit context can be somewhat different from what it is understood to mean in a Western English-speaking context. The bulk of the *Bodhicaryāvatāra* is written in *anuṣṭubh*. This is a simple two-line verse form of 32 syllables, in which less than 50 per cent of the metre is fixed, i.e. only 6 in every 16 syllables are of fixed weight, there being only very minor exclusions for some of the remaining syllables. In other words, it is a verse form which allows considerable flexibility in comparison with others, some of which Śāntideva at times employs. The significance of this flexibility lies not in some modern notion of fluidity, or breaking of traditional norms, but rather in the strict metrical principles which underlie all Classical Sanskrit poetry. The absolute adherence to often highly complex metrical forms was a major feature of Sanskrit poetry and one of the canons by which its success and beauty as poetry would be judged. The Sanskrit poet strives to achieve excellence by employing elaborate and highly distinctive metres as a structure within which he displays other poetic devices, such as assonance, dissonance, punning, and even obscure grammatical forms (thus proving his grasp of the grammar of the language). For those who wish to read more generally on this topic, we can recommend J. Brough's Introduction to *Poems from the Sanskrit* (Harmondsworth, 1968), one of the most imaginative brief introductions to this subject.

Much traditional literature employed the simple *anuṣṭubh* verse, not only for matter which the Western English-speaking world regards as poetry, but for all subjects, including technical manuals of grammar, medicine, astronomy, and even for lexicons! The overall effect of such verse is comparable to a regulated rhythmical prose.

This does not prevent Śāntideva from employing other poetic devices even in *anuṣṭubh* verse, but it is undeniable that the bulk of this text is modest in its poetic aspirations by the standards of Sanskrit *kāvya*, or high poetry. Yet one should not conclude from this that Śāntideva was incapable of the more ambitious poetic style. He does on occasion use elaborate *kāvya* metres, often at the end of a long passage of *anuṣṭubh*. This is a common practice whereby the poet contrasts the bread-and-butter *anuṣṭubh* with more impressive extravaganzas. For Śāntideva it is an opportunity to provide a more elaborate, ornate counterpart to the more plainly didactic material of the bulk of each chapter.

Śāntideva employs his fair share of the poetic devices common to Sanskrit poetry in the *Bodhicaryāvatāra*. We have made a modest attempt to reflect this usage in the English, and have favoured assonances, dissonances, and alliterations. More difficult to render have been the author's word-plays, puns, and (probably intentional) ambiguities. Where English has failed to offer a parallel to a Sanskrit pun, we have sometimes resorted to explanation in a note. There is also a varying texture to his verse, which we have tried to preserve. Sometimes a complex sentence with several relative clauses and subclauses stretches over several verses. By contrast, on occasion a single verse will contain several sentences. The offering verses of Chapter 2 are rich and evocative, whereas the general tenor of Chapter 9 is concise, exacting, and technical. We have generally preserved these features throughout. Another feature of the work is the varying moods evoked from chapter to chapter, and within each chapter. The most condensed are the stages of the Supreme Worship, *anuttara-pūjā*, in Chapters 2 and 3. Remorse over past actions, and fear of death, are repeated refrains throughout this work, but these are alleviated and channelled by evocations of delight, reverence, at times even humour, and, of course, compassion and tranquillity.

Generally Śāntideva's language is clear, perhaps because he eschews a more ambitious poetic style. Even so there are occasional obscurities, arising as often as not from compressions employed to squeeze a statement into a verse of, for example, only thirty-two syllables. Occasionally he makes allusions to issues which would have been well understood by his fellow monks, but which it is easy for us to miss unless we pay special attention to the sense of what he says. Frequently his language is technical, employing a vocabulary and conceptual world familiar to a medieval Indian Buddhist monk, but rather more obscure today. This applies *par excellence* to his unashamedly technical exposition of the perfection of Understanding in Chapter 9. Nor should we overlook the likelihood that, as an author writing in accomplished Sanskrit verse, Śāntideva was born in a brahmin or *kṣatriya* family (the latter implied by the story that he had been a prince), i.e. was from a high-caste background. It is only from this kind of background that he could have acquired the education which is revealed by his literary achievement, a background which in turn determines another strand of allusion and language in his work.

The impression remains of a man writing with great sincerity. His work succeeds in evoking strong responses, and we are probably best advised to seek an explanation of why this should be so by examining the way in which many such people read the *Bodhicaryāvatāra*. Without doubt, most people who are genuinely affected by Śāntideva's work are affected by the sentiments that he expresses there. Many of these have been Buddhists, seeing with what can only be described as the eye of faith. Of course one need not be a Buddhist of any description to appreciate Śāntideva's aspirations, but it has been those who have read his words seeking to apply them to their own experience, enjoying his encouragement, flinching under his castigation, who have responded with the greatest sensitivity to his thoughts and reflections on the Great Work of the Bodhisattva.

The Sanskrit Text of the Bodhicaryāvatāra *and Prajñākaramati's Commentary*

Some readers may be curious to know how translators have had access to Śāntideva's work. This translation is based upon the critical edition of the Sanskrit text of Prajñākaramati's commentary on the *Bodhicaryāvatāra*, the *Bodhicaryāvatāra-pañjikā*, prepared by Louis de la Vallée Poussin and published between 1904 and 1914. His edition was based upon a single manuscript of the commentary, and so he also utilized the Tibetan translation of the same work to help establish an accurate text. Since the commentary, as published, quotes the verses of the main text in full, De la Vallée Poussin's work offers some advance upon, and to some degree replaces, the pioneering edition of the *Bodhicaryāvatāra* alone, published in 1889 by the Russian, Minaev. De la Vallée Poussin had the advantage of utilizing Minaev's work and taking account of Prajñākaramati's explanations, a source of correction not available to Minaev. There are a few places where the commentary omits verses because the text of the *Bodhicaryāvatāra* which Prajñākaramati used differed from that which was transmitted in the manuscripts consulted by Minaev. De la Vallée Poussin records these differences, and we have also incorporated them.

Prajñākaramati's commentary is of variable helpfulness in preparing a translation, despite the expectation often voiced by friends who do not read Sanskrit that it must doubtless be of great interest. This disappointment arises partly through the character of a *pañjikā*-type commentary, which takes as its starting-point the task of commenting upon every word of the main text. This inevitably gives a decidedly grammatical cast to the commentary, which is not without its uses for the translator, of course, but also means that much space is taken by the rather unimaginative provision of synonyms for every term, even (it sometimes feels like 'especially') when completely unnecessary.

The fact remains, however, that for all this Prajñākaramati is not always convincing, and on occasion lets one down with his supply of synonyms—usually when they are most needed. One cannot but suspect that when a difficult term or usage appeared in the text, he observed a discreet silence (it is tempting to follow his example). As for his more discursive comments, it is clear that his main interest was in Chapter 9 of the present work, and indeed it is thought by some that this was the first part of the *Bodhicaryāvatāra* upon which he worked. Roughly one-third of the present bulk of his commentary, and much of his enthusiasm, is devoted to this chapter, although the verses of Chapter 9 only make up about one-sixth of the bulk of the

Bodhicaryāvatāra itself. For the other chapters his remarks are in the main restricted to glosses and explanations of a rather scholastic character—one does not gain the impression that he was touched by the material itself—but these are leavened by references to Mahāyāna scriptures, almost entirely borrowed from Śāntideva's other main work, the *Śikṣā Samuccaya*.

There are passages of Prajñākaramati's commentary which have not survived in Sanskrit; the relevant leaves of the single manuscript which De la Vallée Poussin used for his edition were lost. This affected the following passages: 1.1, 3.23–33, 4.1–45, and 8.109–86. It appears that Prajñākaramati did not comment upon Chapter 10, which is offered by some as an argument that this chapter was not original. These passages are not supplied in De la Vallée Poussin's edition, and for these we have used the text as printed in the rather unreliable edition of text and commentary by Vaidya (1988 reprint), checking readings against a copy of the less accessible Minaev edition held in the Bodleian Library.

NOTE ON THE PRONUNCIATION OF SANSKRIT NAMES

THE following may act as a guide to pronunciation, but for detailed information on the pronunciation of Sanskrit the reader should consult chapter 1 of Michael Coulson's *Sanskrit: An Introduction to the Classical Language* (Teach Yourself Books, 1992).

Pronounce Sanskrit	**as in English**
a	c*u*t
ā	f*a*r
i	s*i*t
ī	m*e*
u	p*u*t
ū	t*oo*
ṛ	r*i*sk
e	pr*ay*
ai	s*i*gh
o	h*o*pe
au	s*ou*nd
c	*ch*urch
v	close to the English *w*
ś	*sh*ame
ṣ	di*sh*
ḥ	as in English, but with a faint echo of the preceding vowel
ṭ etc.	as in English, but with the tongue further back in the mouth
ṅ, ṇ	have a nasal quality
ñ,	ca*n*yon

Pronounce Sanskrit	**as in English**
kh, gh, ch, jh, ṭh, ḍh, th, dh, ph, bh	aspirated, as in 'ho*th*ouse' (*not* 'wi*th*'), 'she*ph*erd', 'clu*bh*ouse', etc.
ṃ	nasalizes the preceding vowel sound, as in French *bon*

ACKNOWLEDGEMENTS

EVERY translation shows a debt. In our case, we are aware of two traditions, without which this project would not have begun. The first is the Buddhist tradition which has continued to pass down and develop the teachings proclaimed by the Buddha nearly two and a half millennia ago. The second is the academic tradition which has allowed us greater access to the former. We are grateful to both. More specifically, for this translation we have benefited from the freely shared knowledge of several individuals: Dr R. Schaturvedi, Dr C. D. Crosby, Romola Dane, Professor R. Gombrich, Dr S. Gupta and Sujata Kana, who generously gave their time to answer queries concerning the interpretation of individual verses; Dharmacari Dharmapriya (Michael Scherk), gave constructive criticism of a draft of the earlier chapters, and reminded us that the English language has a grammar too. Professor Paul Harrison, whose lectures on the translations of Lokaksema (Trinity Term, 1994) provided useful information on the *Ajātaśatru-kaukṛtya-vinodanā*, who also drew our attention to the work of Professor Akira Saito on the Tun-huang recension of the *Bodhicaryāvatāra*, and read our finished typescript meticulously, suggesting a number of improvements. We are indebted to all these people, and to everyone who accepted our unsolicited offer of an opportunity to practise the *pāramitās* of generosity, forbearance, and understanding.

KATE CROSBY AND ANDREW SKILTON

Oxford
May 1994

SELECT BIBLIOGRAPHY

READERS interested in another translation of the *Bodhicaryāvatāra* might look at that made by Stephen Batchelor from the Tibetan translation. Kelsang Gyatso offers a traditional exposition of the text, and another translation from the Tibetan embedded in his commentary. Readers particularly interested in Chapter 9 could consult the translation from the Sanskrit made by B. Alan Wallace, which accompanies a commentary by the present Dalai Lama. For background material concerning the Mahāyāna, readers are recommended the study by P. M. Williams as the most up-to-date and comprehensive. A. Skilton's book provides a broader survey of the history of Buddhism. For an alternative account of the Bodhisattva's career, written by a near contemporary of Śāntideva, we can recommend Meadows's translation, with detailed introduction, analysis, and notes, of Āryaśūra's 'Compendium of the Perfections'. I-tsing's account of his travels in India has been translated by Takakusu. The bulk of this bibliography gives the details of works referred to in our introductory material and annotations.

Batchelor, Stephen, *A Guide to the Bodhisattva's Way of Life* (Library of Tibetan Works and Archives, Dharamsala, 1979).

Bays, G., *The Voice of the Buddha: The Beauty of Compassion*, 2 vol. translation of the Lalitavistara (Berkeley, Calif., 1983).

Bendall, Cecil, and Rouse, W. H. D., *Śikṣā Samuccaya* (London, 1922; repr., Motilal Banarsidass, Delhi, 1971).

Beresford, B. C., *Mahāyāna Purification: The Confession Sūtra with Commentary by Ārya Nāgārjuna*, translation of the Triskhandakasūtra (Library of Tibetan Works and Archives, Dharamsala, 1980).

Birnbaum, Raoul, *The Healing Buddha*, containing a translation of four Bhaiṣajyaguru *sūtras* (Boston, 1989).

Chang, G. C., *A Treasury of Mahāyāna Sūtras* (Pennsylvania State University Press, University Park, Pa., and London, 1983).

Cleary, Thomas, *The Flower Ornament Scripture: A Translation of the Avatamsaka Sutra*, ii, containing translation of the Daśabhūmika Sūtra, pp. 1–123 (Shambala, Boston, 1986).

—— *Entry into the Realm of Reality: A Translation of the Gandavyuha, the final book of the Avatamsaka Sutra* (Shambala, Boston, 1989).

Cowell *et al.*, *The Jātaka or Stories of the Buddha's Former Births*, 6 vols. (Pali Text Society, London, 1895–1907; repr. in 3 vols., Oxford, 1981).

Cowell, Müller, and Takakusu, *Buddhist Mahāyāna Texts* (Dover Publications, New York, 1969), repr. of vol. xlix of 'Sacred Books of the East' series, Clarendon Press, Oxford, 1894.

Dayal, H., *The Bodhisattva Doctrine in Buddhist Sanskrit Literature* (Kegan Paul, Trench, Trubner, London, 1932).

De la Vallée Poussin, L. (ed.), *Prajñākaramati's Commentary to the Bodhicaryāvatāra of Çāntideva, Edited with Indices* (Asiatic Society of Bengal, Calcutta, 1901–14).

Dutt, Sukumar, *Buddhist Monks and Monasteries of India* (George Allen and Unwin, London, 1962).

Emmerick, R. E., *The Sūtra of Golden Light, Being a translation of the Suvarṇabhāsottama* (Pali Text Society, Oxford, 2nd edn. 1990).

Horner, I. B., *Middle Length Sayings*, 3 vols., translation of the Majjhimanikāya (Pali Text Society, London, 1954, 1957, 1959).

—— *The Book of the Discipline* (Pali Text Society, London, 1938, 1940, 1942, 1951, 1952, 1966).

—— *Minor Anthologies*, vol. 3 (Pali Text Society, Oxford, 1975).

Hurvitz, L., *Scripture of the Lotus Blossom of the Fine Dharma: Translated from the Chinese of Kumārajīva* (Columbia University Press, New York, 1976).

Ishida, Chikō, 'Some New Remarks on the *Bodhicaryāvatāra* Chap. V', *Journal of Indian and Buddhist Studies* 37/1 (Dec. 1988).

Johnston, E. H., *Aśvaghoṣa's Buddhacarita or Acts of the Buddha* (Delhi, 1984).

Jones, J. J., *The Mahāvastu*, 3 vols. (Pali Text Society, London, 1949, 1952, 1956).

Kajihara, Mieko, 'On the *Pariṇāmanā* Chapter of the Bodhicaryāvatāra', *Journal of Indian and Buddhist Studies*, 40/2 (Mar. 1992).

Kern, H., *Saddharmapuṇḍarīka or the Lotus of the True Law* (1884, repr. Dover Publications, New York, 1963).

Lamotte, E. 'Passions and Impregnations of the Passions in Buddhism', in L. Cousins *et al.* (eds.), *Buddhist Studies in Honour of I. B. Horner* (D Reidel, Dordrecht, 1974), 91–104.

Meadows, Carol, *Ārya-Śūra's Compendium of the Perfections: Text, Translation and Analysis of the Pāramitāsamāsa* (Indica et Tibetica Verlag, Bonn, 1986).

Müller, M., *Buddhist Mahāyāna Texts* (Clarendon Press, Oxford, 1894; repr., Dover Publications, New York, 1969).

Nārada Thera, *The Dhammapada* (John Murray, London, 1954).

Norman, K. R., *Elders' Verses*, 2 vols., translation of the Thera- and Therī-gāthā (Pali Text Society, London, 1969 and 1971).

Nyanaponika Thera, *The Heart of Buddhist Meditation* (Rider, London, 1975).

Rhys Davids, T. W., *Dialogues of the Buddha*, 3 vols., translation of the Dīghanikāya (Pali Text Society, Oxford, 1899, 1910, 1921).
—— *Buddhist Birth Stories*, translation of the Nidānakathā (repr., Varanasi and Delhi, 1973).
—— and Oldenberg, H., *Vinaya Texts*, Part 1 (1885; repr., Motilal Banarsidass, New Delhi, 1982).
Saito, Akira, *A Study of Akṣayamati(= Śāntideva)'s* Bodhisattvacaryāvatāra *as Found in the Tibetan Manuscripts from Tun-huang*, A Report of the Grant-in-Aid for Scientific Research (C) (Mie, Japan, 1993).
—— 'On the Difference between the Earlier and the Current Versions of Śāntideva's *Bodhi(sattva)caryāvatāra*, with special reference to Chap. 9 (/8) entitled: "Perfection of Wisdom (prajñāpāramitā)"', research paper presented at IXth World Sanskrit Conference held on 9th to 15th January 1994, in Melbourne, Australia.
Skilton, A., *A Concise History of Buddhism* (Windhorse Publications, Glasgow, 1994).
Sweet, Michael, *Śāntideva and the Mādhyamika: The Prajñāpāramitāpariccheda of the Bodhicaryāvatāra*, Ph.D. thesis, University of Wisconsin, 1976 (facsimile, U.M.I. Dissertation Services).
Takakusu, J., *A Record of the Buddhistic Religion* (Oxford, 1896; Delhi, 1966; Taipei, 1970).
Tenzin Gyatso, H. H. Dalai Lama, *Transcendent Wisdom, A Commentary on the Ninth Chapter of Shantideva's Guide to the Bodhisattva Way of Life*, translated, edited and annotated by B. Alan Wallace (Snow Lion Publications, Ithaca, NY, 1988).
Thomas, E., *History of Buddhist Thought* (London, 2nd edn. 1951).
Vaidya, P. L. (ed.), *Bodhicaryāvatāra of Śāntideva with the Commentary Pañjikā of Prajnākaramati* (Mithila Institute, Darbhanga, 1988).
Williams, P. *Mahāyāna Buddhism: The Doctrinal Foundations* (Routledge, London, 1989).

The Bodhicaryāvatāra

1

PRAISE OF THE AWAKENING MIND

THE first chapter of Śāntideva's *Bodhicaryāvatāra* is an extended praise of his subject, the Awakening Mind. He begins, however, with four verses, shared with his *Śikṣā Samuccaya*, in which he makes his initial and traditional obeisance to the Buddhas and Bodhisattvas, and then explains his motives for writing. Thereafter he launches into a lengthy praise of the Awakening Mind itself, emphasizing its rarity and its potency. This culminates in his definition of the Awakening Mind in verses 15–16:

> That Awakening Mind should be understood to be of two kinds; in brief: The Mind resolved on Awakening and the Mind proceeding towards Awakening.

> The distinction between these two should be understood by the wise in the same way as the distinction is recognized between a person who desires to go and one who is going, in that order.

Once this distinction has been made, it leads naturally into a discussion of the virtues of those beings in whom the Awakening Mind has arisen, the Buddhas and Bodhisattvas:

> Such a being, unprecedented, an excellent jewel, in whom there is born a concern for the welfare of others such as others have not even for themselves, how is he born? (v. 25)

The only appropriate response to the magnificence of the conception of the Awakening Mind is to go for refuge to those who embody it, and this is Śāntideva's declaration in the final verse (36). In so doing Śāntideva recapitulates the response to the Buddha, both spontaneous and ritualized, that is incorporated into the fundamental act of religious commitment made by all Buddhists. This act of going for refuge to the Three Jewels, the Buddha, Dharma, and Saṅgha, has spread throughout the Buddhist world as the definitive act whereby people declare themselves to be Buddhists. Śāntideva also implicitly explains why it is that he and other Buddhists go for refuge to the Buddha and Bodhisattvas: because they embody the Awakening Mind.

Praise of the Awakening Mind

1 In adoration I make obeisance to the Sugatas and their sons, and to their bodies of Dharma, and to all those worthy of praise. In brief, and in accordance with scripture, I shall describe the undertaking of the observance of the sons of the Sugatas.

2 Nothing new will be said here, nor have I any skill in composition. Therefore I do not imagine that I can benefit others. I have done this to perfume my own mind.

3 While doing this, the surge of my inspiration to cultivate what is skilful increases. Moreover, should another, of the very same humours as me, also look at this, then he too may benefit from it.

4 This opportune moment is extremely hard to meet. Once met, it yields the welfare of mankind. If the advantage is neglected now, how will this meeting come again?

5 At night in darkness thick with clouds a lightning flash gives a moment's brightness. So, sometime, by the power of the Buddha, the mind of the world might for a moment turn to acts of merit.

6 This being so, the power of good is always weak, while the power of evil is vast and terrible. What other good could conquer that, were there not the perfect Awakening Mind?

7 This is the benefit, seen by the Lords of the Sages meditating for many aeons, whereby deep-welling happiness elates immeasurable masses of beings, through happiness alone.

8 Those who long to transcend the hundreds of miseries of existence, who long to relieve creatures of their sorrows, who long to enjoy many hundreds of joys, must never abandon the Awakening Mind.

9 When the Awakening Mind has arisen in him, a wretch, captive in the prison of existence, he is straightaway hailed

son of the Sugatas, to be revered in the worlds of gods and men.

10 Taking this base image, it transmutes it into the priceless image of the Buddha-gem. Grasp tightly the quicksilver elixir, known as the Awakening Mind, which must be thoroughly worked.

11 You who are accustomed to travelling abroad among the trading towns of the realms of rebirth, grasp tightly this gem that is the Awakening Mind. It is precious, assayed by those of immeasurable expertise, the unique caravan-leaders of the world.

12 Like the plantain stem, all other good things assuredly shed their fruit and then wither, whereas the Awakening Mind is a tree that constantly fruits. It does not wither, but continues to produce.

13 In its protection, as in the protection of a hero, one immediately escapes great dangers, even after committing extremely cruel acts of evil. So why do ignorant beings not seek refuge in it?

14 Like the holocaust at the end of a world age, it completely consumes great evils in an instant. The wise Lord Maitreya related its unmeasured praises to Sudhana.

15 The Awakening Mind should be understood to be of two kinds; in brief: the Mind resolved on Awakening and the Mind proceeding towards Awakening.

16 The distinction between these two should be understood by the wise in the same way as the distinction is recognized between a person who desires to go and one who is going, in that order.

17 Even in cyclic existence great fruit comes from the Mind resolved on Awakening, but nothing like the uninterrupted merit that comes from that resolve when put into action.

18 From the moment that he takes on that Mind to release the limitless realm of beings, with a resolve that cannot be turned back.

19 From that moment on, though he may doze off or be distracted many times, uninterrupted streams of merit like the bursting sky continuously pour forth.

20 This is what the Tathāgata himself explained with proof in the *Question of Subāhu*, for the benefit of beings who are disposed toward the inferior path.

21 Immeasurable merit took hold of the well-intentioned person who thought 'Let me dispel the headaches of beings'.

22 What then of the person who longs to remove the unequalled agony of every single being and make their virtue infinite?

23 Whose mother or father ever has such a desire for their welfare as this, what deities or sages or Brahmās have it?

24 Those beings did not conceive this desire before, even for their own sake, even in a dream. How could they have it for the sake of others?

25 Such a being, unprecedented, an excellent jewel, in whom there is born a concern for the welfare of others such as others have not even for themselves, how is he born?

26 That jewel, the Mind, which is the seed of pure happiness in the world and the remedy for the suffering of the world, how at all can its merit be measured?

27 Worship of the Buddha is surpassed merely by the desire for the welfare of others; how much more so by the persistent effort for the complete happiness of every being?

28 Hoping to escape suffering, it is to suffering that they run. In the desire for happiness, out of delusion, they destroy their own happiness, like an enemy.

29 It satisfies with every happiness those starved of happiness, and cuts away oppressions from those oppressed in many ways.

30 It also drives off delusion. How could there be a holy man its equal, how such a friend, or how such merit?

31 Even if someone returns a favour, he is praised. What, then, can be said of the Bodhisattva, who does good without obligation?

32 People honour someone who gives alms to a few people, saying, 'He does good', because he contemptuously supports their life for half a day with a moment's gift of mere food.

33 What then of the one who offers to a limitless number of beings, throughout limitless time, the fulfilment of all desires, unending until the end of the sky and those beings?

34 The Protector has said that one who harbours in his heart a turbid thought against such a lord of gifts, a son of the Conqueror, dwells in hells for aeons as numerous as the moments of that turbid thought.

35 But fruit outweighing that flows forth for one whose mind becomes serenely confident. For evil action against the sons of the Conqueror requires great force, while pure action comes effortlessly.

36 I bow down to the bodies of those in whom that excellent jewel, the Mind, has arisen, and towards whom even harm will lead to happiness. To those mines of happiness, I go for refuge.

2
CONFESSION OF FAULTS

INTRODUCTION: CHAPTERS 2 AND 3

As has been explained in the Translators' Introduction in the section 'The Structure of the *Bodhicaryāvatāra*', there is manuscript evidence to show that Chapters 2 and 3 were originally one. Since this is confirmed by internal evidence we shall treat them as such here. Together, Chapters 2 and 3 (and perhaps Chapter 1) form a text for an important and widespread Mahāyāna liturgy, known as the *anuttara-pūjā* or 'Supreme Worship'. The history of this liturgy is not fully known, and since the publication of Dayal's study of the Bodhisattva in 1932, in which he discusses the Supreme Worship exclusively in terms of the *Bodhicaryāvatāra*, the assumption that Śāntideva was responsible for its formulation has gained some ground (Dayal, 54–8). In fact, the history of this liturgy goes back several centuries before his time. Śāntideva himself refers, in his *Śikṣā Samuccaya*, to the formulation of the Supreme Worship embodied in the *Bhadracaryā-praṇidhāna-gāthā*, 'Verses on the Vows of Good Conduct' (*Bhadracaryā*), a section of the final chapter of the *Gaṇḍavyūha Sūtra*, which also circulated separately from its parent text. We can infer from the frequency with which the *Bhadracaryā* was copied and quoted, that this provided, for several centuries at least, a widespread model for the Supreme Worship. The date of composition of the *Gaṇḍavyūha Sūtra*, like all Mahāyāna Sūtras an anonymous work, is not known, but we do know that it was first translated into Chinese in the fourth century CE. However, we can push back the use of the Supreme Worship before even this date, because some of its main elements are enumerated, in a ritual context, in one of the very first Mahāyāna Sūtras translated into Chinese, in the late second century CE, by Lokakṣema, i.e. the *Ajātaśatru-kaukṛtyavinodanā*, 'Dispelling the Regret of Ajātaśatru'. Śāntideva was therefore writing according to a well-established liturgical format, for the creation of which he can no longer be credited, although this does not detract from his achievement.

It appears that by tradition the Supreme Worship had seven parts. It is clear, however, that the constitution of these seven parts varied, some being more stable than others, and that we can count up to as many as nine elements used variously to make up the Supreme Worship. The *Bhadracaryā*, for example, records a Supreme Worship consisting of:

1. praise (*vandanā*),
2. worship (*pūjanā*),
3. confession [of faults] (*deśanā*),
4. rejoicing [in merits] (*modanā*),
5. requesting [the teaching] (*adhyeṣaṇā*),
6. begging [the Buddhas not to abandon beings] (*yācanā*), and
7. dedication [of merit] (*nāmanā*).

The *Ajātaśatru-kaukṛtya-vinodanā* mentions: 1. going for refuge to the Three Jewels (*triśaraṇa-gamana*), 2. confession of faults, 3. rejoicing in merit, 4. requesting the teaching, and 5. arousal of the Awakening Mind (*bodhicittotpāda*). The *Dharmasaṃgraha*, a late Mahāyāna compendium of technical terms, follows the same format as the *Bhadracaryā*, but substitutes 'arousal of the Awakening Mind' (*bodhicittotpāda*) for 'begging the Buddhas not to abandon beings'.

That the form of the Supreme Worship was flexible, even to the extent of having less or possibly more than its classical seven parts, is of added significance here, because Śāntideva does not state explicitly what format he had in mind for this part of the *Bodhicaryāvatāra*. Nevertheless, we can provisionally identify the following elements of Supreme Worship in these two chapters:

Chapter 2

1–25	worship, *pūjā*
26	going for refuge, *śaraṇa-gamana*
27–45	confession of faults, *pāpa-deśanā*
46–54	going for refuge, *śaraṇa-gamana*
55–66	confession of faults, *pāpadeśanā*

Chapter 3

1–3	rejoicing in merit, *anumodanā*
4	requesting the teaching, *adhyeṣaṇā*
5	begging the Buddhas not to abandon beings, *yācanā*
6–21	dedication of merit, *pariṇāmanā*
22–33	arousal of the Awakening Mind, *bodhicittotpāda*

Saito reports that the first four chapters (the first three in the Tun-huang recension) show a close correspondence in the two recensions of the *Bodhicaryāvatāra*, so we can only assume for the mean time that this plan is free of later editorial changes and may reflect the intentions of the author. Therefore, although he is without doubt expanding upon the themes of the Supreme Worship liturgy, he has not restricted himself either to seven elements, nor to a simple sequential presentation. If we also look to the chapters adjoining these, i.e. Chapters 1 and 4, the picture is broader and more complex still. Chapter 1, standing as a separate chapter in both recensions, is an extended 'praise', usually the first element in most accounts of the Supreme Worship. The fourth chapter, concerned with strengthening the aspiring Bodhisattva's resolve, has an integral link with the final section of Chapter 3, arousal of the Awakening Mind.

What then is the Supreme Worship, and what is its function? We have already described it as a Mahāyāna liturgy, indicating that it is a ritual expressing the ideals of Mahāyāna Buddhism. More specifically it is concerned with furthering the central religious aspiration of the Mahāyāna Buddhist, namely the arising of the Awakening Mind. It is presumably for this reason that this section as a whole was entitled 'adopting' or 'seizing the Awakening Mind' in the Tun-huang recension. Śāntideva, in the *Śikṣā Samuccaya*, recommends the Supreme Worship as a means of developing merit, this being the necessary counterpart to wisdom or understanding. Together, the pair form the two 'preparations', *saṃbhāra*, without which the Bodhisattva cannot attain full Awakening for the benefit of all beings. More specifically, the Supreme Worship is the means that Śāntideva employs to engender the first of the two kinds of Awakening Mind that he defines in Chapter 1 (vv. 15–16): 'the Mind resolved on Awakening'. This is apparent from the final section of Chapter 3, following his dedication of merit, which begins:

In the same way as bygone Sugatas took up the Awakening Mind, in the same way as they progressed in the Bodhisattva training

So too, I myself shall generate the Awakening Mind for the welfare of the world; and just so shall I train in those precepts in due order.

The wise one who has taken up the Awakening Mind in this way with a serene confidence should continue to encourage his resolve as follows, in order to fulfil his wish. (vv. 22–4)

Thereafter, having strengthened his resolve, he is able to put it into practice in the Bodhisattva training, and to cultivate the second kind of Awakening Mind: 'the Mind proceeding towards Awakening'.

The various elements of the Supreme Worship represent or invoke a sequence of spiritual moods through which the ritual participant is drawn. Despite minor variations in different sources, the sequence of these moods is not arbitrary. One begins with praise (Chapter 1), because this involves reflection upon and appreciation of the virtues of the Awakening Mind. On the basis of this appreciation, one then engages in worship, the active response to what is good, particularly in the form of making offerings to that which is worshipped. Since the Awakening Mind is of incalculable worth, the aspiring Bodhisattva offers everything of value in the universe. A natural extension of this positive response to the Awakening Mind is that one should go to it for refuge (2.26), i.e. commit oneself to its realization. However, the active appreciation and valuation of the Awakening Mind resulting in this act of commitment has a reflexive effect upon the individual, namely the perception of one's own shortcomings. This results in the confession of one's evil, as accumulated in this and previous lives. In part relieved and lightened by this confession, and partly able now to appreciate the good which is achieved by others, one naturally rejoices in their merits. Freed from remorse, and appreciative of others, one can turn one's attention to the teachings of the Buddha which enable one to acquire the Awakening Mind, and so one requests to receive the teaching, indicating one's openness to receive instruction in the Bodhisattva path. At the same time one realizes that the teaching is derived from the Buddhas, and so one begs that they should help oneself and others. Knowing that these actions are themselves productive of much merit, and also aware that this can form a subtle basis for greed and acquisitiveness, one then gives away, in the fullest Bodhisattva spirit, even this merit, dedicating it to the benefit of all beings. Finally, one strengthens one's resolve so as to encourage the arising of the Awakening Mind.

It is of interest to note that the description of the worship in Chapter 2 (vv. 1–25) corresponds closely to that recorded by the Chinese pilgrim monk, I-tsing, when he visited Nālandā in the late seventh century, furnishing us with further evidence for the extent to which life at Nālandā is reflected in the *Bodhicaryāvatāra*, and for the nature of Mahāyāna ritual at this period.

Confession of Faults

1 That I may fully grasp that jewel, the Mind, I worship here the Tathāgatas, and the flawless jewel, the true Dharma, and the sons of the Buddhas, who are oceans of virtue.

2 As many blossoms and fruits and medicinal herbs as there are, as many jewels as there are in the world, and clear refreshing waters;

3 Along with jewel-formed mountains and other places delightful in solitude, the forest groves, creepers brilliant with beautiful flowers their ornaments, and trees, boughs bowed low under the weight of full fruit;

4 And, from the worlds of gods and celestials, scent and incense, magical trees that fulfil every wish and trees laden with gems, lakes adorned with lotuses, where the calls of the geese steal the heart beyond bounds;

5 Plants which grow wild and those which are sown, and whatever else might adorn the honourable, and all those things unowned within the boundaries of the breadth of space;

6 See, in my mind I take hold of all these, and present them to the Bulls amongst Sages, and their sons. With great compassion, tender toward me, may those most worthy of gifts accept these from me.

7 I have no merit, I am completely destitute. I have nothing else to offer in worship. So, through their power, may the Lords resolved on the well-being of others accept this for my well-being.

8 I give my entire self wholly to the Conquerors and to their sons. Take possession of me, sublime beings; out of devotion, I am your slave.

9 You take possession of me. I become fearless. I act for the benefit of beings. I leave behind previous wrongdoing completely; never again shall I do another wrong.

10 In those sweet-smelling bath-houses, where canopies gleam with pearls, over delightful pillars, brilliant with gems, rising up from mosaic floors of clear, brilliant crystal,

11 From many pots, encrusted with enormous gems, filled with exquisitely fragrant water and flowers, see, I bathe the Tathāgatas and their sons, to the accompaniment of songs and music. statues

12 I wipe down their bodies with cloths beyond compare, scented, cleansed of impurities; then I present them with the finest robes, richly dyed and fragrant.

13 With each and every celestial garment, soft, smooth, of many-coloured splendour, and with choice ornaments, I adorn Samantabhadra, Ajita, Mañjughoṣa, Lokeśvara, and other Bodhisattvas.

14 With the costliest perfumes, their fragrance pervading the entire universe of three thousand worlds, I anoint the bodies of all the Lords of Sages brilliant with the lustre of gold well-heated, polished, and cleansed.

15 I glorify the most glorious Lords of Sages with all sweetly scented blossoms, delightful to the mind: celestial flowers, jasmine, blue lotus, and others; and with garlands, alluringly arranged.

16 I envelop them in heady clouds of incense, rich, pervading, and aromatic. I make them an offering of foods, soft and hard, and many kinds of drink.

17 I offer bejewelled lamps, arrayed in rows on golden lotuses, and on the mosaic floors sprinkled with perfume, I strew lovely drifts of flowers.

18 To those formed of goodwill I also offer those shining clouds that are celestial palaces, ornamented at the entrances in the four directions, splendid with pendulous ropes of pearls and precious stones, entrancing with songs and poems of praise.

19 Now, for the Great Sages, I set up splendid, bejewelled umbrellas, encrusted with pearls, fully raised on beautifully formed shafts of gold.

20 Hereafter, may heady clouds of worship arise, and clouds of instrumental music, thrilling every being.

21 May flowers and jewels and other offerings rain down incessantly upon the *caityas*, images, and all the jewels which make up the true Dharma.

22 Just as Mañjughoṣa and others following him have worshipped the Conquerors, so I, too, worship the Tathāgatas, who are Protectors, and their sons.

23 I praise the Oceans of Virtue with hymns that are a sea of notes and harmonies. Let clouds of chanted praise arise no differently among them.

24 With as many prostrations as there are atoms in all the Buddha-fields, I throw myself down before the Buddhas of all three times, before the Dharma, and before the highest assembly.

25 I worship all *caityas* and places associated with the Bodhisattva. I bow down to my teachers, and to spiritual aspirants who are worthy of praise.

26 As far as the seat of the Awakening, I go to the Buddha for refuge; I go for refuge to the Dharma, and to the assembly of Bodhisattvas.

27 To the perfect Buddhas arrayed in all directions, and also to the Bodhisattvas of great compassion, holding my hands together in reverence, I declare:

28 Throughout the beginningless cycle of existence, and again in this very birth, the evil I, a brute, have done or caused,

29 Or anything I, deluded, have rejoiced in to my own detriment, I confess that transgression, tormented by remorse.

30 The harm I have done, in arrogance, to the Three Jewels, or to my mothers or fathers, or to others worthy of respect, with body, speech, and mind;

31 The cruel evil I have wickedly done, corrupted by many faults; O Leaders, I confess it all.

32 How can I escape it? I am continually in a state of alarm, O Leaders. Let death not come too soon to me, before my mass of evil is destroyed!

33 How can I escape it? Rescue me quickly, lest death come swiftly, before my evil is destroyed!

34 This death pays no heed to what is done or undone; a killer of security; not to be trusted by those sick or well; a shattering thunderbolt from nowhere.

35 I did evil in many ways on account of friends and enemies. This I did not understand: I must abandon all and go.

36 Those I loathe will die; those I love will die; I too will die; and all will die.

37 Everything experienced fades to memory. Everything is like an image in a dream. It is gone and is not seen again.

38 Even in this life, as I have stood by, many loved and loathed have gone. But the evil occasioned by them remains, ghastly, before me.

39 Just like them I am a fleeting wraith. This I failed to recognize. In delusion, yearning, and aversion, I did evil many times.

40 Night and day, without respite, more of life is lost. It never gets longer. Surely, will I not die?

41 Though here laid on my bed, though in the midst of family, it is alone that I must endure the agony of the throes of death.

42 For one seized by the messengers of Death, what good is a relative, what good a friend? At that time, merit alone is a defence and I have not acquired it.

43 By clinging to this transient life, not recognizing this danger, heedless, O Lords, I have acquired great evil.

44 Even someone taken away today to have a limb cut off withers, throat parched, gaze wretched. He sees the world in a completely different way.

45 But that is nothing to the feverish horror which grips me, covered in my own uncontrolled excrement, as Death's terrifying messengers stand over me.

46 With cowering glances I search the four directions for deliverance. What saint will deliver me from this great fear?

47 Seeing the directions devoid of deliverance, I fall into total confusion once again. What will I do then in that state of great fear?

48 Right now I go for refuge to the mighty Protectors of the world, who have undertaken the care of the world, the Conquerors who remove all fear.

49 I also go whole-heartedly for refuge to the Dharma they have realized, which destroys the danger of cyclic existence, and to the assembly of Bodhisattvas.

50 Trembling with fear I give myself to Samantabhadra, and again freely I give myself to Mañjughoṣa.

51 Terrified I cry out in anguish to the Protector Avalokita whose conduct overflows with compassion. I have done evil. May he protect me.

52 Seeking deliverance with all my heart I cry out to noble Ākāśagarbha, too, and Kṣitigarbha, and all those of great compassion.

53 I bow down to the Holder of the Vajra. As soon as they see him the ministers of Death and all malign creatures flee, quaking, in the four directions.

54 I have transgressed your command. Now, at seeing the danger, terrified, I go to you for refuge. Destroy the danger, quickly!

55 Even one afraid of passing illness would not ignore the doctor's advice; how much more so one in the grip of the four hundred and four diseases,

56 Of which just one can wipe out all the people in Jambudvīpa; for which no remedy is found in any region.

57 Yet on this I ignore the advice of the omniscient doctor who removes all barbs. Oh, there is no end to my stupidity!

58 I stand with exceeding care even on an ordinary cliff. How much more so above a precipice of a thousand leagues through great expanses of time?

59 Death may not come this very day, but my complacency is ill-founded. Inevitably the time approaches when I shall die.

60 Who has granted me impunity? How shall I escape? It is certain I shall die. How can my mind be at ease?

61 What essence has remained mine from things I once enjoyed, now perished, for which my infatuation led me to ignore the advice of my teachers?

62 Leaving behind this world of the living, along with relatives and intimates, wherever I go I shall go alone. What to me are all those I love or loathe?

63 Rather, at all times night and day, my sole concern should be this: suffering is the inevitable result of wrong. How can I escape it?

64 Whatever evil I, a deluded fool, have amassed, what is wrong by nature and what is wrong by convention,

65 See, I confess all that as I stand before the Protectors, my palms together in reverence, terrified of suffering, prostrating myself again and again.

66 Let the Leaders accept my transgression for what it is. It is not good, O Protectors. I must not do it again.

3

ADOPTING THE AWAKENING MIND

1 I rejoice with delight at the good done by all beings, which abates the suffering of hell. May those who are suffering abide in happiness.

2 I rejoice at the deliverance of embodied beings from the suffering of cyclic existence. I rejoice at the Bodhisattva- and Buddha-nature of the Saviours.

3 I also rejoice at the resolutions of the Teachers, which are oceans bearing happiness to every being, bestowing well-being on all creatures.

4 Holding my hands together in reverence, I beseech the perfect Buddhas in every direction, 'Set up the light of the Dharma for those falling into suffering in the darkness of delusion'.

5 Holding my hands together in reverence, I implore the Conquerors who wish to leave cyclic existence, 'Remain for endless aeons. Do not let this world become blind!'

6 With the good acquired by doing all this as described, may I allay all the suffering of every living being.

7 I am medicine for the sick. May I be both the doctor and their nurse, until the sickness does not recur.

8 May I avert the pain of hunger and thirst with showers of food and drink. May I become both drink and food in the intermediate aeons of famine.

9 May I be an inexhaustible treasure for impoverished beings. May I wait upon them with various forms of offering.

10 See, I give up without regret my bodies, my pleasures, and my good acquired in all three times, to accomplish good for every being.

11 Abandonment of all is Enlightenment and Enlightenment is my heart's goal. If I must give up everything, better it be given to sentient beings.

12 I make over this body to all embodied beings to do with as they please. Let them continually beat it, insult it, and splatter it with filth.

13 Let them play with my body; let them be derisive and amuse themselves. I have given this body to them. What point has this concern of mine?

14 Let them have me do whatever brings them pleasure. Let there never be harm to anyone on account of me.

15 Should their mind become angry or displeased on account of me, may even that be the cause of their always achieving every goal.

16 Those who will falsely accuse me, and others who will do me harm, and others still who will degrade me, may they all share in Awakening.

17 I am the protector of the unprotected and the caravan-leader for travellers. I have become the boat, the causeway, and the bridge for those who long to reach the further shore.

18 May I be a light for those in need of light. May I be a bed for those in need of rest. May I be a servant for those in need of service, for all embodied beings.

19 For embodied beings may I be the wish-fulfilling jewel, the pot of plenty, the spell that always works, the potent healing herb, the magical tree that grants every wish, and the milch-cow that supplies all wants.

20 Just as earth and the other elements are profitable in many ways to the immeasurable beings dwelling throughout space,

21 So may I be sustenance of many kinds for the realm of beings throughout space, until all have attained release.

22 In the same way as bygone Sugatas took up the Awakening Mind, in the same way as they progressed in the Bodhisattva training,

23 So too, I myself shall generate the Awakening Mind for the welfare of the world; and just so shall I train in those precepts in due order.

24 The wise one, who has taken up the Awakening Mind with a serene confidence in this way, should continue to encourage his resolve as follows, in order to fulfil his wish:

25 'Today my birth is fruitful. My human life is justified. Today I am born into the family of the Buddha. Now I am the Buddha's son.

26 'So that there may be no blemish upon this spotless family, I must now act as becomes my family.

27 'As a blind man might find a jewel in heaps of rubbish, so too this Awakening Mind has somehow appeared in me.

28 'This is the elixir of life, born to end death in the world. This is the inexhaustible treasure, alleviating poverty in the world.

29 'This is the supreme medicine, curing the sickness of the world, a tree of shelter for weary creatures staggering along the road of existence.

30 'The causeway to cross over bad rebirths, open to all who travel. It is the rising moon of the mind, mitigating the defilements of the world.

31 'It is the brilliant sun, dispelling the mist of ignorance from the world. It is the fresh butter risen up from churning the milk of the true Dharma.

32 'For the caravan of humanity travelling the road of existence, hungry for the enjoyment of happiness, this is a feast of happiness offered as refreshment to all beings who approach.

33 'Today I summon the world to Buddhahood and to worldly happiness meanwhile. In the presence of all the Saviours, may gods, titans, and all rejoice.'

4

VIGILANCE REGARDING THE AWAKENING MIND

'STRIVE with vigilance' were the Buddha's dying words to his disciples, encouraging them to keep going on the spiritual path, reminding them that vigilance is fundamental to progress. 'Vigilance', *apramāda*, is the opposite of 'negligence', 'intoxication', or 'lack of awareness', *pramāda*. In the previous chapter the aspiring Bodhisattva passionately pledges to become everything needful for all beings and proclaims, 'Today I summon the world to Buddhahood and to worldly happiness meanwhile.' After making such a promise he must not neglect those whose happiness and salvation depend on him.

This chapter, then, takes on a more realistic tone: 'At that time I was intoxicated, speaking without realizing my own limitations' (v. 42); 'I have promised to liberate the universe from the defilements, to the limit of space in the ten directions, but even my own self is not freed from the defilements!' (v. 41). He realizes that, unless he goes on to perfect the Bodhisattva training and persists in his efforts, he will not reach the first stage, *bhūmi*, for a long time (v. 11). Yet it is at that stage that he will have sufficient merit to make vows to transform and liberate the universe (see Introduction to Chapter 10).

Having made the promise to liberate all, he cannot turn back. Though it is appropriate to reconsider rash promises, this undertaking is approved by the Buddhas, who know best. Besides, he would be destined for hell, for having failed so many people, and because hell is inevitable anyway if one does not make the best of this fleeting chance to do good. Once in hell there is little hope of having the mental clarity to do good, so dreadful are conditions there. If this rare opportunity is neglected, it may well be lost for ever.

It is characteristic of Indian religious works designed to inspire the aspiring that they use an array of persuasions. Here the greatest persuasion is the threat of the impending miseries of hellish rebirths, a theme which continues throughout the chapter. One is reminded of the enormity of one's responsibilities—not only was the greatest promise possible made, but it was made to an infinitely vast number of living beings. One is shamed: by the embarrassment of breaking an oath taken publicly; by one's repeated inability to benefit from the help offered by the infinite Buddhas who have gone before; by the knowledge that even the lowest castes endure more difficulties just for their own livelihood than one is prepared to undergo for the most important goal of all. There are repeated reminders of the rarity of this opportunity: one must act now. It is no good making sporadic efforts, for one's progress will be exceedingly slow. The reason one is so far from one's goal is that one is defiled by the moral vices, greed, hatred, and delusion. The destructiveness of these defilements is emphasized: they lead to the Avīci hell whose fire destroys even the mighty Mount Meru on touch.

A more positive mood is engendered in the second part of the chapter. Despair is pointless (v. 24), especially when the 'enemies' who bring one to such straits are, ironically, the vices in one's own mind (v. 29) and will be completely destroyed, never to return, if one can just dislodge them from there the once (vv. 45–7). One must show them no mercy, since they are only more dangerous if indulged (v. 33). Besides, they are mere illusion, 'weaklings to be subdued by wisdom's glare' (v. 46). So, one overcomes the nightmarish horror of being unable to escape approaching hell (v. 27), by stirring up the spirit of an impetuous warrior (vv. 36–7, 42–4). Ultimately, one must realize one has no option: following the Buddha's prescription is the one way to be cured of cyclic existence (v. 48).

The aspiring Bodhisattva persuades himself that he must and can fulfil the vows undertaken in the preceding chapter, and this will lead him to begin, in Chapter 5, his training in the six perfections necessary for Buddhahood.

Saito indicates that there are no major differences between the two recensions of this chapter, and that they both consist of 48 verses. The title of this chapter is given as *nairātmya*, 'Selflessness', in the Tun-huang manuscript in the India Office Library, London.

Vigilance regarding the Awakening Mind

1 The son of the Conqueror who has adopted the Awakening Mind with great resolve in this way should, ever tireless, strive hard not to transgress the training.

2 It is proper to reconsider whether or not one should carry out any rash undertaking, or anything not thoroughly thought through, even if one has already promised to do it.

3 But why hang back from what has been thought through by the Buddhas and their sons, who are great in wisdom, and by me, too, as far as I am able?

4 Moreover, after making a promise of this kind, if I were not to fulfil it in practice and broke my word to all these beings, what would be my future birth?

5 It is taught that a man who has only thought about giving in his mind, but does not actually do so, becomes a hungry ghost, even if the gift were only small.

6 How much worse will it be for me, having proclaimed aloud the unsurpassed happiness with great enthusiasm? After breaking my word to the entire world, what would be my future birth?

7 Only the Omniscient One knows the inconceivable course of action which can still liberate people even when they have abandoned the Awakening Mind.

8 Therefore every error of this kind is all the more serious for a Bodhisattva, since when he errs he deprives every being of benefit;

9 And anyone else who hinders his meritorious actions, even momentarily, will undergo unlimited bad rebirths, because he destroys the benefit for living beings.

10 He would certainly be destroyed, destroying the welfare of just one being; how much more so of the embodied beings dwelling throughout the expanse of space?

11 Swinging back and forth like this in cyclic existence, now under the sway of errors, now under the sway of the Awakening Mind, it takes a long time to gain ground.

12 Therefore I must diligently fulfil what I have promised. If I make no effort today I shall sink to lower and lower levels.

13 Innumerable Buddhas have gone seeking out all sentient beings. Through my own fault I was beyond the reach of their healing care.

14 If even today I continue in such a way that I shall repeatedly attain bad rebirths, disease, and death, have limbs cut off, and be cleaved apart,

15 When shall I find such rare circumstances again: the arising of a Tathāgata, faith, the human state itself, the capacity to practise skilful deeds,

16 Health, and this day, with food and freedom from disaster? In a moment life breaks its promise. The body is like an object on loan.

17 The human state is never achieved again by such acts as mine. When the human state is lost there is only evil. How could there be good?

18 If I do not behave skilfully even when I am capable of skilful deeds, what then will I do when stupefied by the sufferings of the lower realms?

19 For one who does not act skilfully and heaps up evil too, even the idea of a good rebirth is lost for hundreds of billions of aeons.

20 That is why the Fortunate One declared that the human state is so hard to attain: as likely as the turtle poking its neck through the hole of a yoke floating on the mighty ocean.

21 Through an act of evil committed in a single instant, an aeon is endured in the Avīci hell. In the light of evil heaped up through time without beginning, what talk can there be of a good rebirth?

22 Yet having experienced that, one is still not released, since, while experiencing it, one begets more evil still.

23 There is no greater waste of time than this, nor is there greater folly: that after attaining such a fleeting opportunity I do not practise skilful deeds.

24 And if I am sensible of this but, confused, sink down in despair, for a long time I shall lament still more, when summoned by Yama's messengers.

25 Long the intolerable roasting of my body in hell-fire. Long the burning of the untrained mind in the flame of self-reproach.

26 Though I have somehow come to a nigh unattainable place of advantage, and though I understand this, still I am led back to those selfsame hells once more.

27 I have no will in this matter, as if bewildered by spells. I do not understand. By what am I perplexed? Who dwells here within me?

28 Enemies such as greed and hate lack hands and feet and other limbs. They are not brave, nor are they wise. How is it they enslave me?

29 Lodged within my own mind, it is me that they strike down, themselves unshaken. Yet I do not boil with rage at this. Oh, such ill-placed forbearance!

30 If every god and human being were my enemy, even they could not deliver me to the fire of the Avīci hell.

31 Once that has taken hold, not even ash is left, even from Mount Meru. In an instant my mighty enemies, the defilements, cast me there.

32 For the long life of all other foes together is not of such length as that of my enemies, the defilements, which is interminably long, without beginning or end.

33 Everyone becomes well-disposed when they are treated with kindness, but when these defilements are honoured they cause suffering all the more.

34 With all this in mind, while such long-standing enemies, the sole cause of the flowing flood of misfortunes, dwell fearlessly within my heart, how can I take pleasure in cyclic existence?

35 If these gaolers of the prison of existence, who are also the executioners of the condemned in hells and like places, remain in the house of my mind, the cage of greed, how can I be happy?

36 For this reason I shall not cast off the burden here, until these enemies are struck down before my eyes. Once their anger has been aroused, people who are inflated with pride do not sleep until their enemy has been slain, even if he caused only a slight offence.

37 In the vanguard of the battle, violently passionate to kill bringers of darkness destined by nature to suffer death, not counting the pain from blows of arrows and spears, they do not turn away until they have achieved this end.

38 What then when I am striving to kill my natural enemies, who are eternal causes of every pain? Today, even if I suffer a hundred afflictions, what reason do I have to feel the misery of despair?

39 Without cause they display the wounds from the enemy on their limbs, as if they were decorations. Why then, when I am striving to fulfil the Great Cause, do I let my sufferings oppress me?

40 Their minds set only on their own livelihood, fishermen, *caṇḍālas*, ploughmen, and the like withstand such distress as extreme heat and cold. Why have I no endurance though it is for the advantage and well-being of the universe?

41 I have promised to liberate the universe from the defilements, to the limit of space in the ten directions, but even my own self is not freed from the defilements!

42 At that time I was intoxicated, speaking without realizing my own limitations. After that I can never turn back from destroying the defilements.

43 I shall be tenacious in this, and wage war sworn to enmity, except against the kind of defilement that comes from murdering the defilements.

44 I do not care if my guts ooze out! Let my head fall off! But never shall I bow down before the enemy, the defilements!

45 Even if banished, an enemy may acquire retinue and support in another country, and return from there with gathered strength. But there is no such resort for this enemy, the defilements.

46 Based in my mind, where might it go once cast out? Where might it stay and work towards my destruction? I make no effort simply because my mind is dull. The defilements are weaklings to be subdued by wisdom's glare.

47 The defilements do not dwell in objects, nor in the collection of the senses, nor in the space in between. There is nowhere else for them to dwell, and yet they churn up the entire universe. This is but illusion! So, heart, free yourself from fear, devote yourself to striving for wisdom. Why, quite needlessly, do you torment yourself in hells?

48 Making a firm resolve in this way, I shall strive to follow the training as it has been taught. How can someone who could be cured by medicine get well if he does not follow the doctor's advice?

5

THE GUARDING OF AWARENESS

IN this chapter Śāntideva begins his exposition of the Bodhisattva's perfections or *pāramitās*, the means whereby the Bodhisattva attains his goal of Awakening for the sake of all beings. The perfections are six in number: generosity, morality, forbearance, vigour, meditative absorption, and understanding or wisdom, and since their relationship is seen as a progressive one, they are invariably expounded in this order. Since Chapter 6 is Śāntideva's exposition of forbearance, we can look to the fifth chapter for his account of generosity and morality. What we find, however, is a fairly summary definition of these two virtues:

> The perfection of generosity is said to result from the mental attitude of relinquishing all that one has to all people, together with the fruit of that act. Therefore the perfection is the mental attitude itself.
>
> Where can fish and other creatures be taken where I might not kill them? Yet when the mental attitude to cease from worldly acts is achieved, that is agreed to be the perfection of morality. (vv. 10–11)

These are followed by a lengthy account of the qualities of mindfulness and awareness.

Śāntideva maintains that the perfection of generosity is a mental state, rather than necessarily giving anything or everything away. He dwells upon generosity in three places: Chapter 2, the offerings; and Chapters 3 and 10, the dedication of all his merit. All three instances have some connection with the Supreme Worship (see Introductions to these chapters). Since he deals with this virtue in such detail there, perhaps he felt it unnecessary to elaborate further here, and therefore offered only a definition. It would be wrong to assume, therefore, because of his summary treatment in this chapter, that he has neglected this virtue. In a similar manner, the perfection of morality is defined as the mental attitude of withdrawing from all worldly actions. Both definitions underline the central importance of the mind, and so Śāntideva concentrates thereafter on exhortation and advice on protecting one's mind. This is confirmed by the parallel chapter in the *Śikṣā Samuccaya*, which is entitled 'Protection of the Person'. The core of this protection is the practice of mindfulness and awareness.

Let my possessions freely perish, my honour, my body and life, and let other good things perish, but never the mind.

I make this salutation with my hands to those who wish to guard their mind. With all your effort, guard both mindfulness and awareness.

Just as a man weak with illness is not fit for any work, so a mind distracted from these two is not fit for any work. (vv. 22–4)

Mindfulness, *smṛti*, and awareness, *samprajanya*, are two important technical terms found in all phases of Buddhist teaching on meditation. Both are linked to 'calming', *śamatha*, and 'insight', *vipaśyanā*, meditation practice (on which see Introduction to Chapter 8 below). It is possible that the terms *smṛti* and *samprajanya* were synonymous in the earliest tradition, but to some extent they have been defined apart by later tradition, doubtless as the need for a more subtle and precise vocabulary for meditation practice became necessary. *Smṛti* is cognate with the verbal root *smṛ*, to remember, and involves an awareness of the body, one's feelings, one's mental states, and of *dharmas*, the fundamental elements of existence (on which see 5.17 note, and Introduction to Chapter 9), with greater stress upon the faculty of memory, and upon continuity and a sense of the individual's purpose (see *Śikṣā Samuccaya*, Bendall and Rouse, 117–20). *Samprajanya*, cognate with the verbal root *samprajñā*, to know accurately or clearly, covers a similar domain, but with an emphasis more on the immediate awareness and assessment of the position, activity, and so on of the body, the mind, and one's situation (see Bendall and Rouse, 120). Both terms feature frequently in canonical scriptures, the *locus classicus* being the *Satipaṭṭhāna Sutta* 'Discourse on the Foundations of Mindfulness' (Rhys Davids 1910, ii. 327 ff., and Horner 1954, i. 70 ff.; both versions of this *sutta* are also translated with commentary by Nyanaponika Thera, 1975).

As we have already noted above, this chapter is the first to show substantial differences between the canonical and Tun-huang recensions. It is also one of two which have received detailed comparative attention, and the results of this were published by Chikō Ishida in 1988. He was able to establish that the canonical recension contains some fifteen verses not present in the Tun-huang recension: 40, 81, 85, 88–98, and 105. We can see that each of these insertions, with the possible exception of the last, interrupts the flow of the argument of the chapter as a whole:

Verse 40 returns, out of context, to the simile of the mind as an elephant, introduced in vv. 2–3. A very similar line, employing some vocabulary in common, occurs in the *Śikṣā Samuccaya*, as the tenth of twelve mindfulnesses given there (pp. 117–18). Since the following statement in both texts concerns watching the state of one's mind, it may be that the simile in verse 40 was introduced into the *Bodhicaryāvatāra* by association with its context in the *Śikṣā Samuccaya*.

Verse 81, the next insertion in the canonical version, once again is out of context. We have not been able to identify its source.

Verses 85 and 88–98 incorporate a number of rules taken from the monastic rule book, the *prātimokṣa*. The *prātimokṣa* lists all the regulations enjoined upon the members of the monastic community. As such it is therefore the one piece of scripture which every Buddhist monk should know by heart, not least because it is an integral part of the monastic ritual cycle for the monks to gather on the full moon day of each month, and to recite together this rule book. Individuals would then have the opportunity to confess any lapses upon their part, or indeed, to have lapses brought to their attention. This institution, together with the text of the *prātimokṣa*, is attributed to the instigation of the Buddha himself. However, with the passage of time, and under the pressures of geographical dispersal and even schism, there arose a number of distinct *prātimokṣa* traditions, preserved and observed by mutually exclusive ordination lineages. The most easily accessible of these is that of the Theravāda school of South-East Asia, but the texts of those of the Sarvāstivāda, Mūla-Sarvāstivāda, and Mahāsaṅghika schools have been discovered in ancient manuscripts. Those of some other schools, such as the Dharmaguptakas, survive only in translation into other languages, such as Chinese. Not all *prātimokṣas* have necessarily survived.

We have not been able to identify every rule mentioned, nor the particular *prātimokṣa* from which, as a whole, they are drawn. A number of them are given in the *Śikṣā Samuccaya*, drawing from various scriptures, and it is possible that they were introduced from that source because Śāntideva included them in his exposition of the general theme of this chapter in the *Śikṣā Samuccaya*. (Individual instances are mentioned in the notes.) This reference to the monastic rules, directly or indirectly attributable to Śāntideva, seems the least accessible part of this chapter to the non-monastic reader; even more so when one realizes that they are drawn from the section of rules concerned entirely with etiquette, and hence the farthest removed from any issues of morality. Yet, although Śāntideva uses the terms of the monastic discipline, he is not merely quoting rules which must be obeyed mechanically. By emphasizing that this code of discipline is a means of developing mindfulness, in a sense he is bringing these rules to life, both for the monk, for whom they may have become banal from familiarity, and for the layman who has no obligation to observe them. By bringing out their character as a means to a desired end, the guarding of the mind, Śāntideva reveals how the monastic life, as defined by such rules, was solely designed to facilitate the cultivation of particular mental states, and in this way implies the primacy of practice and attainment over and above mere clerical hierarchy and formalism.

Verse 105, recommending the study of the *Śikṣā Samuccaya*, could well have been supplied by the same hand which appears to have incorporated so much of the text of that work into the *Bodhicaryāvatāra*.

Although present in the Tun-huang version, verses 55 and 57 are also given in the *Śikṣā Samuccaya*, but consecutively and with a slight variant in the first verse. Verse 74 also appears in that text, with slight variants.

The Guarding of Awareness

1 One who wishes to guard his training must scrupulously guard his mind. It is impossible to guard one's training without guarding the wandering mind.

2 Rutting elephants roaming wild do not cause as much devastation in this world as the roaming elephant, the mind, let free, creates in Avīci and other hells.

3 But if the roaming elephant, the mind, is tethered on every side by the cord of mindfulness, every danger subsides, complete prosperity ensues.

4 So too tigers, lions, elephants, bears, serpents, and all malign beings, and all the guards of hell, ogresses, demons,

5 All these are bound through the binding of a single mind, and through the taming of a single mind, all are tamed,

6 Since all fears and incomparable sufferings arise from the mind alone. So it was taught by the Teacher of Reality.

7 Who fashioned the weapons in hell so industriously? Who the pavement of scalding iron? And who sired those sirens?

8 Every single thing arises from the evil mind, sang the Sage. So there is nothing dangerous in the three worlds other than the mind.

9 If the perfection of generosity consists in making the universe free from poverty, how can previous Protectors have acquired it, when the world is still poor, even today?

10 The perfection of generosity is said to result from the mental attitude of relinquishing all that one has to all people, together with the fruit of that act. Therefore the perfection is the mental attitude itself.

11 Where can fish and other creatures be taken where I might not kill them? Yet when the mental attitude to cease from

worldly acts is achieved, that is agreed to be the perfection of morality.

12 How many wicked people, as unending as the sky, can I kill? But when the mental attitude of anger is slain, slain is every enemy.

13 Where is there hide to cover the whole world? The wide world can be covered with hide enough for a pair of shoes alone.

14 In the same way, since I cannot control external events, I will control my own mind. What concern is it of mine whether other things are controlled?

15 Even with the help of body and speech, no fruit comes from a dull mind that bears comparison with that from a sharp mind on its own, such as reaching the state of the Brahmā gods.

16 The Omniscient One declared that all recitation and austerity, even though performed over a long time, is completely useless if the mind is on something else or is dull.

17 Those who have not developed this mind, which is recondite and contains the whole sum of dharmas, wander the compass in vain trying to attain happiness and destroy suffering.

18 Therefore I should manage and guard my mind well. If I let go of the vow to guard my mind, what will become of my many other vows?

19 In the same way that someone in the midst of a rough crowd guards a wound with great care, so in the midst of bad company should one always guard the wound that is the mind.

20 Fearing slight pain from a wound, I guard the wound with great care. Why not the wound that is the mind, in fear of the blows from the crushing mountains of hell?

21 The resolute aspirant who maintains this attitude, even when moving in bad company, even amongst young and wanton women, is not broken.

22 Let my possessions freely perish, my honour, my body and life, and let other good things perish, but never the mind.

23 I make this salutation with my hands to those who wish to guard their mind. With all your effort, guard both mindfulness and awareness.

24 Just as a man weak with illness is not fit for any work, so a mind distracted from these two is not fit for any work.

25 What is heard, reflected upon, or cultivated in meditation, like water in a leaky jar, does not stay in the memory of a mind which lacks awareness.

26 Many, though learned, possessing faith, and though absorbed in effort, are befouled by offences due to the fault of lacking awareness.

27 Though they have amassed meritorious deeds, they end up in an evil realm, plundered by the thief, lack of awareness, who comes after the theft of mindfulness.

28 This band of robbers, the defilements, seeks out a point of access. When it has found one, it plunders and destroys life in a good realm.

29 Therefore mindfulness should never be taken from the door to the mind, and, if it does go, it should be reinstated, remembering the torment of hell.

30 Mindfulness comes easily to those fortunate people who practise wholeheartedly, through the instruction of their preceptor, because they live with their teacher, and out of fear.

31 The Buddhas and Bodhisattvas have unobstructed vision in all directions. Every single thing is before them. Before them I stand.

32 Meditating thus, one should remain possessed of shame, respect, and fear. One should recollect the Buddhas in this way at every moment.

33 Awareness comes and, once come, does not go again, if mindfulness remains at the door to the mind in order to act as guard.

34 At first then, I should continually generate such a state of mind as this: I should act at all times as if lacking senses, like a block of wood.

35 One should never cast the eyes to and fro for no purpose. The gaze should be bent low as if continually absorbed in meditation.

36 However, one might occasionally look to the horizon in order to rest the eyes, and if one notices someone within one's field of vision, one should look up to greet them.

37 In order to spot danger on the road and so forth, one may look to the four quarters for a moment. Standing at ease, one may look to the distance, looking behind only after turning right round.

38 One should go ahead or turn back only after looking forward or behind. Likewise, in all situations one should proceed only after ascertaining what is to be done.

39 Having once initiated an action with the intention of keeping one's body in a particular position, thereafter one should from time to time observe how the body is positioned.

40 In this way the rutting elephant, the mind, should be watched with all one's effort, so that, bound to the great post of reflection on the Dharma, it does not break loose.

41 One should so observe the mind, thinking 'Where is mine wandering to?', as never to abandon the responsibility of concentration, even for a moment.

42 If one is not able to do so, in connection with some danger or elation, then one should act at will. For it is taught that the code of moral conduct may be overlooked at a time of giving.

43 One should think of nothing else other than that which one has decided to undertake, with heart fully involved there, until it is completed.

44 For in this way everything is done well. Otherwise neither this thing nor the other would be. Moreover, in that case, the defilement, lack of awareness, would certainly increase as well.

45 One should quell the eagerness that arises for the various kinds of idle chat that often take place, and for all objects of curiosity.

46 Mindful of the teaching of the Tathāgata, fearful, one should abandon immediately any such actions as breaking up clods of earth, ripping grass, and drawing lines in the earth without any purpose.

47 When one wishes to move or to speak, first one should examine one's own mind, and then act appropriately and with self-possession.

48 When one notices that one's own mind is attracted or repelled, one should neither act nor speak, but remain like a block of wood.

49 When the mind is inflated or derisive, full of arrogance and vanity, exceedingly jocose, evasive, or deceiving,

50 When, seeming to advance oneself, it is only deprecating others, contemptuous and scornful, one should remain like a block of wood.

51 My mind seeks acquisitions, reverence, or renown, or again wants an audience and attention. Therefore I remain like a block of wood.

52 My mind longs to hold forth, averse to the good of others, seeking my own advantage, longing only for a congregation. Therefore I remain like a block of wood.

53 It is intolerant, idle, cowardly, impudent, also foul-mouthed, and biased in my own favour. Therefore I remain like a block of wood.

54 Noticing in this way that his mind is defiled or engaged in a fruitless activity, the hero should always firmly curb it with the antidote to that condition.

55 Determined, full of serene confidence, steady, full of application and respect, with humility and timidity, calm, eager to help others,

56 Unwearied by the mutually conflicting desires of the puerile, full of pity, knowing that they are like this as a result of the arising of defilement,

57 See, always in blameless matters I shall keep my mind at the will of myself and other beings, free from delusions, like an illusion!

58 At every moment continuously mindful that it has taken so long to gain the best of opportunities, this is how I shall keep my mind, as unshakeable as Mount Sumeru.

59 Why else does the body offer no resistance when dragged this way and that by vultures greedy for flesh?

60 Why, mind, do you protect this carcass, identifying with it? If it is really separate from you, then what loss is its decay to you?

61 O Fool! You do not identify with a wooden doll even when it is pure. So why do you guard this festering contraption made of filth?

62 First, just in your mind, pull apart this bag of skin. With the knife of wisdom loosen the flesh from the cage of bones.

63 Cracking open the bones, too, look at the marrow within. Work out for yourself what essence is there.

64 Searching hard like this, you have found no essence here. Now explain why it is that you still continue to guard the body.

65 You will not eat it, unclean as it is, nor drink the blood, nor suck out the entrails. What will you do with your body?

66 Of course it is right to protect this wretched body, but as food for vultures and jackals, or as the implement of action for the benefit of humankind.

67 Even as you protect it so, ruthless death will snatch away your body and give it to the vultures. Then what will you do?

68 You do not give clothes and such to a servant if you think he is not going to stay. The body will eat and then go. Why do you make the outlay?

69 On that account, having given the body its wages, Mind, now look to your own needs, for a labourer does not receive all of the wealth he creates.

70 Apply to the body the notion of a ship, on account of the way it comes and goes. At your own command, set the body on course to fulfil the needs of beings.

71 One's own nature mastered in this way, one should always have a smiling face. One should give up frowning and grimacing, be the first to speak, a friend to the universe.

72 One should not throw down stools and other furniture violently with a crash, nor should one pound on doors. One should always delight in silence.

73 The crane, the cat, or the thief achieves his intended goal by moving quietly and gently. The aspirant should move in such a way at all times.

74 One should accept respectfully the advice of those who are able to direct others, who offer unsolicited aid. One should be the pupil of everyone all the time.

75 One should express one's appreciation of all that is well said. When one sees someone doing something meritorious, one should encourage them with praises.

76 One should speak of others' virtues in their absence, and repeat them with pleasure, and when one's own praise is spoken, one should reflect on that person's recognition of virtue.

77 Surely everything is undertaken for the sake of satisfaction, and yet even with money that is hard to find. Therefore I

shall enjoy the pleasure of finding satisfaction in the virtues acquired by others through their hard work.

78 I lose nothing in this world and gain great bliss in the next, whereas animosities lead to the misery of enmity and in the next world great suffering.

79 One should speak confident, measured words, clear in meaning, delighting the mind, pleasing to the ear, soft and slow, and stemming from compassion.

80 One should always look at people directly, as if drinking them in with the eye: depending upon them alone, Buddhahood will be mine.

81 Great good arises from continuous devotion towards the fertile fields that are the Virtuous and our benefactors, and from the application of an antidote in the case of one who suffers.

82 One should be able and energetic, at all times acting upon one's own initiative. In all actions one should not leave any work to another.

83 Each of the perfections, beginning with generosity, is more excellent than its predecessor. One should not neglect a higher one for the sake of a lower, unless because of a fixed rule of conduct.

84 Realizing this, one should always be striving for others' well-being. Even what is proscribed is permitted for a compassionate person who sees it will be of benefit.

85 One should consume in moderation and share with those in difficulty, the helpless, and those observing the vows, and, apart from one's three robes, give away everything.

86 The body serves the True Dharma. One should not harm it for some inferior reason. For it is the only way that one can quickly fulfil the hopes of living beings.

87 Therefore one should not relinquish one's life for someone whose disposition to compassion is not as pure. But for

someone whose disposition is comparable, one should relinquish it. That way, there is no overall loss.

88–9 One should not speak about the Dharma, which is profound and magnificent, to someone who is disrespectful, who, when healthy, wears a turban on his head, or who holds an umbrella, stick or knife, or whose head is veiled; nor to those who are inadequate, or to women without a man present. To the lesser and higher teachings one should show equal respect.

90 One should not restrict someone who is worthy of the higher teaching to the lesser teaching, nor, disregarding the matter of good conduct, beguile them with the Scriptures and spells.

91 It is not desirable to spit out tooth-cleaning sticks and phlegm in public, and it is also forbidden to urinate and so forth on land or into water that is usable.

92 One should not eat with a mouth overfull, noisily, nor with mouth wide open. One should not sit with a leg hanging down, likewise one should not rub both arms at the same time.

93 One should not travel with another's wife if unaccompanied, nor lie down with her, nor sit with her. One should notice and ask about what displeases people and avoid it all.

94 One should not indicate with a finger something that is to be done, but respectfully with the whole of the right hand. One should also point out the road in this way.

95 One should not throw up one's arms and shout at anyone when worked up over some trifle, but instead snap the fingers or the like. Otherwise one would be showing lack of restraint.

96 One should lie down to rest in the preferred direction, in the position in which the Protector passed away. Full of awareness, one should get up promptly, before one is told to do so without fail.

97 The conduct of the Bodhisattvas has been described as immeasurable. In the first place it is essential to engage in conduct that purifies the mind.

98 Three times, day and night, one should recite the *Triskandha*, so that, through recourse to the Conquerors and the Bodhisattvas, one's remaining transgressions cease.

99 One should apply oneself industriously to the trainings appropriate to the various situations in which one finds oneself, whether there at will, or subject to another.

100 For there is nothing from which the sons of the Conqueror cannot learn. There is nothing which is not an act of merit for the good person who conducts himself in this way.

101 One should do nothing other than what is either directly or indirectly of benefit to living beings, and for the benefit of living beings alone one should dedicate everything to Awakening.

102 Never, even at the cost of one's life, should one forsake a spiritual friend who upholds the Bodhisattva vow and is skilled in the meaning of the Mahāyāna.

103 One should also practise towards teachers the correct conduct according to the *Śrīsambhava-vimokṣa*. Both this and other things taught by the Buddha should be understood from the recitation of the Scriptures.

104 The principles of the training are found in the Scriptures. Therefore one should recite the Scriptures, and one should study the fundamental transgressions in the *Ākāśagarbha Sūtra*.

105 The *Compendium of the Training*, the *Śikṣā Samuccaya*, should definitely be looked at repeatedly, since correct conduct is explained there in some detail.

106 Alternatively, one should just look at it briefly, and then with great care at the companion *Compendium of Scriptures*, the *Sūtra Samuccaya*, compiled by the noble Nāgārjuna.

107 One should look in those works at the training, that from which one is prohibited and that which is enjoined, and one should practise it thoroughly in order to guard the mind in the world.

108 In brief, this alone is the definition of awareness: the observation at every moment of the state of one's body and one's mind.

109 I shall express this by means of my body, for what use would there be in the expression of words? For someone who is sick what use could there be in the mere expression of medical knowledge?

6
THE PERFECTION OF FORBEARANCE

FROM this point onwards in the *Bodhicaryāvatāra* Śāntideva allots a complete chapter to each remaining perfection, and in the sixth chapter we come to his treatment of the perfection of forbearance, *kṣānti-pāramitā*.

There is an underlying structure to the chapter, and Śāntideva's argument follows a number of distinct phases. The core of the chapter consists of an exposition of forbearance, *kṣānti*, in three aspects or applications. This is indicated in the *Śikṣā Samuccaya*, where Śāntideva quotes the *Dharmasaṃgīti Sūtra* to the effect that forbearance is threefold in character: forbearance towards the endurance of suffering (vv. 11–21); forbearance as a result of reflection upon the teaching (vv. 22–32); and forbearance of the endurance of injuries from others (vv. 33–75). However, Śāntideva's account of the threefold character of forbearance is set within a larger framework: How does one cope with anger? And why should one avoid it?

Much of his discussion of forbearance revolves around the inappropriateness of anger, for in his view anger and forbearance are to be paired as opposites, as one might an ailment and its antidote. As he points out in the first verse, all the good of all the actions so far described can be destroyed by anger. He is very concerned to make clear the dangers of hatred and the value of patience as its antidote. If the terms of his discussion seem extreme, then perhaps this juxtaposition reflects some insight into human nature on his part. Be this as it may, the first stage of his discussion of forbearance deals with forbearance towards suffering, particularly with physical endurance. A natural extension of this practice is the attempt to understand how it is that one comes to suffer. This leads to the second stage of his exposition, forbearance as a result of reflecting upon the teaching. This takes the form of a discussion of causality, which appears in vv. 22–33. It is immediately apparent, even to a reader unversed in Classical Indian philosophy, that the writer is dealing here with technical arguments, which cannot be understood without some background knowledge. More, much more, of this type of material appears in Chapter 9, which deals with the perfection of understanding, but something should be said here so as to clarify the lines of his argument.

Śāntideva's main concern is to explain, in fact prove (albeit briefly), that all phenomena, including those things which give pain, arise upon conditions. This is of course the main axiom of Buddhism, the crucial insight by which Enlightenment might be defined. Moreover it is used here as the main axiom of Śāntideva's discussion of forbearance, for as he seeks to prove in the following verse, if the actions of people and objects are determined by a network of other conditions, how can any individual person or object be held to blame for the consequence, and, in that light, how can anger be justified?

His argument in these crucial verses is, in brief, as follows:

22–3 Other beings are motivated as impersonally as are illnesses by conditions outside of themselves.
24 We know from experience that we do not decide to become angry, but find ourselves becoming so. This is a reflection of the fact that this anger is conditioned by factors other than our will.
25 Nothing possesses the power of self-willed generation—i.e. all things are conditioned by other, external factors.
26 Nor can we say that the totality of conditions possesses such independent self-willed existence. Therefore, no suffering that we experience is the result of the volition of a discrete micro- or macro-cosmic entity.
27–8 Addressing the fundamental existents of the Sāṃkhya school, Śāntideva points out that the *puruṣa (ātman*, or self) and *prākṛti*, the primal substance (or physical universe in the broadest sense), which are regarded as ultimates because in themselves uncaused, are illogical concepts—something uncaused obviously does not function within the realm of causality, and could be responsible neither for our sufferings, nor for the existence of the phenomenal world, as maintained by the Sāṃkhya.
29–30 Turning to the Vaiśeṣika concept of an ultimately real and permanent self, Śāntideva argues that this too is illogical. As

before, something that is permanent does not operate upon the level of causality. Furthermore, something permanent cannot bring about changes, because to be permanent surely implies being unchanging, yet to meet with other factors and interact with them requires change.

31–3 Therefore we can now appreciate that everything is conditioned by other factors, and thereby is not responsible for its functioning, rather like a magical illusion. Knowing this reality of conditionality, we are free to give rise to conditions now, which in the future will allow us to overcome suffering. Furthermore, we are also able to understand and cope with the provocative behaviour of other people.

These general matters aside, the most ubiquitous object of frustration and anger for most people most of the time is other people, which brings us to the third stage of Śāntideva's exposition of forbearance. In a Buddhist context, especially in a Mahāyāna context, the eschewing of anger must surely seem so fundamental that it hardly needs comment. Yet when we think about it, righteous indignation and the desire for retaliation appear as frequently, if not more so, in a religious context as in any other, and for this reason it is appropriate to note Śāntideva's express concern to deny a toehold for these emotions, both in relation to the topical issue of blasphemy (v. 64), for which Buddhism has no equivalent, and in connection with the perceived inhibition of one's own capacity to practise one's religion (v. 102 ff.).

Undoubtedly the primary reason for the length of Śāntideva's discourse upon the subject of forbearance is the fact that its opposite, anger, is that emotion which most clearly undermines the performance of the Bodhisattva's vow to save all beings. More radically than any other fault, anger alienates one from the very beings whom one has undertaken to save. That this was recognized, and an object of deep concern, in Mahāyāna circles is evinced by an early but important and influential Mahāyāna *sūtra*, the *Upāli-paripṛcchā*, in which comparison is made of the relative danger to one's fulfilment of the Bodhisattva aspiration in faults based in greed and faults based in hatred. Judgement comes down firmly in favour of greed as the lesser of the two failings, for at the very least, when motivated by this, one is left with the possibility of being drawn to other beings, whereas hatred consists in their rejection.

> If while practising the Mahāyāna a Bodhisattva continues to break precepts out of desire for kalpas as numerous as the sands of the Ganges, his offence is still minor. If a Bodhisattva breaks precepts out of hatred, even just once, his offence is very serious. Why? Because a Bodhisattva who breaks precepts out of desire [still] holds sentient beings in his embrace, whereas a Bodhisattva who breaks precepts out of hatred forsakes beings altogether. . . . if he breaks precepts out of hatred, it is a grave offense, a gross fault, a serious, degenerate act, which causes tremendous hindrances to the Buddha-Dharma. (*Upāli-pariprcchā Sūtra*, Chang 1983, 270)

Having dealt with the immediate difficulty of interaction with others, namely accepting injuries that they cause, Śāntideva broadens his discussion so as to address the need to overcome envy of one's fellows—in this case particularly fellow monks (vv. 76–98). He even goes so far as to argue that one's opponents offer one the opportunity to develop this necessary virtue (vv. 99–108) and that for this reason they should be honoured on a par with the Buddhas themselves (vv. 109–18). He concludes this chapter with a lengthy and unacknowledged quotation of material in support of this view drawn from the *Tathāgataguhya Sūtra* (vv. 119–34).

No detailed comparative analysis of this chapter in the two recensions has been made, although Saito indicates that the canonical recension has seven more verses than that from Tun-huang. We do know, however, that the following verses are shared with the *Śikṣā Samuccaya*: 94, 95a, 115, and 119–34. The following verses have partial correspondences in the same text: 10a, 14a, and 19b (the letters 'a' and 'b' refer to the first and second halves of a verse respectively).

There remain a few observations to be made upon more miscellaneous matters. The first of these concerns the terminology that Śāntideva employs in this chapter. The chapter deals with what is known as the perfection of forbearance, *kṣānti-pāramitā*, as it is usually designated. It comes as a surprise, therefore, to find that Śāntideva does not refer to *kṣānti-pāramitā* even once, and further that, out of the sixteen times he explicitly mentions the virtue of forbearance, on twelve occasions the word he chooses to use is *kṣamā*, rather than *kṣānti*. One wonders whether this usage reflects what has come to be understood as a certain ambiguity of denotation with the latter term. It appears that, despite the traditional association of the term *kṣānti* with the verbal root *kṣam*, 'to be patient, to endure, etc.' from which *kṣamā* itself is derived, the term *kṣānti* probably results from an incorrect 'back-formation' of a Prakrit term, *khanti*, into Sanskrit. This not uncommon phenomenon meant that the connotations of the root *kṣam* were thereby mingled with those of the true root of *khanti*, *kham*, meaning 'to be pleased, to be willing to', with the result that one frequently finds *kṣānti* employed in contexts where connotations of willingness seem more appropriate than those of forbearance. The term *kṣamā*, however, remains firmly unambiguous, and perhaps recommended itself to the author for this reason. In order to distinguish (perhaps unnecessarily) between these two terms when they appear in the text, we have adopted 'forbearance' as a translation of *kṣānti*, and 'patience' for *kṣamā*.

One example of word-play which has just about survived 'the great leap' between languages occurs in v. 44, where Śāntideva exploits the primary sense of the root *kup*, to swell or heave with anger, etc., to liken the human body to a swollen boil!

The Perfection of Forbearance

1 This worship of the Sugatas, generosity, and good conduct performed throughout thousands of aeons—hatred destroys it all.

2 There is no evil equal to hatred, and no spiritual practice equal to forbearance. Therefore one should develop forbearance by various means, with great effort.

3 One's mind finds no peace, neither enjoys pleasure or delight, nor goes to sleep, nor feels secure while the dart of hatred is stuck in the heart.

4 Those whom one honours with wealth and respect, and also one's dependents, even they long to destroy the master who is disfigured by hatred.

5 Even friends shrink from him. He gives, but is not honoured. In short, there is no sense in which someone prone to anger is well off.

6 The person who realizes that hatred is an enemy, since it creates such sufferings as these, and who persistently strikes it down, is happy in this world and the next.

7 Consuming the food of dejection prepared by doing the undesirable and thwarting the desirable, biting hatred strikes me down.

8 Therefore I shall destroy the food of this deceiver, since this hatred has no purpose other than my murder.

9 I must not disturb the feeling of sympathetic joy, even at the arrival of something extremely unwelcome. There is nothing desirable in the state of dejection; on the contrary, the skilful is neglected.

10 If there is a solution, then what is the point of dejection? What is the point of dejection if there is no solution?

11 Suffering, humiliation, harsh words, and disgrace: these we desire neither for ourselves nor our loved ones; but for our enemies it is the reverse.

12 Happiness is scarce. Suffering persists with no effort; but only through suffering is there escape. Therefore, mind, be strong!

13 In Karṇāṭa the devotees of Durgā willingly endure to no purpose the pain of burns, cuts, and worse. Why then am I a coward when my goal is liberation?

14 There is nothing which remains difficult if it is practised. So, through practice with minor discomforts, even major discomfort becomes bearable.

15 The irritation of bugs, gnats, and mosquitoes, of hunger and thirst, and discomfort such as an enormous itch: why do you not see them as insignificant?

16 Cold, heat, rain and wind, journeying and sickness, imprisonment and beatings: one should not be too squeamish about them. Otherwise the distress becomes worse.

17 Their own blood for some is valour's boon;
While others' for others produces a swoon.

18 This comes from the bravery or cowardice of the mind. Therefore one should become invincible to suffering, and overpower discomfort.

19 Not even in suffering should a wise person allow his serene confidence of mind to be disturbed, for the battle is with the defilements, and in warfare pain is easily won.

20 Those who conquer the enemy taking the blows of their adversary on the chest, they are the triumphant heroes, while the rest kill what is already dead.

21 The virtue of suffering has no rival, since, from the shock it causes, intoxication falls away and there arises compassion for those in cyclic existence, fear of evil, and a longing for the Conqueror.

22 I feel no anger towards bile and the like, even though they cause intense suffering. Why am I angry with the sentient? They too have reasons for their anger.

23 As this sharp pain wells up, though unsought for, so, though unsought for, wrath wells up against one's will.

24 A person does not get angry at will, having decided 'I shall get angry', nor does anger well up after deciding 'I shall well up'.

25 Whatever transgressions and evil deeds of various kinds there are, all arise through the power of conditioning factors, while there is nothing that arises independently.

26 Neither does the assemblage of conditioning factors have the thought, 'I shall produce'; nor does what is produced have the thought, 'I am produced'.

27 The much-sought-for 'primal matter', or the imagined 'Self', even that does not come into being after deciding 'I shall become'.

28 Since what has not arisen does not exist, who would then form the wish to come into existence? And since it would be occupied with its sphere of action it cannot attempt to cease to exist either.

29 If the Self is eternal and without thought processes, then it is evidently inactive, like space. Even in contact with other conditioning factors, what activity can there be of something which is unchanging?

30 What part does something play in an action if, at the time of the action, it remains exactly as it was prior to it? If the relationship is that the action is part of it, then which of the two is the cause of the other?

31 In this way everything is dependent upon something else. Even that thing upon which each is dependent is not independent. Since, like a magical display, phenomena do not initiate activity, at what does one get angry like this?

32 If it is argued that to resist anger is inappropriate, for 'who is it that resists what?', our view is that it is appropriate: since there is dependent origination there can be cessation of suffering.

33 Therefore, even if one sees a friend or an enemy behaving badly, one can reflect that there are specific conditioning factors that determine this, and thereby remain happy.

34 Were all embodied beings to have their wish fulfilled, no one would suffer. No one wishes for suffering.

35 People cause themselves torment, with thorns and other instruments in a state of intoxication, by refusing food and the like out of anger, and with things that they wish to obtain, such as unattainable women.

36 Some people kill themselves, by hanging themselves, by throwing themselves off cliffs, by taking poison or other unwholesome substances, and by conduct that is devoid of merit.

37 When, under the power of the defilements in this way, they injure even their own dear selves, how could they have a care for the persons of other people?

38 When, driven insane by their defilements, they resort to killing themselves, how is it that not only have you no pity but you become angry?

39 If it is their very nature to cause others distress, my anger towards those fools is as inappropriate as it would be towards fire for its nature to burn.

40 In fact, this fault is adventitious. Beings are by nature pleasant. So anger towards them is as inappropriate as it would be towards the sky if full of acrid smoke.

41 If, disregarding the principal cause, such as a stick or other weapon, I become angry with the person who impels it, he too is impelled by hatred. It is better that I hate that hatred.

42 Previously, I too caused just such pain to living beings. Therefore this is just what I deserve, I who have caused distress to other beings.

43 His the knife, and mine the body—the twofold cause of suffering. He has grasped the knife, I my body. At which is there anger?

44 Blinded by craving I have grasped this boil in the likeness of a human figure, which cannot bear to be touched. In that case, when there is pain, at which is there anger?

45 I do not wish for suffering. Being a simpleton, I do wish for the cause of suffering. When suffering has arisen through my own wrongdoing, how can I become angry with someone else?

46 Just as the infernal forest of razor leaves, just as the winged creatures from hell are really brought into being by my actions, so is this. At which is there anger?

47 Those who injure me are really impelled by my actions. For this they will go to the realms of hell. Surely it is they who are harmed by me?

48 On account of them, because I am patient, my evil is considerably decreased. While on account of me they experience the long-lasting agonies of hell.

49 Really it is I who am harmful to them, and they who aid me! So why, slippery mind, do you turn it the wrong way round and become angry?

50 If I am not to go to the realms of hell, I must possess the virtue of determination. If I protect myself, what in that case is the effect on them?

51 If I did retaliate, they would not be protected and I would fail in my practice, with the result that those in torment would be lost.

52 Since it lacks physical form, the mind can never be harmed by anything, but because it clings to the body it is oppressed by the body's suffering.

53 'Humiliation, harsh speech, and disgrace', this collection does not oppress the body. Why then, mind, do you get angry?

54 Will the disfavour that others show me devour me, here or in another birth, that I avoid it so?

55 It may be that I avoid it because it gets in the way of my material gain, but that will be lost in this life alone, whereas my evil will certainly persist.

56 Better that I die right now than have a long life lived improperly, since, even if I remain here for a long time, the same pain of death awaits me.

57 In a dream one person enjoys one hundred years of happiness and then awakes, while another awakes after being happy for just a moment.

58 Surely the happiness of both ceases once they have awakened. That is what it is like at the time of death for the one who lives long and for the one whose life is short.

59 And though I acquire many possessions, though I enjoy many pleasures over a long time, I shall go empty-handed and naked, like someone who has been robbed.

60 Suppose I destroy evil and perform good while living off my gains? There is no doubt but that someone who grows angry on account of gain acquires evil and destroys good.

61 If that for which I live comes to nothing, what is the point of living, performing only unlovely deeds?

62 If you argue that your dislike of one who speaks ill of you is because he is harming living beings, why then do you feel no anger when he defames others in the same way?

63 You tolerate those showing disfavour when others are the subject of it, but you show no tolerance towards someone speaking ill of you when he is subject to the arising of defilements.

64 And my hatred towards those who damage sacred images and *stūpas* or who abuse the true teaching is inappropriate, since the Buddhas and Bodhisattvas are not distressed.

65 When people harm one's teachers, relatives, and others dear to us, one should, as above, regard it as arising on the basis of conditioning factors and refrain from anger towards them.

66 Whether the cause possesses consciousness or not, distress is inevitable for embodied beings. That distress appears in what is conscious. Tolerate that pain therefore.

67 Some commit offences out of delusion. Others, deluded, grow angry. Who among them should we say is free from blame, or who should we say is guilty?

68 Why did you behave before in such a way that others now trouble you in this way? Everybody is subject to the force of prior actions. Who am I to change this?

69 But realizing this I shall make the effort to perform good actions in such a way that everyone will develop an attitude of friendship, each towards the other.

70 When a house is burning down and the fire has spread towards the next house, any grass or such in which it might spread is dragged off and taken away.

71 So, when the mind is catching alight with the fire of hatred as a result of contact with something, it must be cast aside immediately for fear that one's body of merit might go up in flames.

72 If a man condemned to death has his hand cut off and is spared, is it not good? If through human sufferings one is spared from hell, is it not good?

73 If even this small measure of suffering cannot be tolerated now, then why is anger, the cause of torment in hell, not restrained?

74 In this very same way, on account of anger, I have been placed in hells thousands of times, and I have benefited neither myself nor others.

75 But this suffering is not of that kind, and it will produce great benefit. Delight is the only appropriate response to suffering which takes away the suffering of the universe.

76 If others take pleasure and joy in praising the strength of someone's virtues, why, mind, do you not similarly rejoice in praising it?

77 Such pleasure from your rejoicing is a blameless source of pleasure, not prohibited by the virtuous, attractive to others in the highest degree.

78 What if you do not like it because it is a pleasure only for him? If you were to stop giving wages and the like, both visible and unseen benefit would be lost.

79 When your own virtues are being praised, you want others to be pleased as well. When the virtues of others are being praised, you do not even want to be pleased yourself.

80 After arousing the Awakening Mind out of the desire for the happiness of every being, why are you angry at them now that they have found happiness for themselves?

81 You desire Buddhahood, which is worthy of worship throughout the three worlds, expressly for living beings. Why do you burn inside on seeing them have some slight honour?

82 The person who nourishes someone whom you should nourish is really giving to you. On finding him supporting your family, you do not rejoice, you become irate!

83 What does the person who wishes Awakening upon living beings not wish for them? How can one who is angry at the good fortune of others possess the Awakening Mind?

84 If he had not received that gift it would have remained in the donor's house. In any case it is not yours, so what matters it whether it was given or not?

85 What! Have him suppress acts of merit, and those who are faithful, and even his own virtues? Let him not accept when he is being given donations? Tell, with what are you not angry?

86 Not only do you not grieve at the evil you yourself have done, you seek to compete with others who have performed acts of merit.

87 Suppose something unpleasant does befall your rival. Would your satisfaction make it happen again? It will not happen without a cause, merely by your wishing it.

88 If your wish was fulfilled, what pleasure would there be for you in his suffering? But even were there some advantage in this, what disadvantage would ensue!

89 For this is the horrific hook cast by the anglers, the defilements, from whom you will be bought by the warders of hell and stewed in cauldrons.

90 Praise, good repute, and honour lead neither to merit nor long life, are no advantage to strength or to freedom from disease, nor do they bring me physical pleasure.

91 And this is the kind of thing that would benefit the wise person who knows what is best for himself. One desiring pleasure for the mind could resort to drunkenness, gambling, and the other vices.

92 For the benefit of renown they deprive themselves of benefit. They even kill themselves. Are words fit for food? In death who feels their pleasure?

93 Like a child that howls a wail of distress when his sandcastle is broken, so my own mind appears to me at the loss of praise or renown.

94 Because it lacks consciousness, I must admit that a word cannot praise me. Undoubtedly, the cause of my delight is that another is delighted with me.

95 But what does it matter to me whether another's delight is in me or someone else? His alone is the pleasure of that delight. Not even a trifling part of it is mine.

96 If I take pleasure in his pleasure, let me take it in every single case. Why do I take no pleasure in people who are made happy through their faith in another?

97 Therefore, it is because I am praised that delight is produced in me. In this case, too, because of such absurdity, it is simply the behaviour of a child.

98 Praise and so on give me security. They destroy my sense of urgency. They create jealousy towards those who possess virtue, and anger at success.

99 Therefore those conspiring to destroy things such as my praise, are really engaged in preserving me from descent into hell.

100 The shackle of acquisition and honour is unfitting for me who longs for liberation. How can I hate those who liberate me from that shackle?

101 How can I hate those who have become, as if by the Buddha's blessing, a door closed to me as I seek to enter upon suffering?

102 Nor is anger appropriate in the case of someone who hinders acts of merit. There is no spiritual practice equal to forbearance. Without doubt, this is accomplished through him.

103 In fact, it is through my own deficiency that I fail to practise forbearance here. In this instance I alone create the hindrance when grounds for an act of merit have been provided.

104 If one thing does not exist without another, and does exist when that also exists, then that other thing is really its cause. How can that be called an obstacle?

105 After all, a person in need who turns up at a suitable time is not a hindrance to generosity, nor can it be called a hindrance to going forth when one meets someone who has gone forth!

106 Beggars are easy to find in this world but those who will cause harm are not, because, if I do no wrong, no one wrongs me.

107 Therefore, since he helps me on the path to Awakening, I should long for an enemy like a treasure discovered in the home, acquired without effort.

108 Both he and I, therefore, receive the reward of this forbearance. It should be given to him first, since the forbearance was first occasioned by him.

109 If an enemy deserves no honour, because he did not intend you to achieve forbearance, then why is the True Dharma honoured? It too is the unconscious cause of achievement.

110 If an enemy is not honoured because his intention is to hurt, for what other reason will I be patient with him, as with a doctor who is intent on my well-being?

111 In that case, it is really in dependence upon his malign intention that forbearance is produced, and in that case it is really he that is the cause of my forbearance. I must worship him as the True Dharma.

112 For this reason the Sage has said that the fertile field of living beings is the fertile field of the Conquerors, because many have reached success and spiritual perfection by propitiating them.

113 When the transmission of Buddha-qualities comes equally from both ordinary beings and from the Conquerors, what logic is there in not paying that respect to ordinary beings which one pays to the Conquerors?

114 The greatness of the intent comes not from itself but rather from its effect, and so the greatness is equal. In which case ordinary beings are the equals of the Conquerors.

115 It is greatness on the part of beings that someone with a kindly disposition is honourable, just as it is greatness on the part of the Buddhas that merit comes from serene confidence in the Buddhas.

116 Therefore in one aspect of the transmission of Buddha-qualities, ordinary beings are equal to the Buddhas. Of course, none are fully equal to the Buddhas, who are oceans of virtues with unlimited aspects.

117 If a virtue appears anywhere which is even an atom of those who are a unique mass of the very essence of virtue, then

even the three worlds are not adequate for the purpose of worshipping it.

118 Yet the very best aspect of the development of Buddha-qualities is found in relation to ordinary beings. One should worship ordinary beings in accordance with this aspect.

119 Moreover, for those friends who give immeasurable help without pretext what better recompense could there be than propitiating beings?

120 One should do it for those for whose sake they dismember their own bodies, and enter into the Avīci hell. For that reason, even if people are extremely malignant, all that is skilful should be done for them.

121 How can I act with arrogance rather than servitude towards those very same masters for the sake of whom my Masters, of their own accord, have such lack of regard for themselves?

122 At whose happiness the Lords of Sages become joyful; at whose distress they are sorrowful: to satisfy these creatures is to satisfy the Lords of Sages; to offend them is to offend the Sages, too.

123 Just as no bodily pleasure at all can gladden the mind of one whose body is engulfed in flames, so too those full of compassion cannot come near to feeling joy when living beings are in distress.

124 Therefore, today, I confess as evil the suffering I have caused to all of those of Great Compassion by causing suffering to those people. May the Sages forgive that which has oppressed them.

125 Now, to propitiate the Tathāgatas, with my entire self I become a servant to the world. Let streams of people place their foot upon my head or strike me down. Let the Lord of the World be satisfied.

126 There is no doubt that those whose selfhood is compassion have taken this entire world for themselves. Is it not the

case that they appear in the form of these good people! It is these people who are the Lords. How can I be disrespectful?

127 This alone is the propitiation of the Tathāgatas; this alone is the fulfilment of my own goal; this alone beats back the suffering of the world; so, let this alone be my vow.

128 When a single servant of the king tyrannizes the entire populace, the far-sighted populace has no power to effect change,

129 Because he is not really alone: his potency is the potency of the king. So one should refrain from slighting any impotent person who has caused offence,

130 Since his potency is that of the warders of hell and of the Compassionate Ones. For that reason one should propitiate living beings, just as a servant would a cruel king.

131 What could a wrathful king do that would equal the agony of hell, experienced as a result of causing misery to living beings?

132 What could a gratified king give that would equal Buddhahood, experienced as a result of causing happiness to living beings?

133 Never mind future Buddhahood arising from the propitiation of living beings! Do you not see good fortune, renown, and well-being right here and now?

134 Serenity, freedom from disease, joy and long life, the happiness of an emperor, prosperity: these the patient person receives while continuing in cyclic existence.

7
THE PERFECTION OF VIGOUR

IN Chapter 7 Śāntideva presents his instruction in the perfection of vigour, *vīrya-pāramitā*. His account falls into two sections, the first (vv. 2–30) explaining the opposites of vigour and how to overcome them, and the second dealing with the means for increasing the vigour with which one practises. In so doing he follows the traditional teaching on the 'four correct efforts'—(1) to avoid unskilful mental states arising in the mind; (2) to overcome unskilful states that have arisen in the mind; (3) to develop skilful mental states; and (4) to sustain such skilful states—by dividing his instruction between the unskilful states which drain one's vigour, and the positive or skilful states which reinforce it.

He defines the opposites of vigour: 'Sloth, clinging to what is vile, despondency, and self-contempt' (v. 2), and counters them, from v. 3 to v. 29, with 'the capacity for desire, perseverance, delight, and letting go' (v. 31). Śāntideva's discussion of the cultivation of vigour hinges upon a six-fold classification in terms of desire (*chanda*), pride (*māna*), delight (*rati*), giving up (*tyāga*), dedication (*tātparya*), and control (*vaśitā*). Here desire is, of course, righteous desire, desire for what is good, *dharma-chanda*. Pride makes one willing to act, even alone; it is expressed as a revulsion against the influence of the secondary defilements (*upakleśa*), which incapacitate others; and it determines one's perception of what one is able to do. Delight is an intense pleasure derived from the very actions of the Bodhisattva; and giving up involves the cessation of activity when one cannot be effective (showing the need for a balanced effort). Dedication is maintained through the practice of mindfulness, and self-mastery is the fulfilment of 'power' (*ṛddhi*) that is achieved through a successful cultivation of vigour.

Readers familiar with pre-existing translations of this text and its traditional interpretation may have noted that this analysis departs from the usual interpretation of Śāntideva's account of vigour. This is usually expressed in terms of desire, perseverance (*sthāma*), delight, and letting go (*mukti*). The crucial passage in the text is:

> The capacity for desire, perseverance, delight, and letting go, all lead to the fulfilment of the needs of living beings. Out of the fear of suffering, and while meditating on the praises, one should create desire.
>
> Uprooting the opposite in this way, one should endeavour to increase one's exertion through the capacities of desire, pride, delight, giving up, dedication, and control. (vv. 31–2)

The first of these verses has been taken by commentators, including Prajñākaramati, to indicate Śāntideva's intended plan for his further exposition of vigour, i.e. the remainder of this chapter. If v. 31 contains a plan for the rest of the chapter, then it is difficult to understand why Śāntideva included v. 32, for it would seem to be only repetitious and confusing. However, close attention to each reveals that the two lists are concerned with different issues. The former explains the positive counterparts of the four antitheses to vigour, listed in v. 2, i.e. sloth, clinging to what is vile, despondency, and self-contempt. Thus, sloth is countered by desire; clinging to what is vile, by letting go; despondency, by perseverance; and self-contempt, by delight. From v. 3 to v. 28 the author details the manner in which the opposites of vigour should be dealt with, as negative factors in the mind. In this verse, 31, he retrospectively summarizes their positive countermeasures or antidotes.

Verse 32 clearly states that up to this point one has been concerned with eradicating the opposites of vigour, and also identifies its own list as the capacities by which one cultivates 'exertion' or *utsāha* (Śāntideva's preferred synonym for *vīrya*). This interpretation is confirmed in so far as the plan outlined in v. 32 fits the remainder of the chapter perfectly, in ways which the traditional view does not. The 'plan' in v. 31 mentions perseverance, *sthāma*, as its second item, yet this virtue is never referred to again in the remainder of the chapter. The subject of vv. 46–61 is pride, the second item of the plan in v. 32, but not mentioned in v. 31. The final two items of the second plan are clearly reflected in the concluding verses of the chapter (67–75), which do not fit into the plan in v. 31 at all.

How could this confusion have occurred? One possibility lies in the misperception of clues to the structure in the language of the text. The lists appear similar. Both include desire and delight as their first and third items. The fourth items of each are the synonymous 'letting go', *mukti*, and 'giving up', *tyāga*. Furthermore, the reference to 'letting go', *mukti*, in v. 31, interpreted in its transitive sense as the 'quitting' of an action which cannot be fulfilled, may have been presumed to be echoed in v. 66, which describes this process, and uses the cognate verb *muc* 'to loosen' to do so, and thus might have been seen as establishing a link between the two.

The canonical Tibetan translation of the *Bodhicaryāvatāra* contains an extra verse in this chapter, not appearing in the original Sanskrit, and which forms v. 64 of translations from that language. The Tun-huang recension is nine verses longer than the canonical recension. There has been no comparative study of this chapter in the two recensions. We identified no material in this chapter shared with the *Śikṣā Samuccaya*.

An interesting feature of Chapter 7 is the differentiation of positive and negative aspects of emotions, or motives, which one might suppose should properly be rejected. Śāntideva explains the positive nature of desire (*chanda*), delight or pleasure (*rati*), and pride (*māna*), all reviled in their negative forms, but here explored as sources of the vigour by which the practice of the Bodhisattva's perfections may be fulfilled. Clearly, Śāntideva wishes to show how certain 'base metal' poisons can be sublimated in the service of one's spiritual practice. One might even wonder if Śāntideva wished to shock a little in this respect, for his description of delight in one's spiritual practice borders upon the profane: the Bodhisattva is said to be literally intoxicated and addicted to his actions, and to savour them as does a lover his carnal pleasures, or the gambler the game (v. 62).

We should also note that Śāntideva recognizes a crucial 'gap' between righteous desire and the pride which fuels the Bodhisattva's actions. Thus, in vv. 47–8, he tries to make it clear that, though one may have cultivated considerable righteous desire, one still needs to make a conscious commitment to the Bodhisattva path:

After first assessing the full implications, one should either begin or not begin. Surely, not beginning is better than turning back once one has begun.

This is a habit that continues even in another life, and from its evil suffering increases. Another life and opportunity for action, both lost, and the task not accomplished. (vv. 47–8)

The awesome picture of the Bodhisattva's task painted in the *Vajradhvaja Sūtra* (a section of the *Avataṃsaka Sūtra*, and quoted by Śāntideva in his *Śikṣā Samuccaya*, Bendall and Rouse, pp. 24 ff. and 255 ff.) is clearly something that requires many lifetimes of effort. To undertake it and then back out sets up a pattern of behaviour that is itself productive of further suffering. Only when one has ascertained the 'means' at one's disposal can one be sure of making a skilful and productive commitment. Here, no doubt, pride, as explained in the following verses, will play its own crucial part in one's conviction that such a task is possible to achieve.

The Perfection of Vigour

1 Patient in this way one should cultivate vigour, because Awakening depends on vigour. For without vigour there is no merit, just as there is no movement without wind.

2 What is vigour? The endeavour to do what is skilful. What is its antithesis called? Sloth, clinging to what is vile, despondency, and self-contempt.

3 Sloth comes from idleness, indulging in pleasures, sleep, the longing to lean on others, and from apathy for the sufferings of cyclic existence.

4 Scented out by the trappers, the defilements, you have walked into the trap of birth. Do you not realize even now that you have entered the mouth of death?

5 You do not see those of your own herd as they are killed one by one? You even go to sleep like a buffalo at the butcher.

6 When Yama is sizing you up and at every turn the way is blocked, how can it please you to eat? How can you sleep? How make love?

7 Even if you abandon your sloth as death is swiftly approaching, his implements prepared, it will be too late. What will you do?

8 'I have not started this! This I started, but it remains half-done! Death has come from nowhere! Oh no, I am stricken!'; thinking this,

9 Beholding faces, those of hopeless relatives, eyes red from shedding tears and swollen in the shock of their grief, and those of the messengers of Yama,

10 Tormented by the memory of your own evil, and hearing the hellish bellowings, quaking, from terror your body caked in excrement, what will you do?

11 Realizing you are like a captive fish, how right it is for you to be afraid right now. How much more so when you have committed evil actions and are faced with the intense agonies of hell?

12 So sensitive, touched only by hot water you are scalded. How can you rest at ease like this, when you have committed acts worthy of hell?

13 Hey you, expecting results without effort! So sensitive! So long-suffering! You, in the clutches of death, acting like an immortal! Hey, sufferer, you are destroying yourself!

14 Now that you have met with the boat of human life, cross over the mighty river of suffering. Fool, there is no time to sleep! It is hard to catch this boat again.

15 How can you, after letting go of the most splendid delight, the Dharma, which is an unending stream of joy, find joy in a cause of suffering such as arrogance or ridicule?

16 Freedom from despair, the array of capacities including dedication and control, regarding oneself and others as equal, and the exchange of self and others.

17 Should be practised, and not defeatism from thinking 'How could I possibly achieve Buddhahood?' For the Tathāgata, Speaker of the Truth, spoke this truth:

18 'Even those who were gnats, mosquitoes, wasps, or worms, have reached the highest Awakening, hard to reach, through the strength of their exertion.'

19 How about me, born a human being, able to know good from bad? If I do not forsake the guidance of the Omniscient, why should I not attain Buddhahood?

20 Then again I may be fearful, thinking, 'I shall have to sacrifice a hand or a foot or something'; through lack of judgement, I may confuse the significant with the insignificant in this way!

21 I shall be cut up, sliced open, burned, and split open for innumerable billions of aeons, and still there will be no Awakening.

22 But this limited suffering of mine, the means to perfect Buddhahood, is like the pain of extraction when getting rid of the agony of an embedded thorn.

23 All doctors use painful treatments to restore health. It follows that to put an end to many sufferings, a slight one must be endured.

24 Though such treatment is appropriate, it is not what the best doctor prescribed: he cures by sweet conduct those with the greatest illness.

25 The Guide enjoins giving only vegetables and the like at first. Later, by degrees, one acts in such a way that one is even able to give up one's own flesh!

26 When the understanding arises that one's own flesh is no more than a vegetable, what difficulty is there in giving away one's flesh and bones?

27 One does not suffer from relinquishing evils, nor ail in mind from becoming wise, since affliction in the mind is due to false projections and affliction in the body is due to evil action.

28 The body experiences pleasure as a result of acts of merit. The mind is pleased through learning. When he remains in cyclic existence for the benefit of others what can weary the Compassionate One?

29 Destroying previous evil actions, receiving oceans of merit, by the power of the Awakening Mind alone he progresses more quickly even than the Śrāvakas.

30 Proceeding in this way from happiness to happiness, what thinking person would despair, after mounting the carriage, the Awakening Mind, which carries away all weariness and effort?

31 The capacity for desire, perseverance, delight, and letting go leads to the fulfilment of the needs of living beings. Out of the fear of suffering, and while meditating on the praises, one should create desire.

32 Uprooting the opposite in this way, one should endeavour to increase one's exertion through the capacities of desire, pride, delight, giving up, dedication, and control.

33 I must destroy immeasurable faults, both for myself and for others. The destruction of a single one of those faults takes an ocean of aeons.

34 Yet no trace of an effort is seen on my part to destroy those faults. How does my heart not burst when I am to be allotted immeasurable pain?

35 I must acquire many virtues, both for myself and for others. The discipline of a single one of those virtues might not succeed even in an ocean of aeons.

36 I have never made an effort towards even a trace of virtue. Somehow miraculously attained, I lead my existence pointlessly.

37 I have not found happiness in the great festivals of worship for the Fortunate One, nor have I performed my duties towards the Dispensation, nor have I fulfilled the wants of the destitute.

38 I have not given fearlessness to the fearful, nor have I comforted the afflicted. I became a barb in the womb solely to my mother's suffering.

39 Through my former lack of righteous desire, such misfortunes as these befall me now. Who would reject righteous desire?

40 The Sage has sung that desire is the root of all skilful deeds; in turn, the root of that is ever meditation upon the resulting consequences.

41 Sufferings, feelings of dejection, and many different fears and impediments to their desires befall those who do evil.

42 The heart's delight of those who do good is worshipped with a welcoming reception of fruit wheresoever it goes, as a consequence of their meritorious deeds.

43 But the desire for pleasure of those who do evil is smitten by the weapons of suffering wheresoever it goes, as a consequence of their evil deeds.

44 Born in the womb of lake-growing lotuses, expansive, sweet-smelling, and cool, with thriving splendour granted by the sustenance of the Conqueror's melodious voice, their beautiful forms emerging from the water-born lotuses as they blossom in the rays of light from the Sage, the Sons of the Sugata appear before him in consequence of their skilful deeds.

45 Screaming in agony as his entire skin is ripped away by Yama's minions, his body infused in copper molten in the heat of the oblation-bearing fire, segments of his flesh cleaved away by the hundredfold blows of blazing swords and pikes, he drops repeatedly onto the red-hot ground of iron in consequence of his wrong deeds.

46 So, desire for what is good must be created, meditating carefully on these things. Then one should undertake and develop pride in accordance with the method in the *Vajradhvaja Sūtra*.

47 After first assessing the full implications, one should either begin or not begin. Surely, not beginning is better than turning back once one has begun.

48 This is a habit that continues even in another life, and from its evil suffering increases. Another life and opportunity for action, both lost, and the task not accomplished.

49 One should strive for pride in three areas: action, the secondary defilements, and ability. 'It is I alone who can do it', expresses pride in action.

50 This world is totally subject to the defilements, incapable of accomplishing its own benefit. Therefore I must do it for them. I am not incapable, as is mankind.

51 How is it that another does despised work while I stand by? If I do not do it because of pride, better to let my pride be destroyed.

52 Even a crow acts like Garuḍa when attacking a dead lizard. If my mind is weak, even a minor difficulty is oppressive.

53 When one is made passive by defeatism, without doubt difficulties easily take effect, but exerting one's self and invigorated, one is hard to defeat even for great calamities.

54 So, with a firm mind, I shall make difficulty for difficulty. For so long as difficulties conquer me, my desire to conquer the three worlds is laughable.

55 For I must conquer everything. Nothing should conquer me. This pride should be wedded to me, for I am a son of the lionlike Conqueror.

56 Those beings who are conquered by pride are wretches who have no pride! A person with pride does not fall under the control of a rival. They are under the control of the rival, pride.

57 Led by pride to a bad rebirth, even as a human being their jubilation is destroyed—slaves, eating food scrounged from others, stupid, ugly, and thin.

58 And despised on all sides, sustained by pride, the mortified, even those wretched in the midst of the proud, pray tell of what kind are they?

59 They have pride and are victorious. They truly are the heroes, who bear their pride to victory over the enemy pride; who, slaying the enemy pride though he is ubiquitous, readily present the fruit of their victory to the people.

60 Stood in the midst of the hosts of defilements, one should be a thousand times more hotly proud, invincible to the hosts of defilements, as a lion to herds of deer.

61 Surely, even in great difficulties, the eye will not see a flavour. In the same way too, meeting difficulty, one must not fall under the control of the defilements.

62 One should be addicted solely to the task that one is undertaking. One should be intoxicated by that task, insatiable,

like someone hankering for the pleasure and the fruit of love-play.

63 A task is performed for the sake of satisfaction, notwithstanding that there may or may not be satisfaction. But how can one, for whom the task itself is satisfaction, be satisfied without a task?

64 One cannot get enough of the sensual pleasures in cyclic existence, that are like honey on a razor's edge. How can one get enough of the benign, ambrosial acts of merit, sweet in their result?

65 So, even at the conclusion of one task, one should plunge straight away into the next, as does a tusker, inflamed by the midday heat, immediately on coming to a pool.

66 But when one's energy begins to flag, one should put it aside to take up again, and, when it is completely finished, one should let it go with a thirst for the next and then the next.

67 One should guard against attacks from the defilements, and resolutely attack them, as if engaged in a sword fight with a well-trained enemy.

68 As, then, one would hastily snatch up one's sword in fear did one drop it, so should one snatch up the sword of mindfulness when it drops, remembering the hells.

69 As poison, finding the blood, spreads throughout the body, so, finding a weak point, a fault will spread throughout the mind.

70 One who has undertaken the Vow should be like someone superintended by swordsmen, who is carrying a jar of oil, wholly intent upon it, out of fear of death if he stumbles.

71 So, on the approach of drowsiness or lethargy one should immediately counteract it, as one would jump up immediately were a snake to slide into one's lap.

72 At every single lapse one should burn befittingly with remorse, then reflect, 'How might I act so that this might not happen to me again?'

73 One should look forward to society or a given task with this motive: 'How may I practise the discipline of mindfulness in these circumstances?'

74 Remembering the teaching on vigilance, one should make oneself versatile, as one always prepares oneself prior to undertaking a task.

75 In the very same way that cotton is controlled by the wind as it comes and goes, so one should be controlled by one's endeavour, and in this way one's spiritual power grows strong.

8
THE PERFECTION OF MEDITATIVE ABSORPTION

THE eighth chapter of the *Bodhicaryāvatāra* deals with the penultimate perfection, that of meditative absorption, *dhyāna*. Meditative absorption is a technical term, used by the historical Buddha himself to describe the higher levels of consciousness attained through calming or *śamatha* meditation. From the time of the Buddha, meditation has been a, if not the, major tool used for the task of self-transformation in Buddhism. The English term, meditation, introduces an ambiguity not necessary with the wide vocabulary of meditation used by the Indian Buddhist tradition, for it must do duty covering both the meditational exercises, of which Buddhism employs a large array, and the mental states achieved by the use of these techniques. While attempting to differentiate between these two referents, we also need to understand that Buddhist meditation is said to have two functions: calming, *śamathā*; and insight, *vipaśyanā*, each with their preferred, but also with some shared, techniques of development.

Śamathā meditation is generally concerned with calming and stabilizing the mind, and cultivating positive emotions such as friendliness and compassion. Characteristic techniques employed to achieve these states are the 'mindfulness while breathing' (*ānāpāna-smṛti*) and the 'development of friendliness' (*maitrī-bhāvanā*) respectively. The successful practice of any technique involves a sustained effort to suppress any of the five possible 'hindrances' (*nīvaraṇa*) which might arise and distract the mind of the meditator, and for which task an array of meditations is available. Progress in calming meditation results in the 'rising' of the mind through successively more refined and purified levels of consciousness, known technically as 'meditative absorptions', *dhyāna*. The *dhyānas* are four in number, and are characterized by the successive simplification and purification of the contents of consciousness. The first such meditative absorption is described, in a common formula found in the scriptures, as the mental state which is accompanied by discursive thinking (*vitarka-vicāra*), bliss (*prīti*), and happiness (*sukha*), and is 'born of isolation' (*viveka-ja*). The second is described as arising when discursive thinking dies away, whereupon one's mind becomes tranquil and one-pointed, and one gains meditative concentration (*samādhi*). The third meditative absorption is entered when bliss, which is relatively coarse, dies away and one becomes equanimous, mindful, and aware. In the fourth absorption, awareness of pleasure and pain have subsided and one's mind is 'purified' by mindfulness and equanimity.

By contrast, insight or *vipaśyanā* meditation is concerned with the development of those insights by which the individual is Awakened. The Buddha and all his Enlightened disciples, throughout the ages, have Awakened to a realization of 'the way things really are'. The precise formulation of 'the way things really are' has developed over the course of the centuries (of which more below), but all schools of Buddhism have accepted the realization of this understanding or wisdom as the central and crucial goal of Buddhist practice. Insight meditation is concerned with inculcating a realization in the meditator of just this 'way things really are'. It employs mindfulness (*smṛti*) and awareness (*samprajanya*) as the basis for the analytical investigation of the person and the perceived world, according to any of the standard formulations of the Buddha's understanding. Such analysis might, for example, employ reflection upon the fact that all material and mental phenomena are characterized by three 'marks', *lakṣaṇa*, i.e. impermanence, dissatisfaction, and insubstantiality (sometimes a fourth is added to these, that of foulness, *aśubha*). The desired result of such insight meditation is the direct understanding by experience that this is indeed the case.

The classic account of Buddhist meditation, common to Mahāyāna and non-Mahāyāna forms of Buddhism, enjoins a judicious balance of these two kinds of meditation. The practitioner must acquire some considerable experience of calming meditation, so as to purify and concentrate the mind. However, meditative absorption of the second stage or higher eschews discursive thought, a form of mental activity which is essential for the practice of insight meditation. The meditator therefore trains so as to be able to stay in the first meditative absorption, where discursive thought is still possible, and there engage in the discursive thinking of insight meditation, thus combining the two forms. Combined with the effect of calming meditation, which, as it were, deepens the meditators' experience of themselves and allows them access to a broader spectrum of their psycho-physical being, the insight meditation is able to initiate a radical transformation in the consciousness of the individual. Without the experience of meditative absorption, the reflective process of insight meditation is too liable to distraction, and the meditator's mind is, as it were, too superficial to sustain a transforming insight.

We can now turn to examine Chapter 8 itself, to see how Śāntideva deals with this perfection. However, we should be wary of attributing too much of any analysis of this text of Chapter 8 to the authorship of Śāntideva, since Saito reports that the Tun-huang recension of this chapter has only 58 (one manuscript has 59) verses, compared to the 186 in the canonical recension. In fact it is this chapter alone which accounts for almost 60 per cent of the difference in length between the two recensions. This enormous difference begs further comparative investigation, but this has yet to be done. For the mean time, we shall proceed, taking Chapter 8 as it stands in the canonical recension, and, for ease of reference, taking Śāntideva as the author of the whole.

Since this is Śāntideva's chapter on the perfection of meditative absorption it would be reasonable to expect an account of the techniques and technicalities of calming meditation in the sense just outlined. However, rather than discuss in detail the character and methods for the induction of meditative absorption, he emphasizes the basic principles involved, such as the need truly to leave the world behind, and illustrates them with the most pressing examples. His silence on the technicalities of meditative absorption begs the question of the degree to which calming meditation was practised in his milieu. It would be wrong to assume that this silence implied that his audience was familiar with these techniques and needed no instruction, for the same should also apply to the other practices of the path which he expounds in the *Bodhicaryāvatāra*. It is clear from the accounts of visiting Chinese monks of the period that Nālandā, the monastic university where Śāntideva is said to have composed this work, was very much a competitive worldly environment, open to lay scholars, and used by many as a springboard for a secular career. To be a monk there could not, therefore, entail the life of seclusion which one might associate with monkhood. Achieving the necessary environment and attitude for calming meditation would therefore have required a personal decision and commitment on the part of the individual monk. It is quite possible that the practice of calming meditation was rare, as it is today, for example, amongst the Buddhist monastic communities of Sri Lanka. The idealized descriptions of life in the wilderness that Śāntideva gives support this conjecture.

He begins by pointing out in vv. 1–4 that, unless one gains some degree of meditative absorption, one will not be able to gain insight, and since it is insight which frees one from the influence of the defilements, without absorption one is still their victim.

> Increasing one's endeavour in this way, one should stabilize the mind in meditative concentration, since a person whose mind is distracted stands between the fangs of the defilements. (v. 1)

He continues by stressing the need for the isolation or sequestering of the trainee Bodhisattva's body and mind.

> Distraction does not occur if body and mind are kept sequestered. Therefore, one should renounce the world and disregard distracting thoughts.
>
> The world is not truly renounced because of attachment and the thirst for acquisitions and other rewards. Therefore, to renounce these, anyone with sense would reflect as follows:
>
> Realizing that one well-attuned to insight through tranquillity can destroy the defilements, one should firstly seek tranquillity, and that by disregarding one's delight in the world. (vv. 2–4)

In this he is thoroughly traditional and in keeping with the principles of calming meditation, for 'isolation' or *viveka* is also an inherent quality of and indispensable condition for meditative absorption, which is described time and again as *viveka-ja*, 'born of isolation'. The purpose of this isolation is to free oneself from the greatest distraction, desire (the first of the hindrances).

With this in mind Śāntideva fills his instruction on the isolation of the body (vv. 5–38) with exhortation to give up attachment to loved ones, foolish companions, and competitiveness. It is interesting to note that while the former categories are described in terms appropriate to layman or monk, the terms of the last (vv. 17–25) are strongly redolent of the rivalries which can grow within the monastic community. While he emphasizes the mild asceticism of the forest life (vv. 27–9), he sees the state of bodily isolation as happy and free, and concludes this section by saying:

> Therefore I shall always follow the solitary life, which is delightful and free from strife, leading to the auspicious and calming all distractions. (v. 38)

With this preliminary established he then moves on to the next phase of meditative training, which involves the isolation or withdrawal of the mind (vv. 39–89):

> Freed from all other concerns, my own mind in a state of single-pointed thought, I shall apply myself to taming and increasing the meditative concentration of my mind. (v. 39)

Since it is the passions, *kāmā*, that Śāntideva identifies here as the chief danger for the mind (v. 40), this section is entirely devoted to attacking mental attachment, particularly that of a man for a woman. Apart from demonstrating that the assumed audience for this work was male (the passion of a woman for a man is not mentioned), this passage offers a sustained meditation upon the foulness of the human body, the *aśubha-bhāvanā*. This was not an invention of the author, but rather one of a number of standard meditations devised for the specific purpose of counteracting particular hindrances to meditation. As is clear from even a cursory reading of this passage, the *aśubha-bhāvanā* is designed to eradicate passion and sensuous longing. Śāntideva begins by imagining the body of the beloved as a corpse (vv. 41–8), but soon graduates to reflecting upon the filthiness of the human body (vv. 49–69). This is, of course, repugnant in Western eyes too, but the unpleasant impact of such reflection is doubled in traditional Indian caste society, where the polluting products of the body are avoided at all cost, and where regular contact with them, for example through laundry or leather work, can relegate an entire class of people to the very lowest social status. Equally significant, and poignant and amusing by turns in its authenticity, is the final stage of this section (vv. 70–83), in which Śāntideva expands upon the sheer effort that one has to make if one decides to pander to one's passions. He concludes his account of the practice of isolation with some of the most beautifully evocative verses of the entire work (vv. 85–8).

At this point Śāntideva begins instruction in Mahāyāna meditations specifically concerned with the cultivation of the Awakening Mind, with the words:

> By developing the virtues of solitude in such forms as these, distracted thoughts being calmed, one should now develop the Awakening Mind.
>
> At first one should meditate intently on the equality of oneself and others as follows: 'All equally experience suffering and happiness. I should look after them as I do myself.' (vv. 89–90)

The central thrust of this meditation, which takes up the next thirty verses (vv. 90–119), is that the meditator should reflect upon the equality of oneself and other people, so that one ceases to differentiate between the needs and concerns of either. Although this practice is popularly associated with Śāntideva, it seems to have been overlooked that this meditation incorporates some eight verses from a passage of the *Tathāgataguhya Sūtra* which is quoted at length in the *Śikṣā Samuccaya*. It also includes, as v. 96, the first of Śāntideva's root verses from the same text, and a partial paraphrase in v. 89 of another verse from the *Tathāgataguhya Sūtra* which reads: 'One should make firm the Awakening Mind by practising the equality of self and others' (cf. Bendall and Rouse, p. 315).

The final stage of this specifically Mahāyānist meditation begins with the enigmatic injunction:

> Whoever longs to rescue quickly both himself and others should practise the supreme mystery: exchange of self and other. (v. 120)

In fact, this is exactly what it says it is: a meditation in which one substitutes one's own identity with that of another person.

Taking up the bulk of the remainder of the chapter (vv. 120–73), this passage contains some of the most bizarre and even amusing reflections. Like many Buddhist meditation practices, this involves an act of imagination, but in this case it is employed for remarkable effect. While there is no doubt that Śāntideva expects that the trainee Bodhisattva should really engage in this practice, it is also clear that to some extent the scenario he envisages is purely theoretical and salutary in intention, for the extremes of negative emotion involved, such as envy and pride (v. 140), would surely be detrimental in themselves. One might counter this with the suggestion that his recommendation represents a strong medicine offered to counter a powerful sickness—the sickness of self-identity. One could also interpret this as evidence of the character of the community amongst which the author lived and worked, witnessing the need to counteract a complacency reinforced by the security and social prestige enjoyed by the membership of a major national institution such as Nālandā in the eighth century CE. Whether this is the case or not, the reflections once again take on a monastic colouring, when the spiteful taunts that Śāntideva addresses towards himself from the perspective of another person make frequent reference to jealousy over alms gifts. Most outrageous of all is his suggestion:

> Even if he is given alms we must snatch them from him by force, giving him only enough to live by if he does some work for us. (v. 153)

Did this ever happen between monks in real life, or was it just some twist of the author's imagination?

The latter part of the author's exposition of the exchange of self and others demands that the trainee Bodhisattva envisages himself as a young, newly married wife—a remarkable suggestion in itself (vv. 166 ff.). However, the full impact of this passage could easily be lost on a modern audience. That, in a traditional society, women have a lower status than men is not unusual. The position of the newly married bride in India, however, can be particularly vulnerable to abuse. The ideal bride is completely modest, submissive, and obedient. Often incorporated into the extended household of her husband at the very lowest level, and completely isolated from her own family, she can be subject to the potentially hostile scrutiny of several generations of other women, including her mother-in-law, all of whom she must now serve as well as her husband. The murder and suicide of such unfortunate women still occur in the present day. The treatment that Śāntideva envisages giving himself is the very worst that a husband could offer—bullying, intolerance, selling to others, and physical violence.

The chapter concludes with a short passage on the restraint of one's appetites and the abandonment of interest in one's body (vv. 174–84), followed by a resolve to meditate effectively and to gain insight (vv. 185–6).

This concludes a simple descriptive account of Chapter 8, the perfection of meditative absorption. Our account has shown that the chapter can be understood as falling into two sections; the first dealing with calming meditation, under the heading of the isolation of body and mind, as generally understood in Mahāyāna and non-Mahāyāna forms of Buddhism; the second expounding meditations explicitly concerned with developing the Awakening Mind, and hence exclusively Mahāyāna in orientation. The possibilities of interpretation are not, however, exhausted. The evidence of the Tun-huang recension of the *Bodhicaryāvatāra* suggests that this chapter, more than any other, has been developed at the hand of an editor, and this may account for another layer of interpretation which it is possible to draw from it. For it is also the case that this chapter describes a progressive sequence of insight or *vipaśyanā* meditation. More specifically, it describes meditations concerned with cultivating the liberating insights associated with the non-Mahāyāna and Cittamātra schools of Buddhism. How and why is this so?

In the non-Mahāyāna tradition insight involves the direct realization that the entities of the ordinary world are composite and conditioned, i.e. made up of irreducible elements known as *dharmas*, which mutually condition one another. Insight meditation was therefore geared to the deconstruction of ordinary entities, especially that entity with which we have the greatest problems as non-Awakened beings, the person. Techniques employed for this include the analysis of the human body, and reflections upon its impermanence, insubstantiality, and foulness. In this light, we can see that some of Śāntideva's reflection in the first section of Chapter 8, concerning the isolation of body and mind, amount to insight meditation of this sort.

In some respects the Mahāyāna form of Buddhism arose in contrast to the non-Mahāyāna, and this is especially clear in its concept of the insight which gives rise to liberation. The discourses on the Perfection of Wisdom, the *Prajñā-pāramitā Sūtras*, expound a realization that not only are the entities of the ordinary world composite and conditioned and therefore impermanent and so on, but so too are the elements, the *dharmas*, into which they could be analysed. If one does not pursue one's analysis to this depth, they argue, one cannot gain the liberating insight of full Awakening.

The Mahāyāna, however, was not itself a single entity, and produced two major 'philosophical' schools in India. The Madhyamaka school identified itself with the historical figure of Nāgārjuna (second century CE), albeit retrospectively, and took the Perfection of Wisdom Sūtras as its highest scriptural authority. This retrospective self-definition was made partly by way of contradistinction to the Cittamātra school. The latter saw itself in chronological succession to the Madhyamaka, and as compensating for certain distortions or inappropriate emphases upon the negative character of ultimate truth as described by that school. The Cittamātra refers to itself as 'the third turning of the Dharma wheel', alluding to the alleged 'first discourse' of the Buddha, delivered soon after his Awakening and known to the tradition as 'the first turning of the Dharma wheel'. The Perfection of Wisdom Sūtras, the scriptural focus for the Madhyamaka school, describe themselves as 'the second turning of the Dharma wheel'. For the Cittamātra the ultimate truth was expressed by its own teachings concerning the nature of mind. While it accepted the analysis of most entities and elements, it maintained that the flow of consciousness is itself real, and cannot be analysed into insubstantiality. Although the flow of consciousness is real, the world of subject and objects is a false projection, which can be eradicated by correct analysis. They regarded the absence of duality, i.e. the lack of difference between self and other, as the ultimate truth, their understanding of 'the way things really are'. It is therefore not difficult to see that the meditations offered in the second part of this chapter, concerning the equality and the exchange of self and others, constitute insight meditations leading to just this sort of realization. The obvious ideological context for these practices is the Cittamātra identification of self and other, on the basis of the absence of duality in the flow of consciousness.

If this interpretation is valid, we can conclude that the author(s) of this present chapter used it to describe various insight meditations leading to the realization of deeper and deeper degrees of understanding, *prajñā*, associated with various systems of Buddhist thought. If this has established how our original contention could be correct, it remains to explain why Śāntideva would have done this.

For the Madhyamaka the model of ultimate truth adopted by the Cittamātra was not acceptable, and, ignoring the issue of chronological development, the position adopted by many representatives of this school, of whom Śāntideva was one, was that while the Madhyamaka account of 'the way things really are' was the ultimate truth, the account given by the Cittamātra had a provisional truth, and a functional value. The same attitude is applied to the realizations and ultimate truth about the way things really are held by the non-Mahāyāna. The Madhyamaka therefore accepted the validity of the analyses of the non-Mahāyāna and Cittamātra schools, and organized them as a hierarchy of truths, placing their own view of the way things are at the top of the heap.

This was a predictable resolution of a problem which arose wherever Buddhism was accessible in its greater diversity. Such a scenario required thinkers to develop some system whereby diverse teachings could be synthesized. The usual response, and a characteristically Indian one, was to create a hierarchy, ranking the preferred account of 'the way things really are' as the highest, as ultimate truth. It appears that the non-Mahāyāna schools largely ignored the Mahāyāna developments in scripture and doctrine, but for the Mahāyāna itself, with its inclusive attitude to scripture and doctrine, matters were different. The Mahāyāna schools were aware of their own chronological development, as we have already seen. All Mahāyāna schools accepted the scriptures preserved by the non-Mahāyāna schools. However, they did not accept them as offering a literal account of 'the way things really are', and instead used them as an ideological and practical foundation-stone upon which to build their own accounts of 'the way things really are' and the practices needed to realize that truth for oneself. Such a structure reflects the position in the Buddhist monastic universities, where complex synthetic systems and accounts of the Path to Awakening were developed, incorporating other Buddhist systems and accounts of ultimate truth, but seeing them as only conventional truth (see 9.2 f. and notes).

Therefore the chapter that one expects to be concerned with calming meditation alone involves insight meditation too, but leading to the insights of inferior systems of Buddhist thought, and this is the clue to why Śāntideva included them here. They cannot be included in Chapter 9, in which he expounds his view of the perfection of understanding, because for Śāntideva the perfection of understanding is the Madhyamaka viewpoint alone. Where they are mentioned in Chapter 9 it is to establish their inferiority. Neither the non-Mahāyāna nor the Cittamātra offer the real ultimate truth, but they do offer insights which are preparatory to it. Though an account of the ultimate truth of other schools is inappropriate in his chapter on understanding, they do have a function in his synthetic view of the path, which is a progressive realization of deepening degrees of insight. Hence these inferior truths are expounded within the context of meditative absorption. For Śāntideva the realization of lesser ultimate truths is an aspect of the perfection of meditative absorption, or rather functions as the object of meditative concentration, *samādhi*.

A further reason for Śāntideva to place his meditation upon the equality and exchange of self and other here is to be found in the Madhyamaka understanding of compassion. All schools agreed that the Buddha experienced and gave expression to the highest degree of compassion. Within the Mahāyāna, Enlightenment is universally described in terms of a profound wisdom and a far-reaching compassion. However, the relationship of these two was understood in different ways. From the Cittamātra perspective, compassion arises naturally from the realization of the absence of duality at the level of ultimate truth, that is, the realization of the equality and interconnectedness of self and other. For the Madhyamaka the picture is different, in that the realization of the equality of self and other was not regarded as the ultimate truth, and therefore this natural entrance into compassion is not inherent in their understanding of Enlightenment. For this reason, in the Madhyamaka system, compassion is a virtue in which the Bodhisattva must train, prior to his Enlightenment, so that as a Buddha he is properly equipped. This idea is not so surprising, especially when one remembers the currency of stories concerning *pratyeka-buddhas*, or solitary Buddhas, who were understood to be Enlightened, but who did not teach, presumably from a lack of compassion. Nor is the idea of cultivating compassion foreign to the milieu of the *Jātaka* stories, one of the most popular and widespread teaching mediums used throughout the Buddhist tradition, wherein the Bodhisattva (the historical Buddha-to-be) is shown repeatedly sacrificing life and limb out of a compassionate interest in other creatures (see Cowell *et al.* 1895–1907). Therefore, as a Mādhyamika (i.e. a follower of the Madhyamaka), Śāntideva must build into the Bodhisattva training which he describes a fail-safe method of developing compassion. The connection with compassion is made explicit in the following verses:

> Without exception, no sufferings belong to anyone. They must be warded off simply because they are suffering. Why is any limitation put on this?
>
> If one asks why suffering should be prevented, no one disputes that! If it must be prevented, then all of it must be. If not, then this goes for oneself as for everyone.
>
> You may argue: compassion causes us so much suffering, why force it to arise? Yet when one sees how much the world suffers, how can this suffering from compassion be considered great?
>
> If the suffering of one ends the suffering of many, then one who has compassion for others and himself must cause that suffering to arise. (vv. 102–5)

The need for an object of compassion to help the Bodhisattva complete his training is stated by Śāntideva in the next chapter (see 9.75 and note). This results in the strange inversion by which compassion no longers exists for the sake of beings, but beings are regarded as existing for the sake of the compassion that the Bodhisattva needs to perfect:

If you argue: for whom is there compassion if no being is to be found?

[Our response is] For anyone projected through the delusion which is embraced for the sake of what has to be done. (9.75)

Unlike the insight of Chapter 9, which is mainly concerned with philosophical debate, the insights inculcated in this chapter have a strong affective and moral significance.

The Perfection of Meditative Absorption

1 Increasing one's endeavour in this way, one should stabilize the mind in meditative concentration, since a person whose mind is distracted stands between the fangs of the defilements.

2 Distraction does not occur if body and mind are kept sequestered. Therefore, one should renounce the world and disregard distracting thoughts.

3 The world is not truly renounced because of attachment and the thirst for acquisitions and other rewards. Therefore, to renounce these, anyone with sense would reflect as follows:

4 Realizing that one well-attuned to insight through tranquillity can destroy the defilements, one should firstly seek tranquillity, and that by disregarding one's delight in the world.

5 For what person is it appropriate to be attached to impermanent beings, when that person is impermanent, when a loved one may not be seen again for thousands of lives?

6 Not seeing them one finds no pleasure and cannot remain in meditative concentration, and even when one does see them one is not satisfied. One is tormented by longing, just as before.

7 One does not see things as they really are. One loses the sense of spiritual urgency. One is consumed by that grief, by hankering after contact with the one who is loved.

8 While uselessly preoccupied with that person, life gets shorter by the minute. For a friend who does not last, the everlasting Dharma is lost.

9 Someone who associates with fools invariably goes to a bad rebirth, and someone who disassociates himself is not liked. What is gained from contact with fools?

10 They are friends in a moment, enemies the next. At an occasion for being pleased they get angry. The multitude of people are impossible to satisfy.

11 When given good advice they get angry, and they prevent me from taking good advice. If they are not listened to they get angry and go to a bad rebirth.

12 Superiority causes jealousy. Equality causes rivalry. Inferiority causes arrogance. Praise causes intoxication and criticism causes enmity. When could there be any benefit from a fool?

13 Between one fool and another something detrimental is inevitable, such as self-advancement, complaining about others, or conversation about the pleasures of cyclic existence.

14 So in this way contact with a fool brings harm to the other person too. I shall live apart, happily, my mind undefiled.

15 One should flee far from a fool. One met one should gratify with things that please—not with the intention of intimacy, but rather as would a person who is well disposed but impartial.

16 Taking only what serves the Dharma, as the bumble-bee the nectar from the flower, I shall dwell without acquaintance in any place, as if I had not been before.

17 'I receive plenty of alms, I am honoured and many ask for me': one who thinks this will still die and fears death when it comes.

18 Wherever the mind, deluded about happiness, goes for pleasure, a thousandfold suffering will arise and attend it.

19 Therefore a wise person would not desire it. Fear arises from desire, yet it goes of its own accord. Be firm and bear it impartially.

20 There have been many who have received alms-gifts and many have been popular. It is not known where they have gone with their alms-gifts and popularity.

21 Some detest me. Why am I exultant when praised? Some extol me. Why am I depressed when criticized?

22 Beings have different dispositions. They are not satisfied even by the Conquerors, let alone by the ignorant likes of me. So what's the point of worrying about the world?

23 They blame a person who does not receive alms. They begrudge a person who does. How can there be any pleasure with those who by their nature dwell in misery?

24 The Tathāgatas taught that a fool is a friend to no one, because a fool is not pleased unless his own purpose is served.

25 Joy at the means to one's own good is simply joy at one's own good, just as distress at the destruction of material goods is really caused by the loss of comforts.

26 Trees do not bear grudges nor is any effort required to please them. When might I dwell with those who dwell together happily?

27 Staying in an empty shrine, at the foot of a tree, or in caves, when shall I go, free from concern, without looking back?

28 When shall I dwell in vast regions owned by none, in their natural state, taking my rest or wandering as I please?

29 When shall I live free from fear, without protecting my body, a clay bowl my only luxury, in a robe that thieves would not use?

30 When shall I go to the local charnel ground and compare my own rotting body with other corpses?

31 For this body of mine will also turn putrid in that way, its stench so vile even the jackals will not slink near.

32 Even the bits of bone born together in this single body will be scattered apart; how much more so other people one holds dear?

33 Man is born alone and alone he dies. No one else shares his agony. What help are those one loves, creators of obstacles?

34 As one travelling a road takes lodging on his way, so too one on the path of existence takes lodging in each birth.

35 Before four men bear him out from there with the world lamenting him, he should go forth to the forest.

36 Free from acquaintance, free from conflict, he is quite alone in his body. Having already died to the world, he does not grieve as he dies.

37 Neither do any cause him distress, staying close by him, grieving, nor are there any to distract him from the Buddha and the other recollections.

38 Therefore I shall always follow the solitary life, which is delightful and free from strife, leading to the auspicious and calming all distractions.

39 Freed from all other concerns, my own mind in a state of single-pointed thought, I shall apply myself to taming and increasing the meditative concentration of my mind.

40 For passions bring forth misfortunes in this world and the next: through imprisonment, beatings, and dismemberment in this world; in hells and other lower realms in the next.

41 For whose sake you respectfully greeted messengers and go-betweens many times; for whose sake you hitherto counted the cost of neither misdeed nor disrepute,

42 And even threw yourself into danger and wasted your wealth; on embracing whom you experienced the highest bliss;

43 She is nothing but bones, independent and indifferent. Why do you not willingly cuddle them and feel bliss?

44 You saw that face before; you tried to lift it up when it was lowered in modesty; or maybe it was covered by a veil and you did not see.

45 Now that face is stripped by vultures as if they can no longer bear your frustration. Look at it! Why do you recoil now?

46 Why do you not jealously shield what was shielded even from the glancing eyes of others, now that it is being devoured?

47 Seeing this pile of meat being devoured by vultures and other scavengers, is what is food for others to be worshipped with garlands, sandalwood scent, and jewellery?

48 Although it does not move, you are terrified of a skeleton when it is seen like this. Why have you no fear of it when it moves as if animated by a vampire?

49 They produce both spit and shit from the single source of food. You do not want the shit from it. Why are you so fond of drinking the spit?

50 Taking no pleasure from silky pillows stuffed with cotton because they do not ooze a dreadful stench, those in love are entranced by filth.

51 You had this passion for it when it was covered over, so why dislike it now uncovered? If you have no use for it, why do you rub against the cover?

52 If you have no passion for what is foul, why do you embrace another, a cage of bones bound by sinew, smeared with slime and flesh?

53 You have plenty of filth of your own. Satisfy yourself with that! Glutton for crap! Forget her, that other pouch of filth!

54 You want to see and touch it because you think you like its flesh. How can you desire flesh, which is by its own nature devoid of any consciousness?

55 That mind that you desire can be neither seen nor touched, and what can be is not conscious, so why embrace it pointlessly?

56 It is no wonder that you do not see that the body of another is formed from filth. That you do not understand your own body to be formed from filth is astonishing!

57 Aside from the delicate lotus, born in muck, opening up in the rays of a cloudless sun, what is the pleasure in a cage of crap for a mind addicted to filth?

58 If you do not want to touch something such as soil because it is smeared with excrement, how can you long to touch the body which excreted it?

59 If you have no passion for what is foul, why do you embrace another, born in a field of filth, seeded by filth, nourished by filth?

60 Is it that you do not like a dirty worm born in filth because it's only tiny? It must be that you desire a body, likewise born in filth, because it is formed from such a large amount!

61 Not only are you not disgusted at your own foulness, you glutton for crap, you yearn for other vats of filth!

62 Even the ground is considered impure when pleasant things such as camphor or rice and curries are dripped or spat out onto it.

63 If you are not convinced that this is filth even though it is right before your eyes, look at other bodies, too, discarded and gruesome in the charnel ground.

64 Great is your fear when the skin has been ripped from it. Knowing this how can you still take delight in that very same thing again?

65 Though applied to the body this scent comes from the sandalwood alone, not from anything else. Why are you attracted towards one thing by the scent of something else?

66 Surely it is good if its own natural stench prevents passion towards it. Why do people take delight in what is worthless and smear it with scent?

67 What if the sandalwood smells good? How does that affect the body? Why are you attracted towards one thing by the scent of something else?

68 If, with its long hair and nails, its teeth stained and yellow, bearing blemishes and grime, the naked body is revolting in its natural state,

69 Why is such an effort made to dress it like a weapon, for one's own destruction? The world is a confusion of insane people striving to delude themselves.

70 Apparently you were horrified when you saw a few corpses in the charnel ground. Yet you delight in your village, which is a charnel-ground thronging with moving corpses.

71 Moreover, even though this body is such filth, it is not acquired without a price: the trouble of earning for its sake and torment in hells and other lower realms.

72 An infant is not able to earn money. With what can he get pleasure as a young man? His youth is spent in earning. What can an old man do with pleasures of the flesh?

73 Some who are prey to unwholesome desires, exhausted by a full day's work, on coming home at the end of day just sleep like the dead.

74 Others, on military expeditions, suffer the hardships of living far from home. Though the years pass they do not see the wife and children for whose sake they strive.

75 Deluded by their desires, they sell themselves to get what they never receive. Instead, their life is uselessly wasted doing work for someone else.

76 The wives of others who have sold themselves to carry out commissions have to give birth in places like the jungle and scrubland.

77 In order to live, it seems, they enter battle at the risk of their lives. For the sake of their pride they enter servitude. They are fools made ridiculous by their passions.

78 Some, prey to passion, have limbs cut off. Others are struck by arrows. They are seen being burned to death and slain with spears.

79 Understand that a fortune is an unending misfortune with earning and protecting it and the misery of its loss. In their distracted state those whose thoughts are fixed on wealth have no opportunity to find release from the suffering of existence.

80 For those prey to passion such misery is abundant, whereas enjoyment is paltry, like snatches at bits of grass made by a beast as it draws a cart.

81 For the sake of that snatch of enjoyment which is easy to find even for a beast, this momentary good fortune which is extremely hard to find is lost by one lost to their destiny.

82 This exhausting effort is made for all time for the sake of a puny body which inevitably dies, which falls into hells and other low realms.

83 With a fraction even one hundredth of a billionth of that effort one obtains Buddhahood. For those who follow their passions the suffering involved is greater than the suffering on the Path, and there is no Awakening.

84 No sword, no poison, no fire, no precipice, no enemies can compare with the passions when one remembers the torments in hell and other lower realms.

85 Thus one should recoil from sensual desires and cultivate delight in solitude, in tranquil woodlands empty of contention and strife.

86 On delightful rock surfaces cooled by the sandal balm of the moon's rays, stretching wide as palaces, the fortunate pace, fanned by the silent, gentle forest breezes, as they contemplate for the well-being of others.

87 Passing what time one pleases anywhere, in an empty dwelling, at the foot of a tree, or in caves, free from the exhaustion of safeguarding a household, one lives as one pleases, free from care,

88 One's conduct and dwelling are one's own choice. Bound to none, one enjoys that happiness and contentment which even for a king is hard to find.

89 By developing the virtues of solitude in such forms as these, distracted thoughts being calmed, one should now develop the Awakening Mind.

90 At first one should meditate intently on the equality of oneself and others as follows: 'All equally experience suffering and happiness. I should look after them as I do myself.'

91 Just as the body, with its many parts from division into hands and other limbs, should be protected as a single entity, so too should this entire world which is divided, but undivided in its nature to suffer and be happy.

92 Even though suffering in me does not cause distress in the bodies of others, I should nevertheless find their suffering intolerable because of the affection I have for myself,

93 In the same way that, though I cannot experience another's suffering in myself, his suffering is hard for him to bear because of his affection for himself.

94 I should dispel the suffering of others because it is suffering like my own suffering. I should help others too because of their nature as beings, which is like my own being.

95 When happiness is liked by me and others equally, what is so special about me that I strive after happiness only for myself?

96 When fear and suffering are disliked by me and others equally, what is so special about me that I protect myself and not the other?

97 If I give them no protection because their suffering does not afflict me, why do I protect my body against future suffering when it does not afflict me?

98 The notion 'it is the same me even then' is a false construction, since it is one person who dies, quite another who is born.

99 If you think that it is for the person who has the pain to guard against it, a pain in the foot is not of the hand, so why is the one protected by the other?

100 If you argue that, even though this conduct is inappropriate, it proceeds from the sense of self-identity, [our response is that] one should avoid what is inappropriate in respect of self and others as far as one can.

101 The continuum of consciousnesses, like a queue, and the combination of constituents, like an army, are not real. The person who experiences suffering does not exist. To whom will that suffering belong?

102 Without exception, no sufferings belong to anyone. They must be warded off simply because they are suffering. Why is any limitation put on this?

103 If one asks why suffering should be prevented, no one disputes that! If it must be prevented, then all of it must be. If not, then this goes for oneself as for everyone.

104 You may argue: compassion causes us so much suffering, why force it to arise? Yet when one sees how much the world suffers, how can this suffering from compassion be considered great?

105 If the suffering of one ends the suffering of many, then one who has compassion for others and himself must cause that suffering to arise.

106 That is why Supuṣpacandra, though undergoing torture at the hands of the king, did nothing to prevent his own suffering out of sacrifice for many sufferers.

107 Those who have developed the continuum of their mind in this way, to whom the suffering of others is as important as the things they themselves hold dear, plunge down into the Avīci hell as geese into a cluster of lotus blossoms.

108 Those who become oceans of sympathetic joy when living beings are released, surely it is they who achieve fulfilment. What would be the point in a liberation without sweetness?

109 In fact, though acting for the good of others, there is neither intoxication nor dismay, nor desire for the resulting reward, with a thirst solely for the well-being of others.

110 Therefore, just as I protect myself to the last against criticism, let me develop in this way an attitude of protectiveness and of generosity towards others as well.

111 Through habituation there is the understanding of 'I' regarding the drops of sperm and blood of two other people, even though there is in fact no such thing.

112 Why can I not also accept another's body as my self in the same way, since the otherness of my own body has been settled and is not hard to accept?

113 One should acknowledge oneself as having faults and others as oceans of virtues. Then one should meditate on renouncing one's own self-identity and accepting other people.

114 In the same way that the hands and other limbs are loved because they form part of the body, why are embodied creatures not likewise loved because they form part of the universe?

115 In the same way that, with practice, the idea of a self arose towards this, one's own body, though it is without a self, with practice will not the same idea of a self develop towards others too?

116 Though acting like this for the good of others, there is neither intoxication nor dismay. Even after giving oneself as food, there arises no hope for reward.

117 Therefore, in the same way that one desires to protect oneself from affliction, grief, and the like, so an attitude of protectiveness and of compassion should be practised towards the world.

118 That is why the Protector, Avalokita, empowered even his own name to drive away even such fear as the shyness people have in front of an audience.

119 One should not turn away from difficulty, because by the power of practice the very thing one once feared to hear becomes something without which one has no delight.

120 Whoever longs to rescue quickly both himself and others should practise the supreme mystery: exchange of self and other.

121 If even slight danger causes fear because of overfondness for oneself, who would not detest that self like a fear-inspiring enemy?

122 One who, wishing to fend off hunger, thirst, and weakness, kills birds, fish and animals, or lurks in wait on the highway,

123 One who, motivated by possessions and honour, would even kill his parents, or would take the property of the Three Jewels, who would thereby become fuel in the Avīci hell,

124 What wise person would want such a self, protect it, worship it, and not see it as an enemy? Who would treat it with regard?

125 'If I give, what shall I enjoy?' Such concern for one's own welfare is fiendish. 'If I enjoy, what shall I give?' Such concern for the welfare of others is divine.

126 By oppressing another for one's own sake, one is roasted in hells, but by oppressing oneself for the sake of another, one meets with success in everything.

127 A bad rebirth, inferiority, and stupidity result from the mere desire for self-advancement. By transferring that same desire to others, one achieves a good rebirth, honour, and intelligence.

128 By commanding another to one's own end one attains positions of servitude, whereas by commanding oneself to the benefit of others one attains positions of power.

129 All those who suffer in the world do so because of their desire for their own happiness. All those happy in the world are so because of their desire for the happiness of others.

130 Why say more? Observe this distinction: between the fool who longs for his own advantage and the sage who acts for the advantage of others.

131 For one who fails to exchange his own happiness for the suffering of others, Buddhahood is certainly impossible—how could there even be happiness in cyclic existence?

132 Never mind the next life! Even right here and now the objective of a servant who does not work or of a master who does not pay the wages cannot be achieved.

133 Having forsaken the promotion of one another's happiness, the fountain of happiness now and in the future, by causing mutual distress, the deluded seize upon gruesome suffering.

134 The calamities which happen in the world, the sufferings and fears, many as they are, they all result from clinging onto the notion of self, so what good is this clinging of mine?

135 If one does not let go of self one cannot let go of suffering, as one who does not let go of fire cannot let go of burning.

136 Therefore, in order to allay my own suffering and to allay the suffering of others, I devote myself to others and accept them as myself.

137 Hey Mind, make the resolve, 'I am bound to others'! From now on you must have no other concern than the welfare of all beings.

138 It is not right to look to one's own good with others' eyes and other senses. It is not right to set in motion one's own good with others' hands and other limbs.

139 So having become devoted to others, remove from this body everything you see in it, and use that to benefit others.

140 Creating a sense of self in respect of inferiors and others, and a sense of other in oneself, imagine envy and pride with a mind free from false notions!

141 He is honoured, not I. I do not receive such alms as he. He is praised. I am criticized. I suffer. He is happy.

142 I do chores while he remains at ease. He, it seems, is great in the world. I, it seems, am inferior, without virtues.

143 What can be done by one without virtues? Each person has his own virtues. There are those among whom I am the worst. There are those among whom I am the best.

144 Such things as the failings in my conduct and views, as result from the power of the defilements, are not in my control. I should be cured as far as possible. I agree even to painful treatment.

145 If he cannot cure me, why does he despise me? What use are his qualities to me, when he is the one possessing the qualities?

146 He has no compassion for people who stand in the vicious jaws of an evil rebirth. Moreover, out of pride in his virtues he longs to have victory over the learned.

147 If he regards himself as being on the same level as someone, he will obtain alms-gifts and honour for himself to increase his own advantage, even at the cost of contention.

148 Suppose my virtues were to become apparent to everyone in the world, then no one would even hear of his virtues.

149 Were my faults to be concealed there would be worship for me, not for him. Now I receive gifts of alms easily. I am honoured while he is not.

150 Delighted we shall watch while at last he is crushed, the object of everyone's ridicule, criticized from all sides.

151 Indeed, it seems this wretch even vied with me! Does he have this much learning, wisdom, beauty, good breeding, or wealth?

152 Hearing my own virtues being related on all sides in this way, tingling with delight, I shall drink from the fountain of happiness.

153 Even if he is given alms we must snatch them from him by force, giving him only enough to live by if he does some work for us.

154 We must make him fall from happiness and involve him in continual pain. Because of him we have all suffered the afflictions of cyclic existence hundreds of times.

155 Immeasurable aeons have passed while you sought to realize your own well-being. This mighty effort of yours has led only to suffering.

156 At my entreaty proceed in this way right now without delay. Later you will see the virtues of this, for the word of the Sage is true.

157 This condition, without success, happiness, or Buddhahood, would not have come to pass if you had done this before.

158 Therefore, just as you have formed the notion 'I' regarding others' drops of sperm and blood, you must also develop that notion regarding other people.

159 Acting as the other person, take away from this body every useful thing you see in it, and use that to benefit others.

160 'He is well-situated, another badly off. The other is lowly. He is exalted. The other works. He does not.' In this way engender jealousy towards yourself.

161 Make yourself fall from happiness and involve yourself in the suffering of others. Saying, 'When does he do anything?', point out his pretence.

162 Even if a mistake is made by someone else, on his head alone let it fall, and, even if his error is only minor, inform on him to the 'great sage'.

163 Tarnish his reputation with reports of the superior repute of others and set him to do tasks for people as if he were a despised slave.

164 He should not be praised for his chance share of virtues, for he is full of faults. Act so that no one might know of his virtue.

165 In brief, whatever malicious act you performed upon others in order to benefit yourself, cause that same predicament to befall yourself for the benefit of living beings.

166 He should be given no encouragement at all which might make him talkative. He should be made to behave like a new bride: modest, timid, and guarded.

167 'Do this! Stay like that! You must not do this!' This is how he should be subjugated and punished if he disobeys.

168 If, despite being instructed in this way, you do not do it, you it is, Mind, that I shall punish. All faults rest with you.

169 Where are you off to? I can see you. I shall knock all the insolence out of you. Things were different before, when I was ruined by you.

170 Give up now any hope that you may still get your own way. Unworried as you are by repeated molestation, I have sold you to others!

171 If I do not give you away joyfully to living beings, you will hand me over to the guards of hell. There is no doubt.

172 Long have I been tormented, handed over by you in that way many times. Recalling those iniquities I shall strike you down, you slave to your own wants.

173 If you are pleased with yourself you should take no pleasure in yourself. If the self needs protection it is inappropriate to protect it.

174 The more this body is protected, the more fragile it becomes, the more it degenerates.

175 And when it has degenerated in this way, even the entire wealth-bearing earth is not adequate to fulfil its longings. So, who will grant its desire?

176 One who longs for the impossible is tormented and his hopes are shattered. Whereas, for one who does not hope for anything, there is fulfilment unimpaired.

177 Therefore do not give rein to the ever increasing desires of the body. It is really good not to take something when one wants it.

178 This ghastly impure form, which is devoid of motion and is impelled by another, is to end up lost in ashes. Why do I cling to it?

179 What do I want with this contraption, whether it is dead or alive? What is so special about its clay and other elements? Hah! You do not violate your identification of it as yourself!

180 One partial to the body earns suffering to no purpose. What purpose has hostility or kindness for something equal to a block of wood?

181 Whether protected by me in this way, or devoured by vultures and other scavengers, it feels neither affection nor dislike. Why do I create affection for it?

182 At its ill-treatment, rage; at its worship, pleasure; if it knows neither for itself, for whose sake my exertion?

183 Those who are fond of this body are said to be my friends. Why are those who are fond of their own body not also dear to me?

184 Therefore, without regret, I abandon my body to the benefit of the world. For this reason, though it has many faults, I carry it as a tool for the task.

185 So enough of worldly affairs! I shall follow the learned ones, remembering the teaching on vigilance, warding off sloth and torpor.

186 Therefore, in order to tear down the obscuring veil, I shall concentrate my mind in meditation, constantly on the proper object, dragging it from false paths.

9
THE PERFECTION OF UNDERSTANDING

ALL other teaching was in preparation for the perfection of Understanding—so Śāntideva explains in the first verse of the chapter by that name. Understanding of the ultimate truth is, then, the most important of the perfections, and also, of course, the most difficult, if not impossible, to define. In recognition of the ineffability of the salvific 'omniscience' of Buddhas, proponents of the Madhyamaka school of Buddhist philosophy, to which Śāntideva adhered, refused to make any philosophical statements of their own. All intellection and verbalization are part of conventional truth or reality, rather than of ultimate truth. What one must realize is the emptiness, *śūnyatā*, of all phenomena, including everything perceived as constituting the universe. It includes philosophical views and statements of truth not only of other religions, but even those of Buddhism itself, such as the Four Truths of the Nobles, found in the teaching of the historical Buddha's first sermon (see v. 40). It even includes Enlightenment.

The teaching of *śūnyatā* is propounded by the *Prajñā-pāramitā Sūtras*, the Perfection of Wisdom Sūtras, which are accepted by the Madhyamaka school as the highest scriptural authority. The *Prajñā-pāramitā Sūtras* propound the 'emptiness' of all phenomena, but pay particular attention to the categories of constituents into which the psycho-physical organism called man is analysed. These constituents, *dharmas*, their arising and cessation, were initially set forth by the pre-Mahāyāna tradition as suitable objects of meditation in order to develop the Understanding that there is no permanent, unchanging, entirely satisfactory entity with which to identify. To realize this was to realize the truth. The regularization and organization of these teachings was the object of a secondary body of scripture, known as the *Abhidharma*, or 'ancillary doctrine'. However, these categories and this truth seem themselves to have become the objects of reification, and to have been perceived as ultimates, particularly by Ābhidharmikas, those who expounded the *Abhidharma*, and who maintained that the lists of such categories contained the ultimate truth. The *Prajñā-pāramitā Sūtras* seem to have arisen in reaction to such tendencies, attempting to rectify such wrong views by reasserting exhaustively the emptiness of all phenomena. For something 'to exist really' it must be permanent, unchanging, and independent of other factors. The Madhyamaka continued this tradition of asserting *śūnyatā*, emptiness, by demonstrating the inherent inconsistencies of all statements purporting to be true.

The chapter on the perfection of Understanding in the *Bodhicaryāvatāra* is a deluge of such refutation. A number of opponents are lined up, each to be rebutted in turn as their particular views become relevant to Śāntideva's line of argument. It is the nature of such works as this that one knows the winner from the outset. For the audience it is just a matter of watching how skilfully each opponent is rebutted, how smooth the turn to the next. No opponent is taken all the way through the argument. Each is dismissed once he has served Śāntideva's purpose. Opponents are refuted on their own grounds, their theories shown to be flawed and often made laughable; or they are taken under the wing of the author and shown that, did they but understand their own theories properly, they would realize they were in agreement with the Madhyamaka in what is really relevant.

Even to refute is to make a statement and take a position of some kind. The statements most characteristic of the Madhyamaka are such as these:

> . . . nothing exists without a cause, nor contained in individual or combined causes.
>
> Neither has anything come from another, nor does it remain, nor does it go . . . (vv. 141–2)
>
> It follows that there is no cessation and there is no coming into existence at any time. Therefore none of this entire universe has come into existence or ceased. (v. 149)

The arguments which lead to these conclusions are, in places, extremely difficult to understand, especially as it is not possible to be sure of the original line of reasoning: there is debate within the Buddhist tradition over the interpretation of individual verses and even disagreement whether some arguments are put forward by the opponent or the Mādhyamika. Moreover, the exacting style of this chapter derives from the competitive scholastic debates which took place daily at such monastic universities as Nālandā. According to the Chinese monk Hsüan-tsang, who visited Nālandā in the first half of the seventh century CE, even monks of moderate renown who had managed to pass the exacting entrance examination were certain to be humbled and to forfeit their renown at such debates (Dutt 1962, 328 ff.). The abstruse character of this chapter is therefore deliberate and a mark of its success.

In some places in our translation we have chosen to differ from the interpretation of received tradition, especially where that interpretation seems far-fetched. For example, the argument of the Cittamātra ('Mind-only') opponent in v. 24 is traditionally understood to refer to mind-reading, which is one of the supernormal powers of a Buddha. The debate at this point is whether or not the mind can perceive itself. According to the Cittamātra there must be a real mind which is the basis of the illusory world and that illusion is the product of and perceived by the unenlightened mind. 'If someone with the necessary causal conditions such as concentration can see the consciousness of others from afar, therefore it must be possible to clearly behold one's own consciousness which is so near' (Batchelor 1979, 131). Taken in this way, the argument in the verse is that, if the mind of a Buddha can perceive the mind of another, mind must be able to perceive mind, thus proving that the mind can perceive itself.

However, we understand the argument as an assertion that the mind is aware of itself by inference: it knows that it exists because it perceives, otherwise what would be perceiving?

It illuminates itself by seeing what is in indirect contact with the cause.

We think that our interpretation makes better sense of the Sanskrit, fits the flow of the debate, and better justifies the refutation by the Mādhyamika. Yet there is no support for our interpretation in the commentarial tradition on this verse and it is radically different from the traditional interpretation. Is it really possible for the tradition to have 'got it wrong'? Can we be justified in rejecting the interpretation offered by Prajñākaramati? To answer this we shall look at that tradition.

The earliest commentaries on the *Bodhicaryāvatāra* known to us were probably written in the tenth to eleventh centuries CE, that is, three centuries after its composition. These commentaries are based on the canonical version. However, the substantially different and shorter version of the *Bodhicaryāvatāra* recovered from Tun-huang seems to have been mentioned in a ninth-century Tibetan catalogue (see Saito 1993, 13). The Tun-huang version contains some verses identical to those in the canonical version, some additional to them, and some which are similar but not identical, as well as excluding many verses present in the canonical version (see below). By the time of the commentaries available to us, then, there was already considerable discrepancy between the two versions of the text.

Although these commentaries show no awareness of the existence of another version and the canonical version is accepted as the product of a single author, uncertainty is expressed regarding certain verses in this chapter: Prajñākaramati gives two variant readings for v. 52, and denies the authenticity of a series of verses: 49–51. Even if Prajñākaramati and the later commentators had access to an unbroken tradition of commentary on the text reaching back to its original composition, the text clearly underwent a great deal of change, as did its interpretation.

Commentaries were composed for a combination of reasons. They preserved the text and provided it with meaning at different levels, from the grammatical to the spiritual. The text was, and is, used as the basis for spiritual instruction, but the meaning given to the text was coloured by the religious perspective of the individual commentator and of his milieu. This led to the inclusion in the main body of the text of additional material, perhaps originally commentarial, considered important or relevant by that tradition. Thus, for example, the canonical recension of the *Bodhicaryāvatāra* contains a section, not found in that from Tun-huang, refuting the existence of a creator god (vv. 118–25), and possibly indicating the increased importance of monotheistic beliefs in the centuries after Śāntideva's time or in the geographical region where such material was incorporated.

It is characteristic of the Indian commentarial style to read as much as possible into the basic text. Some types of commentary on Hindu scriptures even read entire words, sentiments, and references into the individual letters of a word. While no such extreme occurs here, it remains true that the tradition has provided a considerable amount of material, which may be far removed from the intentions of the original author. At the same time, though one may attempt to recover his intention, one can at best make an informed guess and cannot be certain that any conclusions are correct. (No autograph manuscript of a medieval Indian Buddhist text has survived to the present day.) So, as far as Śāntideva's intention is concerned, an absolute 'truth' cannot be reached. Yet the interpretations of different traditions are true for them, because they are relevant to the aims and world view of those traditions. In making this translation we are not representing any particular Buddhist tradition, and our approach has been to try to provide the simplest possible reading of the text in the hope that this also corresponds most closely to the author's intent.

Existing translations of this chapter into English, French, and German supply varying, sometimes copious, amounts of additional commentarial material within the translation itself, without which the verses of the text are deemed to be incomprehensible. (Verse 24 quoted above is a mild example of this method.) With the exception of stage directions, we have avoided such additional material in our translation, since we feel it can distort and sometimes confuse the line of argument. It also totally obscures the literary character of the original text. Though terse, the verses do, in our opinion, contain all the arguments and these do make sense by themselves. This terseness is characteristic of texts of Indian philosophical debate. A word or two referring to a particular argument, belief, or analogy would conjure up the whole in its entirety for a scholar familiar with contemporary philosophical positions and their rebuttal. This terseness, combined with the fact that it deals with philosophical issues, explains why most of the difficulties and differences of interpretation of the *Bodhicaryāvatāra* relate to this chapter.

While we feel that the additional material provided by existing translations does on occasion distort the line of argument, it is undeniable that the line of argument has in any case become distorted in transmission. From comparison with the Tun-huang version it is clear that in places the argument would flow more smoothly without the additions present in the canonical recension. The general structure is untidy. For example, there is debate with the Sāṃkhya school in two different places in the current recension. Admittedly, this is only an aesthetic failing, but one which we suspect the author would have preferred not to allow. Furthermore, there is confusion as to whether certain arguments expressed are those of the Mādhyamika philosopher, i.e. Śāntideva, or of his Cittamātra opponent. The Cittamātra school of Buddhist philosophy is closely related to the Madhyamaka school, responding to its perceived shortcomings (see Introduction to Chapter 8), and it is, therefore, understandable that they are difficult to distinguish. Nevertheless, it seems likely that matters were clearer prior to some of the additions made to the canonical recension. It is in any case interesting to compare and speculate. Since Saito's work on this chapter is not easily accessible, we reproduce below a summary of part of the table in which he compares this chapter from the two recensions by listing which verses have equivalents, approximate equivalents, or are absent from the other version (Saito 1994, 9–13). He uses the numbering of the Sanskrit editions, which we have taken the liberty of readjusting (on the numbering, see below). We are assuming that his mention of the canonical version's 20cd to 21ab is a reference to the verse included in error by Minaev. Thus our '21' is Saito's '22', etc., whereas our numbering prior to 21 is the same as his. In our lists the letters a and b refer to the two halves of a Sanskrit verse.

The following verses of the canonical version have equivalents in the Tun-huang version:

3 5 7a 9b–10a 11a 12–14a 15 18a 19a 21 23a 30–31a 34 36–37 53–54 56–59 74 81 83 85 87 99a 100b–101 103–104 141b 143 145ab 147–148 151–152 164a.

The following verses of the canonical version have approximate equivalents in the Tun-huang version:

1 2 4 6 9a 10b 11b 14b 16a 17a 18b 19b 20b 22 24–25 32a 33 35 42 55 68a 75 78 79b 80 82 84 86 99b–100a 102 142 149–150 153–155 167.

The following verses of the canonical version have no equivalents in the Tun-huang version:

7b–8 16b 17b 20a 23b 26–29 31b 32b 38–41 43–52 60–67 68b–73 76–77 79a 88–98 105–141a 144 145b–146 156–163 164b–166.

Saito also gives the reverse information for the Tun-huang recension of this chapter, which reveals that it in turn contains verses not in the canonical recension. Most of these come in the section to which Saito gives the subheading 'Examination of Selflessness' (vv. 57–77 in the canonical recension). The total number of verses in the Tun-huang recension of this chapter is 92, making it much shorter than the canonical recension, which has 167 verses.

An outline of the structure of this chapter in the canonical recension, the basis of our translation, is given below. We have given more detailed assistance and explanation in the notes to this chapter:

Introduction of topic: Understanding v. 1

The existence of two levels of truth or reality vv. 2–8

Refutation of Hīnayānist (non-Mahāyāna) re process of gaining merit vv. 9–10

Refutation of Mind-only vv. 11–34

Refutation of Hīnayānist vv. 35–56

Refutation of an entity 'I', vv. 57–87:
- on basis of analysis, accepted by Hīnayānist, of body into teeth, hair, blood, etc. vv. 57–9
- against Sāṃkhya theory of a Self characterized by consciousness vv. 60–7
- against Nyāya definition of Self vv. 68–9
- concerning moral consequences in absence of a Self vv. 70–1
- as the mind vv. 73–4
- concerning the problem of the practice of compassion vv. 75–6
- by analysis of the body down to atoms which are also analysed vv. 77–87

Refutation of an entity 'sensation' vv. 88–101

Refutation of an entity 'mind' vv. 102–5a

Conclusion that no entities really exist v. 105b

Nature of the existence of two truths vv. 106–11a

Impossibility of establishing causality or non-causality, vv. 111b–49:

- between consciousness and object of consciousness vv. 111b–15
- including impossibility of existence without causes vv. 116–17
- of God vv. 118–25
- of atoms v. 126a
- of the Sāṃkhya theories of the three constituents of primal matter and the consequence being present in the cause vv. 126b–37
- concluded, and taken as proof of emptiness vv. 138–49

Spiritual relevance of the established emptiness vv. 150–3

Resolve that all beings should understand emptiness v. 154a

The horrors of cyclic existence, the result of not realizing emptiness vv. 154b–65

Resolve to bring all beings to the understanding of emptiness vv. 166–7

The refutation of the ultimate existence of a personal entity, 'I', or of any other entity, contained in vv. 57–105, follows the structure of the four 'foundations of Mindfulness', the *sati-paṭṭhāna* (in Pali). These are the subject of the two *Sati-paṭṭhāna Suttas* in the Pali Buddhist canon and form one of the most fundamental Buddhist meditation practices for the development of mindfulness and Understanding. The four are the body (*kāya*), sensations (*vedanā*), mind (*citta*), and all phenomena or possible objects of the mind (*dharma*). Though this last category is stated in v. 105b, it could be taken as the subject of the entire remaining debate.

According to the *Sati-paṭṭhāna Suttas*, by observing each category and applying various analyses to them, one realizes that they are not fixed entities, that they all arise and cease. In Śāntideva's work various opponents are refuted through the analyses of these four categories. Moreover he takes the analyses beyond the traditional limit to their logical extreme. He establishes that even the resulting products of analysis can be reduced to nothing by further analysis and are therefore 'empty'. Even their arising and cessation will be stated to be ultimately empty later on in the argument (v. 149). Thus Śāntideva takes a traditional Buddhist analysis and uses its own methods to draw out from it the Madhyamaka truth of 'emptiness' (*śūnyatā*).

The main opponents in this chapter are either fellow Buddhists of other schools of Buddhist philosophy: the Hīnayānist (i.e. the non-Mahāyāna), including the Ābhidharmika, and the Mind-only; or proponents of orthodox schools of Brahmanical Hindu philosophy: the Sāṃkhya and the Nyāya-vaiśeṣika. Most attention is given to the Hīnayānist, the Mind-only, and the Sāṃkhya. Madhyamaka developed in reaction to the Hīnayānists, who do not accept realization of emptiness as the liberating Understanding. Mind-only accepts emptiness, but, in reaction to Madhyamaka, posits the real existence of a mind which underlies both cyclic existence and Enlightenment. The Madhyamaka did not accept this development (see the Introduction to Chapter 8). The argument probably engages with those opponents most strongly represented in the monastic university environment.

We have identified the speaker as the Mādhyamika or as an opponent with the help of stage directions in square brackets. There are exceptions to this when Śāntideva makes it clear in his text that he is presenting the opponent's view by such phrases as 'if you argue that . . .', 'if you claim that', or 'What if . . .?'

The Sanskrit editions accessible to us (see p. xl) contain various errors in the numbering of the verses. There are 167 verses, but the final number counted by all of them is 168. This results from a mistake, reproduced by Minaev (1890) from the text recorded in a manuscript before him, which had copied the equivalent of a single verse twice—a common scribal error. Verses 20b and 21a of his edition are not found in some manuscripts or in the Tibetan translation. Although De la Vallée Poussin (1901–14) and Vaidya (1988) point out this error (albeit with a rather confused regurgitation of De la Vallée Poussin on the part of Vaidya), they both retain the numbering originally provided by Minaev. We have not. Nor have we retained the occasional numbering of three-line and one-line verses that they offer in an attempt to redress the marked limp, where sentences straddle verses, created by the insertion of verses and half verses into the text during the course of its history (see Saito 1994, pp. 2–3). We begin at the beginning, counting each verse as one verse until we reach the end. Thus we finish at v. 167, and with the advantage that our numeration corresponds to that of translations from the Tibetan.

A few other works have been published on, or including, this chapter (see the General Introduction, n. 17). The most readable of them is H.H. the Dalai Lama, *Transcendent Wisdom* (1988). Additionally, available in facsimile is Michael Sweet's Ph.D. thesis *Śantideva and the Mādhyamika: The Prajñāpāramitā-pariccheda of the Bodhicaryāvatāra*, University of Wisconsin (U.M.I. Dissertation Services, Ann Arbor, Michigan, 1976). This provides the most material, including a translation of the commentary by Prajñākaramati.

The Perfection of Understanding

1 It is for the sake of understanding that the Sage taught this entire collection of preparations. Therefore, in the desire to put an end to suffering, one should develop understanding.

2 It is agreed that there are these two truths: the conventional and the ultimate. Reality is beyond the scope of intellection. Intellection is said to be the conventional.

3 In the light of this, people are seen to be of two types: namely, the spiritually developed and the spiritually undeveloped. Of these, the world-view of the undeveloped is invalidated by the world-view of the spiritually developed.

4 Even the views of the spiritually developed are invalidated by the superior understanding of those at successively higher levels, by means of an analogy which is accepted by both parties, irrespective of what they intend to prove.

5 Ordinary people see existent things and also imagine them to be real, that is to say, not as an illusion. It is in this regard that there is disagreement between the ordinary person and the spiritually developed.

6 Even the objects of direct perception, such as visible form, are only established by popular consensus and not by a valid means of knowledge. That consensus is wrong, like, for example, the popular view that impure things are pure.

7 The Protector taught in terms of existent things in order to guide people.
If it is objected on the basis of conventional usage that in reality these entities are not momentary,

8 [the fact is that] there is no fault in the use of conventional truth by the spiritually developed. They understand reality better than ordinary people do. Otherwise ordinary people would invalidate the definition of women as impure.

9 Merit comes from a Conqueror who is like an illusion in the same way as it would if he was truly existent.
[Hīnayānist] If a living being is like an illusion, how then is it reborn once dead?

10 [Mādhyamika] Even an illusion persists for as long as the concurrence of its causes.
How does a being truly exist simply because there is a continuum of states that last a long time?

11 [Cittamātra] If consciousness does not exist, then there is no evil in, for example, murdering an illusory man.
[Mādhyamika] On the contrary, good and evil arise when one is endowed with the illusion of consciousness.

12 [Cittamātra] An illusory conscious mind is not possible, since spells and the like cannot produce such an illusion.
[Mādhyamika] Illusion is also of different kinds, arising from different causes.

13 Nowhere is there a single cause which has the power to produce everything.
[Cittamātra] If one liberated according to ultimate truth remains subject to cyclic existence according to conventional truth,

14 Then, in that case, even a Buddha would be subject to cyclic existence. So what is the point of the path of conduct leading to Awakening?
[Mādhyamika] Because illusion is not stopped unless its causes are stopped,

15 Whereas, even according to conventional truth, it is not possible when its causes are destroyed.
[Cittamātra] When even false perception does not exist, by what is illusion perceived?

16 [Mādhyamika] When, according to you, illusion itself does not exist, what is perceived?
[Cittamātra] It is an aspect of the mind itself, even if it is different from reality.

17 [Mādhyamika] If illusion is the same as the mind, what is seen by what? Moreover, it is taught by the Protector of the world that mind does not perceive mind.

18 As a knife blade cannot cut itself, so it is with the mind. If you object that it illuminates itself, as does a light,

19 [our response is that] a light-source itself is not illuminated, because it is not concealed by darkness.
[Cittamātra] Unlike clear crystal, a blue object is not dependent on anything else for its blueness.

20 This shows that something is either dependent on another or independent.
[Mādhyamika] When something is not blue it cannot make itself blue by itself.

21 A light is said to illuminate once this action is cognized by a cognition. Intellection is said to illuminate once this is cognized by what?

22 Whether the mind is luminous or not, talking about it is pointless since it is never seen by anything, like the beauty of a barren woman's daughter.

23 [Cittamātra] If there is no self-perception, how is consciousness remembered?
[Mādhyamika] Memory comes from connection with another experience, as with the shrew's poison.

24 [Cittamātra] It illuminates itself by seeing what is in indirect contact with the cause.
[Mādhyamika] A jar seen by applying sight-restoring lotion would still not be the lotion itself.

25 How something is seen, heard, or cognized is not what is contested here, but it is refuted here that projection is real, as that is the cause of suffering.

26 [Mādhyamika] If illusion is the same as the mind it is false to claim that it is also different. If it exists as a thing in its own right, how is it the same? If it is the same, then it does not exist in its own right.

27 Just as illusion can be seen even though it does not really exist, so it must be with the thing that sees, the mind. If you claim that cyclic existence must be based on something real or else it would be just like space,

28 [our reply is] How could something non-existent gain causal efficiency by being based on something real? For, according to you, the mind is reduced to isolation, accompanied by things which do not exist.

29 If the mind is without external objects, then everyone is a Tathāgata. That being so, what virtue is gained even if 'mind-only' is posited?

30 [Cittamātra] Even if the similarity to illusion is recognized, how does defilement cease, when lust for a woman who is an illusion still arises in the one who created her?

31 [Mādhyamika] That happens because the influence of the defilements and what is cognized has not been destroyed in her creator, so that at the time of seeing her the influence of emptiness in him is weak.

32 The influence of phenomena is removed by employing the influence of emptiness, and even that is later eradicated by inculcating the realization, 'nothing really exists'.

33 [Cittamātra] If it is concluded that the entity which does not really exist cannot be perceived, then how does a non-entity which is without basis remain before the mind?

34 [Mādhyamika] When neither entity nor non-entity remains before the mind, since there is no other mode of operation, grasping no objects, it becomes tranquil.

35 As the wishing-gem and the magical tree fulfil desires, so the appearance of the Conqueror is seen because of his vow and the people who need to be trained.

36 Just as a pillar empowered by an expert on poisons, who then dies, will continue to neutralize venom and other poisons even when he is long dead,

37 So too the 'pillar' that is the Conqueror, empowered by following the path to Awakening, continues to achieve all ends even after that Bodhisattva has attained Enlightenment.

38 [Hīnayānist] How could worship offered to something which has no consciousness be fruitful?
[Mādhyamika] Because it is taught that it is the same whether he is present or has attained Enlightenment,

39 And, according to scripture, fruit comes from that worship, whether it is conventionally true or ultimately true, in the same way that worship offered to an existing Buddha is said to be fruitful.

40 [Hīnayānist] Liberation comes from understanding the Truths. What is the point of understanding emptiness?
[Mādhyamika] The reason is that scripture states that there is no Awakening without this path.

41 [Hīnayānist] Surely Mahāyāna scripture is not established!
[Mādhyamika] In what way is your scripture established?
[Hīnayānist] Because it is established for both of us.
[Mādhyamika] It was not established for you at first!

42 Apply your criterion for the acceptance of it to Mahāyāna scripture also. If something is true because accepted by two different parties even texts such as the Vedas would be true.

43 If your objection is that Mahāyāna scripture is controversial, reject your own scripture since it is contested by non-Buddhists, and any part in that scripture contested by your own people or others.

44 The dispensation is rooted in the monkhood and the monkhood itself is imperfectly established. Even the Enlightenment of those whose minds grasp onto entities is imperfectly established.

45 If your objection is that liberation results from the destruction of the defilements, then it should happen immediately afterwards. Yet one can see the power over them even of undefiled action.

46 If you put forward the argument that they have no craving leading to grasping,
[our response is:] Even if their craving is undefiled, does it not exist as delusion?

47 Feeling causes craving, and they do have feeling. A mind which has objects will get stuck on one or another.

48 Without emptiness a mind is fettered and arises again, as in the meditative attainment of non-perception. Therefore one should meditate on emptiness.

49 You accept that whatever text might be in accordance with the Discourses was spoken by the Buddha. So why are the Mahāyāna scriptures not accepted as equal in value to your own Discourses?

50 If the whole lot is faulted because one part is not accepted, why not treat the lot as spoken by the Conqueror because a single part is the same as in the Discourses?

51 Who will bar acceptance of the teaching over which those led by the Great Kāśyapa hesitated, simply because you do not understand it?

52 Remaining in cyclic existence for the benefit of those suffering through delusion is achieved through freedom from the two extremes, attachment and fear. This is the fruit of emptiness.

53 So, that being the case, there is no valid objection to the emptiness position. Therefore, emptiness should be meditated upon without reservation.

54 Since emptiness is the countermeasure to the darkness of the obscuration of what is cognized and the obscuration by the defilements, how is it that one who desires Omniscience does not make haste to meditate upon it?

55 Granted that something which causes suffering causes fear—but emptiness allays suffering! So why does it cause fear?

56 Granted, too, fear may come from any quarter whatsoever if there is something called 'I'. If your position is that there is no 'I', who can be afraid?

57 The teeth, hair, or nails are not I, nor is the bone, nor am I the blood, neither the mucus nor the phlegm, not the pus nor the synovial fluid.

58 I am neither the marrow nor the sweat. I am neither the lymph nor the intestines. I am not the rectum, nor am I the excrement or the urine.

59 I am neither the flesh nor the sinews. I am neither heat nor wind. I am neither the orifices nor, in any way, the six consciousnesses.

60 If I were consciousness of sound, then sound would be perceived at all times. But without something to be conscious of, what does it perceive on account of which there is said to be consciousness?

61 If not being conscious of anything is consciousness, it follows that a block of wood is consciousness. This proves that there is no consciousness in the absence of something to be cognized.

62 Why does what is conscious of a colour not also hear it at the same time? [If you argue that] When it has no connection with sound there is also no consciousness of such from that,

63 [we respond:] How can something whose nature is to perceive sound perceive colour?
[Sāṃkhya] One person is regarded both as a father and a son.
[Mādhyamika] But they do not really exist,

64 Since neither 'goodness', nor 'passion', nor 'darkness' are either the son or the father. Moreover, its essential nature is not observed in connection with the perception of sound.

65 If you argue: It is the same thing taking on a different guise, like an actor. He too does not remain constant. The one thing has different natures.
[We respond that] It has an unprecedented kind of uniformity.

66 If the different nature is not the true nature, then please describe what its own form is. If it is the nature of consciousness, then it follows that all people are one and the same.

67 What is conscious and what is unconscious would also be one and the same thing because both are equally existent. After all, if difference is false, then on what basis is there similarity?

68 That which is not conscious is not 'I' because it lacks consciousness like an object such as a cloth. If it is a conscious thing because it possesses consciousness it follows that when it stops being conscious of something it perishes.

69 If the Self is in fact unchanged, what is achieved by its having consciousness? It is agreed that the nature of something which is unconscious and does not partake in any activity in this way is the same as space.

70 If you argue that the connection of action and consequence is not possible without a Self, for 'If the agent of the action has perished who experiences the consequence?',

71 [our response is:] For both of us it is established that the action and the consequence of the action have a different location. Moreover, since the self does not have any function in this, surely arguing this point is irrelevant here.

72 The one who provides the cause is connected with the consequence? Such an occurrence is never seen. It is taught that there is an agent and an experiencer of the consequence in terms of a unity of the continuum of consciousnesses.

73 The past or future mind is not 'I' since that does not exist. If the present mind is 'I' then, when it has ceased, the 'I' does not exist any more.

74 Just as the trunk of a banana tree is nothing when split into pieces, in the same way too, the 'I' is not a real entity when hunted out analytically.

75 If you argue: for whom is there compassion if no being exists?,

[our response is] For anyone projected through the delusion which is embraced for the sake of what has to be done.

76 [Objection] Whose is the task to be done, if there is no being?
[Mādhyamika] True. Moreover, the effort is made in delusion, but, in order to bring about an end to suffering, the delusion of what has to be done is not prevented.

77 However, egotism, which is the cause of suffering, increases from the delusion that there is a Self, and, if this is the unavoidable result of that, it is better to meditate on no-Self.

78 The body is not the feet, not the calves, not the thighs, and the body is not the buttocks. It is not the stomach nor the back either, nor is it the chest nor arms.

79 It is not the hands nor the sides either, nor the armpits, nor is it the shoulder area. The body is not the neck nor the head. What among these, then, is the body?

80 If you argue that the body is present in part in all of these, [our response is that] it is only the parts that are present in the parts, so where does it occur itself?

81 If the body did exist in its entirety in the hands and all these other parts, then there would be just as many bodies as there are hands and other parts.

82 The body is not inside. It is not outside. How can the body be in the hands and other parts? It is not separate from the hands and other parts. How, then, is it to be found?

83 So there is no body. Yet, under the influence of delusion, there is the belief in a body regarding the hands and other parts, because of their particular configuration, just as one might believe there is a person when looking at a post.

84 As long as the combination of causes lasts, that post looks like a person. In the same way, as long as it lasts in respect of the hands and other parts, the body continues to be seen in them.

85 In the same way, since it is an assemblage of toes, which one is the foot? The same goes for a toe, since it is an assemblage of joints. A joint can also be analysed into its own constituents.

86 Even the constituents can be analysed down to atoms. The atom too can be divided according to the directions. The division of a direction, since it is without parts, leaves space. Therefore the atom does not exist.

87 What person who analyses things thoroughly would take delight in a form which, as has been demonstrated, is like a dream? And since the body, as demonstrated, does not exist, then what woman or what man is there?

88 If suffering really exists, why does it not afflict people when they are cheerful? If tasty food or the like is a pleasure, why does it not please someone afflicted by grief, for example?

89 If it is not experienced because it is overcome by something stronger, how can the nature of a sensation be attributed to that which does not have the nature of an experience?

90 [Objection] Surely suffering continues at a subtle level, its grossness removed?
[Mādhyamika] If the next sensation is purely one of contentment, then that subtlety must also be subtlety of contentment.

91 If suffering does not arise when causes of the opposite have arisen, surely the resulting notion of 'a sensation' is in fact a superimposition of our imagination?

92 For that reason this analysis is practised as an antidote to that superimposition. For spiritual practitioners are nourished by the meditative absorptions which grow in the field of false imagination.

93 If a sense organ and an object are separated by a space, how can there be contact between the two? Furthermore, if they are not separate they are one, so what is in contact with what?

94 One atom cannot enter another atom because each is the same, without free space. If one thing does not enter the other they cannot combine. If they do not combine there is no contact.

95 How can there be contact for something which has no parts? If you understand how there can be contact without parts, demonstrate it.

96 Moreover, it is impossible for consciousness, which has no physical form, to have contact, nor for an assemblage since it is not a real thing, as was concluded from earlier analysis.

97 When, as this shows, there is no contact, how can sensation arise? For what purpose is this vexation? From what and for whom is there affliction?

98 Since there is no one to experience sensation and sensation does not exist, why, after realizing that this is the case, O craving, do you not burst asunder?

99 There is seeing and touching by a self which is like a dream or illusion. Sensation is not perceived by the mind because it is produced simultaneously with it.

100 What happens earlier is remembered by what arose later, not experienced. It does not experience itself and it is not experienced by another.

101 Moreover, there is no one who experiences sensation, therefore, in reality, there is no sensation. So who, in this bundle devoid of self, can be afflicted by it?

102 The mind is not positioned in the sense faculties, nor in form or the other aggregates, nor in the space in between. The mind is found neither internally nor externally, nor anywhere else either.

103 What is not in the body nor elsewhere, neither intermingled nor separate anywhere, that is nothing. Therefore living beings are inherently liberated.

104 If consciousness exists prior to what is cognized, on what basis does it come into existence? If you argue that

consciousness arises simultaneously with the object perceived, on what basis does it come into existence?

105 If it arises after the thing to be cognized, then from what does the consciousness arise? In this way, it is demonstrated that no phenomenon comes into existence.

106 [Objection] If, this being the case, conventional truth does not exist, then how can there be two truths?
[Mādhyamika] In fact it does exist according to the conventional truth of another.
[Objection] How can there exist a liberated being?

107 [Mādhyamika] He is false imagination in the mind of another, but he does not exist because of conventional truth on his own part. After something has been established it exists; if not, it does not even exist as a conventional truth.

108 The pair imagination and what is imagined are mutually dependent, just as all analysis is expressed in terms that are commonly understood.

109 [Objection] But when, as a result of analysis, there is further analysis by means of analysis, there is no end to it, since that analysis can also be analysed.

110 [Mādhyamika] But when the thing which is to be analysed has been analysed there is no basis left for analysis. Since there is no basis it does not continue and that is said to be Enlightenment.

111 But whoever holds that these two both truly exist is on extremely shaky ground. If an object does exist on the strength of consciousness, how does one arrive at the existence of consciousness?

112 If the existence of consciousness is established on the strength of the existence of the object of which it is conscious, how does one arrive at the existence of the object? If they exist on the strength of each other's existence, neither of the two can exist.

113 If there is no father without a son, how can there be a son? If there is no son there is no father, so neither of them exist.

114 [Objection] A shoot grows from a seed. The seed is indicated by that shoot. Why is the existence of an object of consciousness not verified by the consciousness which results from it?

115 [Mādhyamika] The existence of the seed is verified by a consciousness which is not the same as the shoot. How is the existence of consciousness cognized so that it verifies the object of consciousness?

116 Ordinary people, through direct perception, observe all sorts of causes, since the distinct parts of a lotus, such as the stalk, result from distinct causes.

117 If you ask what caused the variety of the causes, [the answer is:] it results from the variety in the preceding causes. If you ask how the cause results in its consequence, [the answer is:] they resulted through the power of the preceding causes.

118 [Nyāya-Vaiśeṣika] God is the cause of the world.
[Mādhyamika] Then explain what God is. If he is 'the elements', so be it, but then why the fuss over a mere name?

119 Moreover, the earth and other elements are not one, nor permanent. They are inert and not divine. One can walk on them. They are impure. That is not God.

120 Space cannot be God, because it is inert. Nor is the Self, because its existence was disproved above. If creativity belongs to what is beyond conception, what can be said of the inconceivable?

121 What does he want to create? If a Self, surely that is something eternal? God, consciousness resulting from a cognizable object, and the nature of earth and other elements, are without beginning.

122 Suffering and happiness are the result of action. So say what he created. If you argue that the cause has no beginning, how could there be a beginning to its effect?

123 How come he does not create continuously, if he is not dependent on anything else? There is nothing else whatsoever which was not made by him, so on what might he depend?

124 If you argue that God is dependent on a combination of conditions, then again he is not the cause. He would have the power neither to refrain from creating if the combination of conditions were present, nor to create if they were absent.

125 If you argue that God creates without desiring to create, it follows that he is subject to something other than himself. Even if he creates out of the desire to create, he is subject to desire. In what way does this creator have omnipotence?

126 Those who claim that atoms are permanent have also been refuted above. Followers of Sāṃkhya maintain that primal matter is the permanent cause of the world:

127 The constituents of nature, that is, goodness, passion, and darkness, present in equilibrium are called primal matter. The universe is explained by their disequilibrium.

128 But it is not possible for a single thing to have three separate natures, so it does not exist. Likewise the constituents do not exist, since they too would each be made up of three constituents.

129 Furthermore, in the absence of the constituents, the existence of sound and other sense objects is beyond possibility. Moreover, sensations such as pleasure are not possible in something which has no consciousness, such as cloth.

130 If you argue that it is of the nature of existent entities to cause those sensations, surely existent entities have already been analysed away? Moreover, you hold that it is pleasure and the like which are the cause and not, therefore, cloth and other material objects.

131 If sensations such as pleasure came from things such as cloth, in the absence of those things there would be no

sensations such as pleasure. Furthermore, feelings such as pleasure are never seen to have any permanence.

132 If the manifestation of pleasure really exists, why is the feeling not perceived?
[Objection] That same sensation becomes subtle.
[Mādhyamika] How can it be both gross and subtle?

133 [Objection] Relinquishing the state of grossness it becomes subtle. It is the state of grossness or subtlety which is impermanent.
[Mādhyamika] Why not accept the impermanence of everything, as of them?

134 If you argue that the grossness is not separate from the feeling of pleasure, it is evident that pleasure is impermanent. If you accept that something non-existent cannot come into existence because of its non-existence,

135 You accept, even against your will, the coming into existence of something manifest which does not exist. If you accept that the result is in the cause, someone eating rice is eating dung!

136 Cotton seed would be bought at the price of cloth and worn as clothing! If you argue that ordinary people do not see this because of ignorance, one who understands this reality is in the same position.

137 Anyway, even ordinary people know about that. In what way do they not see it? If you argue that there is no validity in the knowledge of ordinary people, even the direct perception of something manifest is not real.

138 [Objection] If a means of knowledge is not a means of knowledge, surely knowledge gained by that means is false. Therefore, the emptiness of phenomena is not in reality ascertained.

139 [Mādhyamika] When there is no perception of something falsely projected as existent, there is no understanding of the non-existence of that entity. For it follows that, if an entity is not real, the negation of it is clearly not real.

140 Therefore, in a dream, when a son dies, it is the projection 'he does not exist' that prevents the projection of his existence from arising, but that is also false.

141 Therefore, with this kind of analysis, nothing exists without a cause, nor contained in individual or combined causes.

142 Neither has anything come from another, nor does it remain, nor does it go. What is the difference between an illusion and this which is taken by fools to be real?

143 Reflect on this: What is created by illusion and what is created by causes? Where does each come from and where does it go?

144 How can there be real existence in something factitious like a reflection, which is only seen in conjunction with something else and not seen in its absence?

145 For a phenomenon which already exists, what purpose would be served by a cause? Also for something which does not exist, what purpose would be served by a cause?

146 Even hundreds of billions of causes will not produce any change in something which does not exist. How can something in that state become existent? And what else can come into existence?

147 If something is not an existent thing at the time when it is a non-existent thing, when does the existent thing become existent? For that non-existent thing does not go away while the existent thing has not been produced.

148 And while the non-existent thing is not gone there can be no opportunity for the existent thing. Something which exists does not become non-existent, since this would have the contradictory consequence that one entity would have two natures.

149 It follows that there is no cessation and there is no coming into existence at any time. Therefore none of this entire universe has come into existence or ceased.

150 Rather, the states of existence are like dreams, on analysis the same as the trunk of a banana tree. There is in substance no difference between those who have attained Liberation and those who have not.

151 When all things are empty in this way, what can be received, what taken away? Who can be honoured or humiliated by whom?

152 From what can there be happiness or misery, what can be liked and what loathed? What craving can there be? For what is that craving, when examined as to its true nature?

153 On analysis, what world of living beings is there? Who, then, will die in it? Who will come to exist? Who has existed? Who is a relative? Who is whose friend?

154 May all of my kind accept that everything is like space. They get angry in disputes and delight in celebrations.

155 With feelings of grief, vexation, and despair; with mutually inflicted lacerations and amputations, because of their evil actions, they lead their lives miserably, longing for their own happiness.

156 After coming again and again to a good rebirth and enjoying pleasures again and again, they die and fall into hells and long, severe afflictions.

157 There are many pitfalls in existence, but there is not this truth there. There is mutual contradiction between the two. Reality could not be like this.

158 There, too, are oceans of misery, unending and savage, beyond compare. Likewise strength is meagre there. There, too, life is short.

159 There, too, because of the concerns of livelihood and health, in hunger, fatigue, and exhaustion, in sleep, in misfortunes, and in fruitless association with fools,

160 Life passes quickly, pointlessly, while solitude is hard to find. There, too, how could there be a way of preventing habitual distraction?

161 There, too, Māra strives to make us fall into great misfortune. There, because of the profusion of false paths, doubt is hard to overcome,

162 And the opportune moment is difficult to obtain again. The appearance of Buddhas is exceedingly rare and the flood of defilements hard to check. Oh, what a succession of suffering!

163 Oh misery! The extremely grievous condition of these beings who stay in the oceans of sufferings, who do not see their own wretched state though they stand in such extreme wretchedness!

164 Just like one who dowses himself with water again and again but must each time re-enter the fire again, so they consider themselves fortunate, though they are also extremely wretched.

165 As people live like this, pretending they will not grow old or die, horrific misfortunes approach, with death the foremost of them.

166 When shall I provide relief for those tormented in the fire of such suffering, with offerings of happiness flowing from the clouds of my merit?

167 When shall I teach emptiness and the accumulation of merit, by means of conventional truth, without reliance on projection, respectfully to those whose views are based on projection?

10
DEDICATION

INSTRUCTION has been given in all six perfections in the preceding chapters. Śāntideva now concludes the *Bodhicaryāvatāra* with a series of vows or *praṇidhāna*, in which he dedicates to the benefit of all beings the merit that he has generated through the training.

By the good that is mine from considering 'Undertaking the Way to Awakening', the *Bodhicaryāvatāra*, may all people adorn the way to Awakening. (10.1)

The sequence of vows which follows this opening declaration is not the first that he has made, however, for the bulk of Chapter 3 consists of similar dedications, introduced by the avowal:

With the good acquired by doing all this as described, may I allay all the suffering of every living being. (3.6)

Whereupon Śāntideva gives a further fifteen verses of dedication of merit. This section of Chapter 3 in fact constitutes the penultimate section of the liturgy of the Supreme Worship, and the 'good' referred to there is that arising from his performance of the previous sections of that ritual. Should we see the vows of Chapter 10 as needless duplication, resulting from the pious if repetitive excesses of a devout poet?

The key to understanding this second, and indeed the first, section of dedication lies in Śāntideva's definition of the Awakening Mind. In the first chapter he explains that the Awakening Mind is twofold:

That Awakening Mind should be understood to be of two kinds; in brief: the Mind resolved on Awakening and the Mind proceeding towards Awakening.

The distinction between these two should be understood by the wise in the same way as the distinction is recognized between a person who desires to go and one who is going, in that order. (1.15–16)

The merit produced by the former is great, but not as great as that produced by the latter:

> Even in cyclic existence great fruit comes from the Mind resolved on Awakening, but nothing like the uninterrupted merit that comes from that resolve when put into action. (1.17)

We can see therefore that the first section of dedication, in Chapter 3, involves the dedication of the merit which Śāntideva has generated through the arising of the first kind of Awakening Mind, 'the Mind resolved on Awakening'. When he reflects that he has now been born in the family of the Buddha (3.25) it is through the arising of this resolve. The second section of dedication, here in Chapter 10, involves the dedication of the merit generated through the second kind of Awakening Mind, 'the Mind proceeding towards Awakening'. As we have already explained, the dedication in Chapter 3 occurs as a part of the liturgy of the Supreme Worship, and so we can now see that Śāntideva employs this liturgy as the means whereby he encourages the first kind of Awakening Mind to arise. It follows from this that the merit he dedicates in Chapter 10 is the 'uninterrupted' merit that comes from the second kind of Awakening Mind, and that the means of its 'proceeding' towards Awakening is the practice of the perfections by the aspiring Bodhisattva.

The character of the two sets of vows reflects this difference. In Chapter 3 the vows are of a more limited scope: Śāntideva offers his own body to all creatures; he vows to provide sustenance, assistance, and guidance to all. Yet these vows remain very much in the realm of cyclic existence. He offers help to beings within the world. In Chapter 10, on the other hand, the Bodhisattva's vows are on a far grander scale, because he can dedicate the far greater merit acquired by putting his resolve for Awakening into action:

> Through my merit may all those in any of the directions suffering distress in body or mind find oceans of happiness and delight. (10.2)

Now he even has the power to transform the hells of cyclic existence with the glory of the various celestial Bodhisattvas, such as Samantabhadra, Mañjughoṣa, and Kṣitigarbha, and to transform cyclic existence itself into a Pure Land.

The grandeur of these vows reflects the grandeur of the Bodhisattva ideal in the Buddhist tradition and echoes vows made by previous Bodhisattvas earlier in their careers, particularly those of Dharmākara, the Bodhisattva who became the Buddha Amitābha. Amitābha is the Buddha of Sukhāvatī, the 'land of happiness', also known as the 'Pure Land' (see 10.4 and note). The larger *Sukhāvatī-vyūha Sūtra* (Cowell, Müller, and Takakusu 1969) relates how, in a previous life as the Bodhisattva Dharmākara, he made a series of vows describing the characteristics of Sukhāvatī. It was the realization of these vows that enabled him, through the power of his merit, to create Sukhāvatī, and it is interesting to note that a few of those vows occur here in Chapter 10, such as the vows that women become men (v. 30), and that all beings have immeasurable life (v. 33).

The making of such vows has then an added significance, for they are not only the expression of pious wishes, but the seeds of a spiritual reality which for many Mahāyāna Buddhists formed an important dimension of their own religious world. It is possible that the shorter *Sukhāvatī-vyūha Sūtra* was composed as early as the first century BCE, and it is known that Amitābha was the centre of a popular cult from the early centuries of the common era. In the form of the Pure Land schools of China and Japan, the power of Sukhāvatī and of Dharmākara's vows are felt even today. However, the significance of making such vows was not limited to the perspective of the *Sukhāvatī-vyūha Sūtras* alone, for the *Daśabhūmika Sūtra* also gives a list of ten such vows, quoted by Śāntideva in the *Śikṣā Samuccaya*, which are undertaken by the Bodhisattva when he enters upon the 'stage of delight', *pramuditā-bhūmi*, the first of the stages of the Bodhisattva's career (Bendall and Rouse, 265 ff.). In other words, the making of vows in this way came to be incorporated into the description of the Bodhisattva's career. The implication here is that Śāntideva envisages at this point that the aspiring Bodhisattva has finally entered upon the first of the Bodhisattva stages, i.e. through his training in the perfections he has become a Bodhisattva. In the account of the Bodhisattva stages given in the *Daśabhūmika Sūtra* each stage involves, amongst other things, the perfection of each perfection, beginning with that of generosity in the first stage, the stage of 'delight'. How appropriate that it is here that the Bodhisattva makes his vows by the power of his own merit, i.e. he dedicates or gives away all the merit that he has accumulated in his training.

This interpretation is consistent with the concern he expresses in Chapter 4 that, without sufficient merit and not strengthening his resolve, he will take too long to reach the first of the Bodhisattva stages, or *bhūmis*:

> Swinging back and forth like this in cyclic existence, now under the sway of errors, now under the sway of the Awakening Mind, it takes a long time to gain ground. (4.11)

The sense of the verse depends upon a double meaning, for both 'stage' and 'ground' translate the single term *bhūmi*.

As a further reflection of the extent to which Śāntideva was working within his milieu, we should note that other images in this chapter come from other Buddhist *sūtras*. The appearance of Kṣitigarbha (v. 13) conjures up the vows that he had made, as an aspiring Bodhisattva, to save all those in hell, as described in the *Kṣitigarbha Sūtra*. The streams gushing from Avalokiteśvara to satisfy the hungry ghosts (v. 18) are also described in the second chapter of the *Kāraṇḍavyūha Sūtra*.

After the culmination of the dedication of his merit with the wishes for the welfare of the Buddhas, Bodhisattvas, Pratyekabuddhas, and Śrāvakas in vv. 48–50, the author begins a separate section in vv. 51–8, the final part of the work. Here he turns to his own concerns and makes repeated requests for his own welfare and progress. This explains why he refers here to the 'stage of delight' which is assumed for the preceding part of the chapter:

> Through adoption by Mañjughoṣa, may I always gain entry into the spiritual community and the recollection of former births, until I reach the 'stage of delight'. (10.51)

In Chapter 1 Śāntideva explained that he was compiling the *Bodhicaryāvatāra* 'in order to perfume' his own mind; in other words, by contemplating the Bodhisattva's training and the arising of the Awakening Mind, he hoped that he would influence his own mind, and dispose himself to follow the same training. He has now finished this contemplation, and makes a personal plea that he himself should realize this training, as he has described it. For, as he exclaims at the end of Chapter 5, what is the point of advice if one does not act upon it?

These verses also differ from the rest in that they introduce Mañjughoṣa in a distinctly emphatic manner. Mañjughoṣa is mentioned individually here four times, whereas previously he was just one of several Bodhisattvas, usually headed by Samantabhadra. The *Śikṣā Samuccaya* also ends with devotional verses to Mañjuśrī, and, until comparison is made with the Tun-huang recension, there remains the possibility that these final verses of the *Bodhicaryāvatāra* were added on the model of the *Śikṣā Samuccaya*. The Tun-huang recension is eight verses longer than this recension.

Dedication

1 By the good that is mine from considering 'Undertaking the Way to Awakening', the *Bodhicaryāvatāra*, may all people adorn the path to Awakening.

2 Through my merit may all those in any of the directions suffering distress in body or mind find oceans of happiness and delight.

3 As long as the round of rebirth remains, may their happiness never fade. Let the world receive uninterrupted happiness from the Bodhisattvas.

4 Let the embodied beings, in however many hellish states are found in the world spheres, enjoy the happiness and delight of Sukhāvatī.

5 Let those afflicted by cold find warmth; let those afflicted by heat be cooled by oceans of water pouring from the great cloud of Bodhisattvas.

6 May they experience the sword-leaved forest as the splendour of the divine grove, and may the thickets of torturing thorns grow into magical trees that fulfil every wish.

7 May the regions of hell become glades of delight, with lakes scented by a profusion of lotuses, splendid and delightful with the chorus of song from grey geese, ducks, *cakravākas*, swans, and other water-birds.

8 Let the heap of hot coals be a heap of jewels, and let the red-hot earth be a crystal mosaic, and the 'crushing' mountains of hell become celestial palaces of worship filled with Sugatas.

9 Let the rain of burning coals, heated rocks, and daggers from this day forth be a shower of flowers; and let the warring with these weapons, one against the other, now be merely playful—a tussle with flowers.

10 Let those who are overwhelmed by the 'torrential' river of hell whose waters burn like fire, all their flesh fallen away, their bones the colour of the jasmine flower, attain divine bodies and come to stand with celestial damsels in the 'slow-curving' river of heaven, by the power of my skilful deeds.

11 May the servants of Yama, and the gruesome crows and vultures, watch in fear as, without warning, here the darkness disperses on all sides. 'Whose is this gentle radiance bringing forth happiness and pleasure?' Wondering this, gazing upwards, may they see in the sky the blazing Vajrapāṇi and, their vileness vanished from the force of his delightfulness, may they go to join him.

12 A shower of red lotuses falls mingled with fragrant waters. It is seen to quell the unquenched fires of hell. 'What is this?' they think, suddenly refreshed by joy. May those in hell see the one who holds a red lotus in his hand.

13 'Come, come quickly! Put away fear, brothers! We are alive! See, some prince in the robes of a monk has come to us, resplendent, bringing fearlessness.' By his power all affliction is removed, streams of bliss gush forth, the perfect Awakening Mind is born, so too compassion, the mother of protection for all beings.

14 'Look at that one! His lotus feet are honoured by the crowns of hundreds of deities. His gaze is moist with compassion. On his head rains down a stream of many flowers let fall from the upper storeys, delightful with the singing of a thousand divine damsels, eloquent with praise.' On seeing Mañjughoṣa before them, may those in hell immediately send up a roar of delight.

15 In this way, through my skilful deeds, may those in hell rejoice at beholding these clouds, bearing cool, sweet-scented breezes and showers of well-being, on which Bodhisattvas are revealed, with Samantabhadra at their head.

16 May the intense pains and fears of those in hell be allayed. May those dwelling in all evil realms be freed from those states of woe.

17 May the risk for animals of being eaten by each other go away. May the hungry ghosts be as satisfied as the men of Uttarakuru.

18 May the hungry ghosts be fed, may they be bathed, may they always be refreshed by the streams of milk flowing from noble Avalokiteśvara.

19 May the blind see forms, may the deaf always hear, and may expectant mothers give birth as did Māyādevī, free from pain.

20 May they receive clothing, food and drink, garlands, sandalwood balm, and ornaments, and everything the heart desires conducive to well-being.

21 May the fearful become fearless and those oppressed by grief find joy. May those who are anxious be rid of their anxiety and feel secure.

22 May health come to the sick. May they be freed from every fetter. May those weak find strength, their minds tender toward each other.

23 May every region be hospitable to all those who travel the roads. With whatever aim they set out, may their plan succeed.

24 May those embarked on sea voyages succeed in their heart's desire. May they come safely to shore and rejoice with their families.

25 May those who fall upon the wrong path in the wilderness meet with a merchant caravan and, free from weariness, may they proceed without fear of thieves, tigers, or other predators.

26 May gods provide protection for the young and elderly who are without protector, and for those asleep, drunk, or heedless, at risk of illness, or in a jungle.

27 Freed from all inopportune births, full of faith, wisdom, and compassion, perfect in appearance and conduct, may they always be able to recall their former births.

28 May they possess inexhaustible treasure like Gaganagañja, 'Sky-treasure'. May they be free of extremes, free from irritation, and their actions self-directed.

29 May those beings lacking in vigour be greatly invigorated. May those wretches who are deformed attain perfect beauty.

30 May all those in the world as women make progress, becoming men. May the lowly gain high status, but remain free from pride.

31 By this merit of mine may all beings without exception desist from every evil deed and always act skilfully.

32 Never lacking the Awakening Mind, concerned solely with the path to Awakening, adopted by Buddhas, not subject to Māra's tricks,

33 May all beings have immeasurable life. May they always live happily. May the very word 'death' perish.

34 May every quarter become a place of delight with gardens of magical trees that grant every wish, teeming with Buddhas and the heirs of the Buddhas, enthralling with the sound of the Dharma.

35 May the ground in every place be smooth and level like the palm of a hand, free from grit and stones, and made of beryl.

36 May the circles of the great assembly of Bodhisattvas be seated all around. May they emblazon the surface of the earth each with their own radiant hue.

37 Let embodied beings hear, unwearied, the sound of the Dharma from winged birds, from every tree, from light rays, and from the sky.

38 May they constantly meet with Buddhas and the Buddhas' kin. May they worship the Teacher of the Universe with unending clouds of worship.

39 May the god send timely rain, and may crops flourish. May the populace prosper, and may the king be righteous.

40 May medicines be potent, and the spells of the mutterers be effective. May ogresses, demons, and their like be overwhelmed with compassion.

41 May no being suffer, nor be wicked, nor diseased, neither contemptible nor despised. May no one be dejected.

42 May the monasteries be well appointed, humming with recitation and study. May the *Saṅgha* always remain undivided and may the purpose of the *Saṅgha* be fulfilled.

43 May monks experience solitude and take pleasure in their precepts. Their minds supple, devoid of all distraction, may they experience meditative absorption.

44 May nuns receive support, be free of bickering and harassment, and may the ethical conduct of all those who enter the spiritual community remain unbroken.

45 May those whose conduct is wrong be shaken up by the need to change. May they always delight in putting an end to evil action. May they reach a good rebirth, and once there may their resolve remain unbroken.

46 May they be learned and cultured, receive support, and be given food. May the flow of their mental states be pure, and their renown be proclaimed in every direction.

47 May the universe attain Buddhahood in a single, divine embodiment, without tasting the torment of hell, without the need for laborious effort.

48 May all Perfect Buddhas be worshipped in many ways by every living being. May they be happy to the highest degree in the inconceivable bliss of Buddhahood.

49 May the desires of the Bodhisattvas for the welfare of the world meet with success. May what the Protectors intend for living beings be completely fulfilled.

50 May Pratyekabuddhas and Śrāvakas be happy, ever worshipped with great respect by gods, titans, and men.

51 Through adoption by Mañjughoṣa, may I always gain entry into the spiritual community and the recollection of former births, until I reach the 'stage of delight'.

52 May I remain full of strength whatever the posture I adopt. In all my lives may I acquire the means for the solitary life.

53 When I desire to see or ask anything, may I see without obstruction the Protector Mañjunātha himself.

54 May my own conduct emulate that of Mañjuśrī, who works to achieve the welfare of all living beings throughout the ten directions of space.

55 As long as space abides and as long as the world abides, so long may I abide, destroying the sufferings of the world.

56 Whatever suffering is in store for the world, may it all ripen in me. May the world find happiness through all the pure deeds of the Bodhisattvas.

57 The sole medicine for the ailments of the world, the mine of all success and happiness, let the Dispensation long endure, attended by support and honour.

58 I bow down to Mañjughoṣa through whose inspiration my mind turns to good. I honour the spiritual friend through whose inspiration it grows strong.

NOTES TO THE TEXT

CHAPTER 1

1.1 The term Sugata is an epithet of a Buddha, an 'awakened being', one who is no longer subject to the cyclic existence of rebirth and suffering, *saṃsāra*. The truth awakened to and taught by a Buddha is called the Dharma. The spiritual community of those aspiring to achieve Buddhahood by practising these teachings is termed the *Saṅgha*. Collectively these are known as the Three Jewels (*triratna*) or the three refuges (*triśaraṇa*). By tradition, an author pays homage to these at the beginning of his work.

Dharmakāya, 'the body of Dharma(s)', can be interpreted at different levels. At one level, it is the collection of the truths that the Buddha realized and taught. In a physical sense this is the body of the *sūtras*, the texts recording the Buddha's teachings, in contrast to the Buddha's physical body. But the *Dharmakāya* is also the collection of qualities exemplified by the Buddha. Further still, as a result of his wisdom he is free from delusion, and therefore represents the true nature of things.

'Scripture' translates the word *āgama*, which is used as the term for each section of the *sūtrapiṭaka*, or 'collection of discourses', in the Buddhist canon. *Āgama* also means 'tradition', in the sense of 'what has come down (i.e. has been inherited) [from the Buddha]'.

1.2 The expression 'perfume' is not only a poetical metaphor. It is also a technical term used to explain the means whereby the ethical character of actions, *karma*, can influence future experience and behaviour. See 9.31.

1.3 Ethically appropriate actions are considered to be 'skilful', *kuśala*, because they involve judgement and understanding as well as good intention, and they lead toward ever greater degrees of spiritual competence.

1.4 'The opportune moment' is birth as a human being and contact with the Buddha's teaching. See 4.15–16.

1.5 The concept of 'merit' is found throughout Indian religious culture. It is a kind of good fortune, acquired, in a Buddhist context, through skilful actions of three kinds: generosity, good or ethical conduct, and meditation.

1.10 The same metaphor occurs in the *Gaṇḍavyūha Sūtra* (see 1.14 note), where the Awakening Mind is said to transmute the ordinary being into a Buddha, in the same way that an elixir transmutes copper into gold. Quicksilver, used in alchemy, has first to be worked (*vedhanīya* 'must be struck'), as does the Awakening Mind, for the process of transmutation to take place.

1.12 After the banana plant has fruited it dies and is replaced by another sucker growing from the underground stem.

1.14 Indian cosmogony describes an endless sequence of evolution and devolution of the universe. 'A world age' is a single such cycle, which is brought to its conclusion by an all-consuming conflagration.

In the second half of the verse, the author refers to the tale of Sudhana's spiritual quest described in the *Gaṇḍavyūha Sūtra*, the final book of the *Avataṃsaka Sūtra* (see Cleary 1989). In his quest Sudhana meets with a number of spiritual friends including Maitreya, the future Buddha and ultimate personification of spiritual friendship. Maitreya gives Sudhana a lengthy account of the qualities of the Awakening Mind (ibid. 352–65).

1.20 The *Question of Subāhu*, or *Subāhuparipṛcchā*, is a canonical scripture to be found in the *Ratnakūṭa* collection of Mahāyāna sūtras. 'The inferior path', or *Hīnayāna*, is the term given by the Mahāyāna to non-Mahāyāna Buddhism.

1.23 The Brahmās are amongst the highest gods in Buddhist cosmogony, but, since they are still subject to death and rebirth, they are spiritually inferior to a Buddha.

1.29 'It' is the Awakening Mind.

1.36 Śāntideva uses a term for 'bodies' which also means 'bodily relics', i.e. the physical remains of earthly Buddhas and Bodhisattvas who have died. These were and still are worshipped.

For the manner in which harm to a Bodhisattva can lead to happiness, see the story of Supuṣpacandra, summarized in 8.106 note. Going for refuge, usually to the Three Jewels (see 1.1 note), is a fundamental expression of religious commitment made by Buddhists (on which see Introduction to Chs. 2 and 3).

CHAPTER 2

2.6 In Sanskrit literature terms for powerful animals, such as bull, lion, and elephant, are used to express majesty and superiority. Here Śāntideva uses the term *muni-puṃgava* 'sage-bull', i.e. 'the best of sages', which is a common epithet for a Buddha.

2.11–19 This sequence of visualized offerings follows rituals performed within a temple, in which a Buddha image is first bathed, dried, clothed, and perfumed, and then offered flowers, incense, and lamps.

2.13 Samantabhadra, 'Universal Good', is a Bodhisattva associated with compassion. He is the protector of the *Lotus Sūtra (Saddharmapuṇḍarīka Sūtra)*, and he assists Sudhana in the final stage of his progress to Enlightenment in the *Gaṇḍavyūha Sūtra*, on which see 1.14 note.

Ajita, 'the Unconquered', is an epithet of Maitreya, on whom see ibid.

Mañjughoṣa, 'Gentle-Voiced', is a form of Mañjuśrī, on whom see General Introduction, p. xi.

Lokeśvara, 'Lord of the World', is an epithet of Avalokiteśvara, 'The Lord who looks down [to see the suffering of the world]'. He is the ultimate personification of compassion. He is the central figure in the *Heart Sūtra (Prajñā-pāramitā-hṛdaya Sūtra)* and the *Kāraṇḍavyūha Sūtra*. The *Lotus Sūtra* devotes a chapter to the benefits that he bestows upon those in imminent danger.

2.21 A *caitya* is an object of veneration, such as a relic mound, sacred tree, or holy site connected with an incident in the life of the Buddha or his disciples. The images referred to here are representations of Buddhas or Bodhisattvas. The 'jewels which make up the true Dharma' are understood by Prajñākaramati to be the twelve divisions of the Buddhist scriptures. These are an ancient analysis of the scriptures according to literary form.

2.22 In a previous life as king Ambararāja, Mañjuśrī devoted his time and his kingdom to making unlimited offerings to the Buddhas, and encouraged all his subjects to do likewise. The episode is described in the *Mañjuśrībuddhakṣetraguṇavyūha Sūtra*. (Chang 1983, 172–6)

2.23 The Oceans of Virtue are the Buddhas and Bodhisattvas.

2.24 A Buddha-field is the area of a Buddha's spiritual influence. Beings in a particular Buddha-field may benefit from that Buddha's spiritual guidance and accumulated merit. In Mahāyāna Buddhism there are an infinite number of Buddhas, each with his own Buddha-field. See also 5.81 and note, and Introduction to Ch. 10.

The highest assembly stands for the third of the 'jewels', the Saṅgha (see 1.1 note). Prajñākaramati takes this to be a reference to the assembly of Bodhisattvas alone.

2.25 'Bodhisattva' here refers to the historical Buddha before his Awakening. Hence the places referred to are identifiable sites mentioned in connection with his early life and also in the *Jātaka* stories, i.e. the tales of the Buddha's former lives, which became sites of pilgrimage.

2.26 'The seat of the Awakening' is a translation of *bodhimaṇḍa*, literally 'essence of Awakening'. The term refers to the place or seat of the historical Buddha's Awakening at Bodh Gaya, in the modern Indian state of Bihar. Tradition has it that Buddhas always attain Enlightenment at the same location, and so Śāntideva implies, 'Until I become a Buddha . . .'

2.27 'Holding hands in reverence' is the *añjali*, the Indian gesture of salutation and greeting, made with hands held, palms together, in front of the chest.

2.30 Śāntideva refers to his 'mothers and fathers' from this and previous lives.

2.32 The skilfulness or unskilfulness of any action, *karma*, determines good or bad consequences for the person who performed it. If death occurs before one has 'used up' the accumulated evil consequences of one's past actions, they will determine the character of the next rebirth which is experienced, projecting one into a realm of suffering, such as hell.

The authenticity of this verse is disputed by modern editors, because it is missing from one of the Sanskrit manuscripts of the *Bodhicaryāvatāra* and also from the canonical Tibetan translation.

2.42 Yama, or Death, is the pan-Indian lord of the realms of the dead. He is a grim figure, depicted as an angry male, dark-skinned and red-eyed, holding a noose with which he draws away the dead. He is also the judge who dispenses punishment in the hell realms, and is usually depicted as such in representations of the 'wheel of life'.

2.46 'Saint', not in the sense of a canonized person, but of a good or holy person, a *sādhu*.

2.51 Avalokita is another epithet of Avalokiteśvara, on whom see 2.13 note above.

2.52 Ākāśagarbha, 'space-store', is a Bodhisattva associated with generosity. Kṣitigarbha, 'earth-store', is the ultimate embodiment of altruism, by virtue of the vow he made in earlier lives to save all those tormented in hells. In one life he made this vow when he was a pious woman distressed by the agonies her late mother was undergoing in hell as a result of lack of faith. In another life he made the vow as a pious king worried about the sufferings in store for his unruly subjects. At present he has taken on numerous embodiments and appears in hells to help the beings there towards Enlightenment. He will continue doing so until the arrival of the future Buddha, Maitreya.

2.53 The 'Holder of the Vajra' is a synonym for Vajrapāṇi, the Bodhisattva associated with vigour. He has peaceful and wrathful forms, and in the latter he is depicted as a heavily built dark blue-black striding male figure, surrounded by fire. He holds in one hand a *vajra*, a type of religious implement representing a thunderbolt, which symbolizes his ability to remove obstacles—hence his name.

2.55 According to Prajñākaramati, there are one hundred ways of dying prematurely apart from death from old age. Each of these one hundred and one manners of death can be caused by a single one of the three humours, wind, bile, and phlegm, or a combination of these, hence the number four hundred and four. Anyone stuck in the infinite cyclic existence will naturally be afflicted by all of these at one time or another.

2.56 Jambudvīpa is the name given to the southern continent, which includes India. This world is made up of four continents, according to traditional Indian cosmogony.

2.64 Prajñākaramati understands what is 'wrong by nature' to be transgressions of the moral precepts, such as abstention from taking life or stealing, and what is wrong 'by convention' to be transgressions of the rules of monastic discipline undertaken by Buddhist monks. Śāntideva could well have had in mind a broader understanding of what constitutes conventional morality, such as the laws of the society within which the Buddhist community operates.

CHAPTER 3

3.3 The 'resolution' of a Buddha is the initial resolution to attain Awakening for all beings, which occurs when the Awakening Mind arises.

3.8 An 'intermediate aeon' is a period of famine and destruction occurring either during or between major world ages. On 'world age' see 1.14 note.

3.10 'All three times', i.e. past, present, and future.

3.15 The phrase 'achieving every goal' immediately evokes the personal name of the historical Buddha, Sarvārthasiddha, which means 'one who has accomplished every goal'. This is the name used in some accounts of his life rather than the name Siddhārtha, which means 'one who has accomplished his goal'.

3.17 Each of these metaphors is well used within scripture: protector and caravan-leader for the Buddha; boat, causeway, and bridge for the Dharma.

3.19 Each of these mythical items is said to fulfil every wish, being similar in connotation to Aladdin's lamp.

3.20 There are four 'basic elements', *mahābhūta*: earth, water, fire, wind.

3.22–3 Early in the history of Buddhism a standard scheme of the historical Buddha's career as a Bodhisattva had been developed. This was thought to apply to all Buddhas, past and future. All Buddhas-to-be initially take the vow to become a Buddha in the presence of another Buddha, and then spend innumerable lifetimes perfecting the qualities of a Buddha. The story of the historical Buddha first making this vow is told in the *Cariyāvaṃsa* of the Pali canon (see Horner 1975). The *Jātaka* tales describe episodes from past lives in the training career of the historical Buddha (see Cowell *et al.* 1895). All the biographies of the Buddha employ the main features of this standardized biography. See *Buddhacarita* (Johnston 1984), *Lalitavistara* (Bays 1983), *Mahāvastu* (Jones 1949, 1952, 1956), *Nidānakathā* (Rhys Davids 1973).

3.30 The light of the moon is traditionally considered soothing after the intense heat of the sun during the day.

CHAPTER 4

4.4 The promise referred to here is that of the Bodhisattva to achieve perfect Buddhahood in order to help all beings.

4.5 This and the following verse are a reference to the *Saddharma-smṛty-upasthāna Sūtra*, quoted in the *Śikṣā Samuccaya* (Bendall and Rouse 1922, p. 13). The hungry ghosts, or *pretas*, are the occupants of one of the six realms of existence in Buddhist cosmology. (See note to v. 18 below.) This is a realm of acute suffering, the hungry ghosts characterized by bellies swollen with hunger, their mouths and throats the size of a pin-hole. They are tortured by incessant and insatiable greed. Any food or liquid that they do manage to obtain turns to excrement or liquid fire.

4.6 The 'unsurpassed happiness' is Enlightenment for all.

4.11 Śāntideva puns here with the term *bhūmi*. Meaning literally 'ground', it is also used in Mahāyāna Buddhism to denote specific stages of attainment in the career of the Bodhisattva. Having undertaken the vow to achieve full Buddhahood, the Bodhisattva must progress through successively higher *bhūmis* or stages which bring him closer to that goal. There are differing systematizations of these stages, but that followed by Śāntideva is the ten-stage system, as given in the *Daśabhūmika Sūtra*, *The Discourse on the Ten Stages* (see Cleary 1986). The first stage is the *pramuditā* stage of 'delight' at the realization that one will achieve Buddhahood and save infinite beings from suffering (see 10.51 and Introduction to Chapter 10; see further Dayal 1932).

4.16 The last two of the favourable circumstances, having food and freedom from disaster, are particularly relevant for the monastic community who depended on lay patronage for food. If there was a disaster such as a famine or war, lay people would be too concerned with their own physical survival to be able to support the monastic community in their spiritual life.

We have taken the reading *kāyo yācitakopamaḥ*, giving 'The body is like an object on loan', rather than the *kāyopācitakopamaḥ* of De la Vallée Poussin's edition, for which we see no meaning.

4.18 'The lower realms' translates the term *apāya*, and refers to the realms of the animals, the hungry ghosts, the beings in hell, and the titans. There are reckoned in all to be six, sometimes five, realms of existence in Buddhist cosmology. In addition to those above there are also the heavenly realms and the human realm. The discrepancy between the two totals occurs when the realm of the titans is included as a part of the heavenly realm, rather than as separate from it. The cycle of existence, *saṃsāra*, is made up of these realms, and beings are reborn in one or the other of them according to the ethical character of their actions in previous births.

4.20 The simile of the turtle is common for the rarity of human birth. It appears in the early Buddhist canon, where it is sometimes more fully elaborated. For example, in verse 500 of the *Therīgāthā* of the Pali canon the turtle is also blind (see Norman 1969).

4.21 The Avīci hell is the most fearful of the hells of Buddhist cosmology. By popular etymology its name means 'without intermission', perhaps assuming that the tortures experienced there are ceaseless. The hells are not places of eternal damnation, however, since although one may endure them for very long periods as a result of unskilful actions, it is also possible to leave them (when the effects of those actions are exhausted) and to be reborn in another realm of existence.

4.24 On Yama, see 2.42 note.

4.27 A spell, or *mantra*, is a verbal formula which, through repetition, will obtain magically some specified end, either secular or spiritual. They are used throughout Indian religious culture, no less in Buddhism than in Hinduism.

4.31 Mount Meru is the great mountain at the centre of the world in Indian Buddhist cosmology.

4.32 In the Buddhist tradition there is no beginning to time, nor is there any moment of creation for the universe, and speculation upon these subjects, far from providing any spiritual illumination, is thought at best to be irrelevant to the spiritual life, at worst an obstacle to it. *Saṃsāra*, the cycle of existence, has been fuelled since beginningless time by the defilements, which are themselves rooted in *avidyā*, ignorance.

4.35 That the defilements of one's mind are also the executioners in hell is consistent with the scholastic rather than popular position that hell and its minions are merely products of one's own corrupt mind.

4.40 The author chides himself on two counts here. It is not only that these people are able, for their own personal livelihood, to endure great hardships which the author is not able to endure though it be for the welfare of the entire world. The people mentioned also all belong to the lowest and most despised sections of society according to the Brahmanical caste system, and so manage greater things than the high-caste author, though they are supposedly inferior to him. *Caṇḍālas* were traditionally 'untouchables', who did work associated with dead bodies: as executioners, and at cremation grounds.

4.43 Any destructive act, based in greed, hatred, or delusion, leads to an increase in the defilements, and so the author wryly adds that he is not bothered by any defilements which might result from destroying defilements.

4.47 Śāntideva refers here to the standard Buddhist physiology of sense perception. This is explained in terms which leave no place for any concept of an unchanging or permanent self, *ātman*. Our awareness of the world is understood in the Buddhist tradition as being made up of distinct but instantaneous moments of consciousness. These arise when the necessary conditions are present: namely, an object, and a sense organ. These three, object, sense organ, and the concomitant moment of consciousness, account completely for our experience of the world. Hence, if, as Śāntideva suggests, the defilements can be expelled from the mind, i.e. the moments of consciousness which make up the mind-continuum of the individual, there is nowhere else for them to go, since as moral qualities they cannot dwell in objects of perception, or the organs of sense. Morality is essentially intentional in Buddhist teaching, and so objects which do not possess or generate intention cannot engage in ethical activity.

4.48 From the earliest times the Buddha was likened to a doctor who offered a medicine, Awakening, to cure the ills of the world. The Four Truths of the Nobles, the most ubiquitous of Buddhist teachings, are themselves couched as a medical diagnosis of the sickness of the world, which is suffering. The first Truth, that there is suffering, is the diagnosis of the condition. The second Truth, that suffering arises from causes, is a statement of the causes of the condition. The third Truth, that there can be an end to suffering, is a prognosis that the condition is curable. The fourth Truth, describing the path to end suffering, is the prescription of treatment. (See Horner 1954–9, iii. 43–4; also Birnbaum 1989, a study of healing symbolism, particularly in the Mahāyāna.)

CHAPTER 5

5.2 The analogy of the mind to a rutting elephant is traditional, for example *Dhammapada* 326. During the period of rut, or sexual excitement, male elephants are extremely dangerous and fight each other for females, causing considerable destruction.

5.6 'Teacher of Reality', or *tattvavādin*, is used here as an epithet of the Buddha.

5.7 The commentary explains that the women referred to here are the women who appear in the hells on and below the thorny silk-cotton trees wherein adulterers try to clamber! See 4.35 note.

5.8 One need look no further than the first verse of the *Dhammapada* for a statement to this effect 'sung' by the Buddha: 'Things are controlled by the mind, have mind as their chief, are made by the mind. If one speaks or acts with a mind made bad, then suffering follows one like the wheel the foot of the draught.' See also 5.17 below and note.

5.9 The perfection of generosity is the first of the perfections, *pāramitās*, which are cultivated by the Bodhisattva so as to gain full Buddhahood. From this point on Śāntideva begins his exposition of the *pāramitās*.

5.10 In this verse Śāntideva defines the perfection of generosity. The fruit referred to here is the fruit of such generosity. This is understood not in the concrete sense of gifts made in return, but in the sense of the *puṇya* or merit (a sort of non-material 'good fortune'), which such skilful action builds up for the donor. This definition counteracts the possibility of 'spiritual materialism', whereby someone might engage in acts of generosity with an essentially selfish motive, thinking only of the benefit to themselves in terms of merit attained (cf. 8.97–8 and note). This has an undoubted relevance to Śāntideva's social context, in which, as had been done for many centuries before, *dāna*, generosity, was defined in terms of giving material goods to the monastic community on the understanding that this led to a substantial reward of merit for the donor.

'Mental attitude' here translates *citta*. See Translators' Introduction, p. xxxvi.

5.11 In this verse Śāntideva defines the perfection of ethical conduct. Buddhist ethics are essentially concerned with intention.

His concern is that involvement in the world at any level inevitably leads to unskilful actions, unless one's intention is fundamentally transformed. There is no point in trying to remove all potential victims of one's unskilful behaviour. One must rather change the behaviour itself.

The rather obscure exclamation is probably an oblique reference to a tradition which sought to explain how the Buddha, thought to be perfect in himself, came to have certain unpleasant experiences, as described in the scriptures. Recourse was made to past lives in which he had performed some bad action which inevitably resulted in unpleasant consequences for him, even if those results were only experienced after his enlightenment. The reference here is to a past life in which he had watched a fisherman with his catch and had taken pleasure in the sight of him killing the fish. This was said to have resulted in him experiencing a headache once he was enlightened. One suspects that this verse and the next go together, contrasting gratuitous and vicarious violence with 'justified' violence, respectively.

The concepts of 'cessation' and 'freedom from passion' are both contained in the Sanskrit term *virati*, here translated as 'to cease from worldly acts'.

5.15 Śāntideva refers in this verse to the benefits of calming meditation (see Introduction to Chapter 8). While the meditative absorptions themselves are described in terms of subjective experience, the Buddhist tradition also describes cosmological realms which are the objective correlates of these internal states. In other words, the level of consciousness which a person experiences determines their experience of the world, and of the cosmological realm which they occupy. The realms which are correlated in this way with the meditative absorptions are the heavenly realms occupied by the deities of Buddhist cosmology. The higher of these realms are the abodes of *Brahmā*, the highest deity, and were regarded as the pinnacle of mundane existence. Typically these are to be reached through the practice of a set of four calming meditations, the *brahma-vihāras*, or 'abodes of Brahmā'. These involve the cultivation of *maitrī*, love, *karuṇā*, compassion, *muditā*, sympathetic joy (at another's happiness), and *upekṣā*, equanimity (both with regard to one's affective response to pleasure, discomfort, etc., and in the sense of achieving an equal response of the first three emotions towards all beings). Experience of these realms is said to be subtly blissful, and hence very attractive, yet it all remains a part of cyclic existence, and does not lead to Awakening. In the Buddhist tradition, even gods are the victims of past actions and are as in need of spiritual Awakening as any other being. See also 6.81 note.

5.16 Recitation, *japa*, refers to the recitation of scriptures or spells, *mantras* (see 4.27 note). Austerity, *tapas* (literally 'heat'), was generally forbidden to the Buddhist monk or nun as one of the extremes which the Buddha's Middle Way avoided, the other extreme being that of hedonism. The early canon records, in various places, a total of 13 *dhūtaguṇas* (Pali: *dhūtaṅgas*), or minor austerities, which were allowed the monk, including living in the open, wearing only rag robes, eating only one meal a day, living in a cemetery, or sleeping only in a sitting position. Sometimes the term *tapas* is used as a synonym for religious practice in general.

5.17 Prajñākaramati suggests that the *citta*, mind, is the *bodhicitta*, which is imperceptible to foolish people, i.e. those who do not pursue the religious life. The use of the term *dharma* is ambiguous here. It could mean that the mind (of Awakening, i.e. the *bodhicitta*) is the sum of all Teachings, or it could refer to *dharmas* as the fundamental irreducible units to which phenomenal experience can be reduced. These are largely mental in character, and their enumeration was one of the main concerns of the *Abhidharma*, a body of literature which grew up in the centuries immediately following the Buddha. The mind is therefore the whole sum of *dharmas* in the sense that all phenomena are understood as inseparable from the mind. This idealist tendency in Buddhist teaching was present from the earliest period but was brought to its most sophisticated expression by exponents of the Yogācāra school.

5.18 Śāntideva uses the term *adhiṣṭhita*, here translated as 'manage'. This term, with its cognate forms, has a technical usage in the training of elephants, referring to a stage in the process of inducing a wild elephant to perform one's will. It is also very widely used in Mahāyāna scriptures to denote a form of benevolent blessing, or controlling power, exercised by a Buddha or Buddhas upon a favoured Bodhisattva.

5.25 'Memory' here translates *smṛti*, elsewhere translated as 'mindfulness'.

Śāntideva refers here to the three levels of understanding or wisdom. The first is that which is merely 'heard', *śruta*, i.e. has been learnt from a teacher or from the scriptures, 'heard' in both cases because the scriptures were disseminated primarily by recitation. The second level is that 'reflected upon', *cintita*, i.e. wisdom or understanding developed by the individual through their own intellective reflection. The third level is that of 'cultivation in meditation', *bhāvanā*, and refers to the levels of insight or wisdom that can be cultivated through the practice of meditation, particularly *vipaśyanā* meditation. (See Introduction to Ch. 8.) These three types of understanding are seen as progressively higher, and as reflecting the necessary stages of training for the Buddhist. This process begins with simply hearing the teachings of the Buddha; progresses to an intelligent and informed application of those principles to one's own experience; and culminates in the attainment by the individual, through meditation particularly, of those insights which informed the original teaching of the Buddha.

5.30 According to the monastic code (*vinaya*), a monk is assigned to his preceptor, *upādhyāya*, when he receives full ordination. The relationship between them is characterized as that between father and son, the preceptor taking responsibility for the spiritual welfare of the monk. One may or may not live with one's preceptor, but in the absence of the preceptor one is assigned an instructor, *ācārya*, with whom one is expected to live, and whose duties correspond with those of the preceptor. Here Śāntideva uses the term teacher, *guru*, rather than instructor.

5.32 According to Prajñākaramati, one should experience shame, *trapā*, at the thought of any kind of unskilful, unwholesome action; respect, *ādara*, towards the Buddha's teaching; and fear, *bhaya*, at the possibility of transgressing it.

In this verse Śāntideva introduces the practice of 'recollection' or *anusmṛti* of the Buddha and his qualities. This can be performed in various ways. One such practice is the recitation of the *buddha-vandanā*, or 'praise of the Buddha(s)': 'This is what the Fortunate One is like: worthy, fully awakened, endowed with knowledge and virtue, in a good state, knower of the worlds, the unsurpassed trainer for individuals who need to be trained, teacher of gods and men, Awakened, the Fortunate One.' The term *anusmṛti* is cognate with *smṛti*, and means a guided remembering of a specific object.

5.35 Śāntideva here, as elsewhere in the remainder of this chapter, repeats the injunctions of minor rules of the *vinaya*, or monastic discipline. These will not be noted unless they require some special explanation.

5.36 'Field of vision' translates *ābhāsa*, which has a technical usage denoting the field of operation of the senses.

5.40 This verse is not in the Tun-huang recension. The use of the term *dvipa* is very apt here. Commonly this word is an epithet for an elephant, literally meaning 'one who drinks twice', with trunk and then mouth, but it could also be analysed as 'one who protects twice', i.e. the mind, which provides itself with the two protectors, mindfulness and awareness.

5.41 Concentration, *samādhāna*, is not an act of will, in which one forces the mind onto a single object, but rather a disciplined but harmonious and organic integration of the mind achieved through the practice of mindfulness and calming meditation. (See Introduction to Ch. 8.)

5.42 The kind of elation envisaged here by Prajñākaramati is that from participation in a Buddhist festival, the worship of the Three Jewels, or arising from experience of a *samādhi*, or meditative concentration. There is possibly the same instruction given in the *Śikṣā Samuccaya*, but mistranslated by Bendall and Rouse (1922, p. 117).

'It is taught' may be a reference to the *Akṣayamati Sūtra*, which Śāntideva quotes on this point in the *Śikṣā Samuccaya* (Bendall and Rouse, 12). The *Akṣayamati Sūtra* is now lost in its Sanskrit original, but a translation from the Chinese has been published in Chang 1983, 415–26.

5.45 Abstinence from 'idle chattering' is the sixth of the 'ten paths of skilful conduct', or *daśa-kuśala-karma-patha*, a set of ten ethical precepts governing acts of the body, speech, and mind, enjoined from the earliest stratum of the canon. They are, to abstain from unskilful actions of the body, viz. harming living beings, taking what is not given, sexual misconduct; of speech, viz. lying, harsh speech, spiteful speech, idle speech; and of the mind, viz. covetousness, ill will, and wrong views.

5.46 These three activities are specifically prohibited for the orthodox brahmanical householder by Hindu law books (e.g. *Viṣṇusmṛti* 71.41 ff.) which stipulate 'good manners' for a well-educated person. They are permitted if for a useful purpose, such as agriculture—in the case of the first two—and as an act to purify the earth at the beginning of ritual—in the case of the last. Drawing a line in the earth wounds it, and may harm living creatures, but in the purificatory ritual the wound is soothed by the pouring of water. Drawing a line in the earth outside this context may be an involuntary gesture of being overwhelmed by an emotion, or of telling a lie. Although Śāntideva uses the language found in the Hindu law books, there are approximate equivalents in the extant Buddhist monastic codes.

5.49 Prajñākaramati's commentary suggests that, amongst other reasons, the mind can become inflated in the sense of being intoxicated from hearing the Dharma.

5.52 'Congregation' translates *pariṣat*. The literal meaning of the term is 'seated around', referring to those who sit around a teacher. It is used to denote the four 'congregations' or assemblies of the traditional Buddhist community, i.e. the laymen and laywomen, and the monks and nuns.

5.54 This is a standard principle of Buddhist meditation. The pupil should be guided by the teacher to engage in meditation techniques which counteract specific character traits of the pupil. Thus lust would be counteracted by the meditation on the foulness of the body (see 8.45 ff.), or hatred would be counteracted by the development of friendliness through *maitrī bhāvanā*.

5.55 This verse and v. 57 are quoted together in the *Śikṣā Samuccaya* (Bendall and Rouse, p. 127) from the *Sāgaramati Sūtra*.

5.57 The author enjoys a pun which can be only faintly reflected in translation. He undertakes to maintain his mind 'free from delusion' or literally 'free from pride', *nirmāna*, just like 'an illusion, or a magical display', *nirmāṇa*. There are several levels of meaning to this word play: a magical display has no self-will, because it has been created and is directed in its actions by the magician; a magical display is free from delusion or pride because it is not capable of intentional action, and therefore cannot engage in unskilful actions; the archetypal magical display for the Mahāyāna Buddhist is the *nirmāṇa-kāya*, the Magically Created Body, of the Buddha. The last is an allusion to the late Mahāyāna teaching that the Buddha has three bodies, *kāya*, and that of these the physical body of the historical Buddha was a magical display, *nirmāṇa*, created through compassion to teach beings in this world.

5.58 On 'best of opportunities' see 4.15–16. *Sumeru* is a synonym for Meru. See 4.31 note.

5.61 On the impurity of the body, see 8.63 ff.

5.62 With the image of the knife of understanding, *prajñā-śastreṇa*, Śāntideva plays upon the double association of the knife of the anatomically knowledgeable surgeon or butcher, and the sword of wisdom, held in the right hand of the Bodhisattva Mañjuśrī, which cuts away delusion.

5.65 Throughout this and the preceding verses, Śāntideva plays upon the Indian high-caste phobia of the 'polluting' body and its products, as well as any fear for the integrity of the physical body.

5.71 To speak first is a sign of respect, both within and outside the monastic community.

5.74 Literally one should accept such advice 'with the head'. This refers to bowing the head in acknowledgement or to showing respect by touching with one's head the feet of someone revered or placing revered objects on one's head. The head is the highest part of one's being, in all senses, and by performing such an act one subordinates the best of one's self to that which is revered. This verse appears with variants in the *Śikṣā Samuccaya* (Bendall and Rouse, 319).

5.75 The 'well said' is a frequent synonym for the Buddha's teaching, and expresses one significant difference between the Mahāyāna and non-Mahāyāna views of the Dharma. In the latter, it is understood that everything said by the Buddha is 'well said', i.e. is true and to the benefit of beings. The Mahāyāna tradition consciously introduced an inversion, saying that everything 'well said' was the word of the Buddha, i.e. that any teaching which was true and to the benefit of beings should be respected to the same degree as those teachings preserved in the canon of scripture attributed to the historical Buddha. The general thrust of this inversion was to create a more inclusive attitude to what constituted the Buddhist teaching, in itself an appropriate expression of the doctrine of *upāya*, or skilful means. Such a reinterpretation of the Buddha's teaching was also vital for the Mahāyāna followers who revered the Mahāyāna *sūtras* which had begun to circulate by about the first century BCE, and which, since they were not universally incorporated into the material attributed to the historical Buddha, were rejected as 'mere poetry' by the non-Mahāyānists. Dharmasvāmin, a

Tibetan pilgrim travelling in India in the thirteenth century, was asked to discard a Mahāyāna scripture that he was carrying before he would be allowed access to a non-Mahāyānist monastery at Bodh Gaya, the place of the Buddha's Enlightenment. Here Śāntideva plays with the ambiguity of the Mahāyānist position. Of course, as a pious Buddhist, one should express one's appreciation of the Buddha's teaching, but one should also express satisfaction with whatever accords with that teaching, whatever its source.

5.81 This verse is not in the Tun-huang recension. Prajñākaramati suggests that 'the Virtuous' refers to the Buddhas and Bodhisattvas; that the 'benefactors' are our parents and so on; and that 'one who suffers' refers to those who are sick, and so on. He also glosses 'antidote', *pratipakṣa*, as 'the cultivation of the realization of emptiness as an antidote to the defilements'.

The description of the Buddhas and Bodhisattvas, and one's worldly benefactors (often the monastic community itself is described in this way) as 'fields' is a common agricultural metaphor. Such people are fields in which one sows a crop of good actions of one's own, viz. devotion, generosity, etc., and from which one harvests a crop of fruit, *phala*, in the form of merit, *puṇya*.

5.83 'A fixed rule of conduct' is glossed by Prajñākaramati as *śikṣā-saṃvara*, 'the bond of the training' of the Bodhisattvas.

5.85 This verse is not in the Tun-huang recension. In a parallel passage quoted from the *Ratnamegha Sūtra* in his *Śikṣā Samuccaya*, Śāntideva lists those with whom one should share as fellow monks, those who suffer, and those in difficulty (Bendall and Rouse, 127). The giving away of the three robes is forbidden in the *Bodhisattva-prātimokṣa*, quoted ibid. 143.

According to the ancient rules governing the monastic community, the individual monk was allowed an absolute minimum of possessions only. These included three robes and a belt to hold up the lower of these, a bowl in which to receive begged food, needle and thread, razor, water-strainer, and medicines. However, at least from the time of the emperor Aśoka (3rd century BCE), the monastic community had been the recipient of extensive lay and royal patronage, becoming a considerable property-owner. I-tsing, a Chinese monk who travelled in India in the second half of the 7th century CE, reports that Nālandā, the monastic institution where Śāntideva composed this work around that time, held lands containing over two hundred villages.

Members of this community had access to its central treasury of money, with the permission of the three treasurers. Furthermore, individual monks of high standing travelled in sedan chairs, with attendants to carry their baggage. Thus, while the rules governing individual possessions remained in place, *de facto* many monks became the heirs of considerable estates, which they would administrate on behalf of the community as a whole. Combined with a literalism by which some monks consider permissible anything which is not specifically forbidden in the letter of the *Vinaya*, one can imagine that by Śāntideva's day there was considerable scope for circumventing monastic regulations.

5.88 This verse, and those that follow up to and including 98, are not in the Tun-huang recension. These are minor monastic regulations. As one can infer, these are concerned to prevent one from teaching to people who are unreceptive. The various potential modes of unreceptivity are implied by the accoutrements. It would be acceptable to teach someone under these circumstances if they were ill. (See Horner 1942, 140 ff.)

5.89 The 'inadequate' are understood by Prajñākaramati to be 'those with unsophisticated minds, or those whose disposition is inferior'. The need for a monk to be chaperoned when teaching women is to protect both parties from exploiting with sexual intent the opportunity of privacy. The monk is required to be strictly celibate. The lesser teachings referred to here are those of the so-called Hīnayāna. The higher teachings are those of the Mahāyāna.

5.90 The prohibition against giving the lesser teaching to one suitable for the higher teaching may be a reference to the *Kāśyapaparivarta Sūtra* passage quoted in the *Śikṣā Samuccaya* (Bendall and Rouse, 55). Prajñākaramati explains that the second reference is to the practice of telling people that they will be purified by reciting this *sūtra* (scripture) or that *mantra* (spell) irrespective of how they behave. A *sūtra* is a text that purports to contain a discourse by the historical Buddha. For *mantra* see 4.27 note.

5.91 The first rule is given, phrased slightly differently, in the *bodhisattva-prātimokṣa* quoted in the *Śikṣā Samuccaya* (Bendall and Rouse, 125). The second rule is given separately, ibid. 124.

5.92 Rubbing both arms at the same time is a gesture of threat or challenge. This verse is quoted in the *Śikṣā Samuccaya* (Bendall and Rouse, 125) and ascribed to the *Prātimokṣa*, although it does not occur in the Pali *Pāṭimokkha*.

5.93b The displeasure of society is the prime reason given in the *Vinaya* for the instigation of many monastic rules. This injunction reveals the symbiotic relationship of the monastic and lay communities, whereby, in return for merit earned, the laity feeds and clothes the monks. The price paid by the monks for this arrangement is that the monastic community itself is assessed by a vigilant laity who are keen to see that their generosity is not wasted on lax monks. A similar statement is made in the *Śikṣā Samuccaya*, ibid. 125.

5.96 The monk is enjoined to imitate the Buddha at his death, or final emancipation, *parinirvāṇa*, at which he lay with his head to the north, on his right side, his head on his right hand, left hand stretched out along his left thigh, and his robes wrapped closely around his body. The Buddha's *parinirvāṇa* has frequently been depicted in paintings and sculpture. The subject is not considered morbid, but an inspiring representation of the point at which the Buddha was finally released from the cycle of existence, *saṃsāra*.

5.98 The *Triskandha* is probably a reference to the *Triskandha-dharma Sūtra*, The Discourse on the Teaching of the Three Heaps, which is a short Mahāyāna *sūtra* that survives only in Tibetan and Chinese translations. It consists of an extended confession of faults to the thirty-five 'Buddhas of confession', and ends with a brief rejoicing in merit and dedication to Enlightenment. For a translation of this work from the Tibetan, see Beresford 1980, 17–21. In the *Śikṣā Samuccaya*, Śāntideva quotes this rule from the *Ugradatta paripṛcchā*, which defines the 'Three Heaps' as 'confession of sin, delight in merit, solicitation of Buddhas', see Bendall and Rouse, 1922, 263–4. Prajñākaramati merely glosses this reference by mentioning confession of faults, rejoicing in merit, and the maturation of Awakening, so that, while he may have had this particular *sūtra* in mind, other formulations of the same sentiments were in use.

5.102 'Spiritual friend' translates *kalyāṇamitra*. The 'Bodhisattva vow' has received various formulations. See Introduction to Ch. 10.

5.103 Teacher, *guru*, is used by Śāntideva as a synonym for the *kalyāṇamitra* of the previous verse. The *Śrīsambhava-vimokṣa* is the 53rd chapter of the *Gaṇḍavyūha Sūtra* (see 1.10 note). There the spiritually advanced boy and girl, Śrīsambhava and

Śrīmatī, explain to the pilgrim Sudhana the indispensable role of spiritual friends and the attitude that one should have towards them.

5.103 'Scripture' translates *sūtrānta*, which is a parallel term for *sūtra*, i.e. a canonical 'discourse'.

5.104 The *Ākāśagarbha Sūtra* is one of the *sūtras* in the *Mahāsaṃnipāta Sūtra* collection. The Sanskrit text is not known to survive, except for the passage referred to here, which Śāntideva quotes at length in his *Śikṣā Samuccaya* (Bendall and Rouse, 61–70). This describes eight fundamental transgressions, *mūlāpatti*, for the Bodhisattva: 1. Teaching profound *sūtras* to those incapable of understanding them, thereby putting them off the higher path (the Mahāyāna); 2. Teaching the lesser path (the Hīnayāna) to those capable of the higher; 3. Teaching the higher path and neglecting the monastic rules and the discipline; 4. Discouraging people from following the lesser path; 5. Discrediting others and boasting of oneself, including boasting of having attained psychic powers (such powers are regarded as a natural by-product of calming meditation, particularly of experience of the fourth meditative absorption; see Introduction to Ch. 8); 6. Showing off a mere book-learning of the Mahāyāna, but claiming it is based on personal insight; 7. Cultivating political contacts who exploit the wealth of the religious community and then appropriate that wealth; 8. Falling away from spiritual discipline under external pressures, and honouring those who are corrupt in their discipline.

5.105 This verse is not in the Tun-huang recension. A similar statement is made, however, in the *Śikṣā Samuccaya* itself (Bendall and Rouse, 17).

5.106 Nāgārjuna was the great teacher of the 2nd century CE who is regarded by tradition as the founder of the Madhyamaka tradition, to which Śāntideva adhered. Renowned as a 'second Buddha', he is associated with the 'discovery' and promulgation of the Perfection of Wisdom Sūtras. The interpretation of this verse is discussed by Ishida (1988).

CHAPTER 6

6.1 This verse lists topics already covered in the previous chapters: worship, i.e. the Supreme Worship, in Chs. 2–3, and generosity and proper conduct in Ch. 5.

6.2 This may be an allusion to *Dhammapada* 184a: *khantī paramaṃ tapo titikkhā*, 'Long-suffering forbearance is the highest spiritual practice.' 'Spiritual practice' is a translation of the term *tapas*, which means literally 'heat', and refers, in the broader Indian religious context, to austerities, both in the sense of generating internal heat and enduring extreme external heat. Śāntideva therefore uses a term for spiritual practice which in itself implies great endurance, but in the Buddhist context with the added sense of patience. In this last respect, the use of this term illustrates the Buddhist tendency to ethicize and psychologize pan-Indian religious concepts.

6.3 The dart or arrow is a frequent metaphor for the piercing emotions of greed and hatred. The most famous instance, and one undoubtedly known by Śāntideva, is that in which a person is struck by a poisoned arrow (i.e. by the sufferings of cyclic existence) but, instead of letting the surgeon get on with removing it, hinders him with questions about the provenance and type of the arrow (i.e. with metaphysical questions). (See Horner 1957, ii. 99–100.) The image also appears in the well-known 'Wheel of Life', a diagram illustrating the nature of causality. Here, in the outer circle, as a symbol of feeling, *vedanā*, a person is shown with an arrow in the eye. See Thomas 1951, 58–70.

6.9 On 'sympathetic joy' see 5.15 note. On 'skilful' see 1.3 note.

6.10 This verse also occurs in the *Śikṣā Samuccaya* (Bendall and Rouse, 176).

6.13 Durgā is a fierce goddess, one of the principal forms of the wife of the Hindu deity Śiva. Even to this day, blood sacrifices are offered to her and devotees mutilate themselves, e.g. by piercing their flesh with hooks, or taking burning-hot bowls in their hands, to gain her favour, particularly for material gain. Karṇāṭa was an area of south India corresponding to an area which includes the modern-day state Karnataka.

6.14a Similar in the *Śikṣā Samuccaya* (Bendall and Rouse, 176).

6.15 Some of these irritations take on greater significance for someone trying to meditate.

6.19b Similar in the *Śikṣā Samuccaya* (Bendall and Rouse, 319).

6.21 This is 'the intoxication of youth, wealth, etc.', according to Prajñākaramati, although there is also a widespread and early enumeration of three intoxications: of youth, health, and life.

Prajñākaramati also glosses 'longing' as: 'devotion', *bhakti*; 'faith', *śraddhā*; and 'serene confidence of mind', *citta-prasāda*.

6.22 This verse and the next two involve an extended pun revolving around the use of the verbal root *kup* and its derivatives, which encompass connotations of agitation, bilious ill-humour, and downright anger. Excess of bile gives rise to physical ailments as well as anger, according to traditional Indian medicine.

6.25 The notion of a single cause for any event is rejected in Buddhist thought from the earliest period. Every phenomenal event arises on the basis of numerous conditioning factors, the nature of which, at least in terms of a general typology, was described in the *Abhidharma*, the section of some Buddhist canons which sought to systematize and organize the teachings from the Scriptures (see 5.17 note). While individual actions might be singled out as skilful or unskilful, the 'result' of that action in the life of the individual person cannot be predicted with any great exactitude, since it will be affected by numerous other contributory conditions, reflecting other actions on the part of that person.

6.27 'Primal matter', *pradhāna*, is considered by Sāṃkhya philosophers to be the material cause of all phenomenal existence. The 'Self', *ātman*, is the ultimately real essence of an individual according to many non-Buddhist Indian philosophies. The sarcastic tone of this verse reflects Śāntideva's disdain for these philosophical theories which are rejected in Buddhist thought. While he offers preliminary arguments against both in the next verse, Śāntideva engages in a more detailed refutation of their existence in Ch. 9. See 9.56 ff. (on the self) and 9.127 ff. (on primal matter).

6.28 These arguments are both based on the premise held by *ātmavādins*, 'those who hold a doctrine of a Self', that a Self is necessarily permanent and unchanging. If it is permanent it must always have existed, so there can never have been a time, prior to its existence, at which it forms the intention of coming into existence. If it does exist and is involved in 'the sphere of action' or the material world, since it is unchanging, this involvement must be part of its nature and so it cannot change and stop doing this.

6.30 Śāntideva refers to the perceived conjunction of an agent and an action attributed to that agent. If the agent does not change in the course of the action then it is not involved in it in any meaningful way. If, as some maintain, the action is continued within the agent, then both have the same status, and there is no causal relationship.

6.32 Śāntideva envisages a non-Buddhist response to his argument that takes the view that, since Buddhists deny the existence of an enduring 'self', their arguments against anger are incoherent, since they presume a world of enduring entities, or selves. Śāntideva's reply is both doctrinally based and pragmatic. Suffering arises through causes and conditions, and does not need a 'self' upon which to be inflicted. Also, the fact is that there is suffering, and there are conditions which give rise to it which can be controlled. Suffering needs to be dealt with regardless of one's metaphysical outlook. On dependent origination, see 9.46 note and Thomas 1951, 58–70.

6.35 Śāntideva lists examples of self-torture motivated by each of the three root poisons, delusion, hatred, and greed, in that order. People tormenting themselves with thorns possibly refers to self-torture in a state of religious hysteria, another reference to cults such as that of Durgā. The term used for intoxication, *pramāda*, is the antithesis of mindfulness and awareness, for which the term *apramāda* is often used. The refusal of food is a widespread form of emotional blackmail in Indian society.

6.41 The scenario envisaged is of somebody being attacked by someone else with a weapon.

6.46 See 4.35 note.

6.48 The speaker has committed evil in the past and must therefore undergo the evil consequences of those actions in the form of suffering. If he does not react unskilfully to others who are the agents of that suffering, the overall evil still to be worked off is reduced.

6.64 The author refers to sacred images of the Buddhas or Bodhisattvas. A *stūpa* is a funerary monument built to contain bodily relics of spiritually advanced people, most typically of the Buddha. They were extremely popular, being raised at all the pilgrimage sites associated with the life of the Buddha. The concept of blasphemy is foreign to Buddhism, and the Buddha is recorded as unambiguously forbidding righteous indignation to his followers, even when he or they, or the teaching, was abused by outsiders (see *Brahmajāla Sutta*, Rhys Davids 1899).

6.65 One should reflect as directed in the preceding passage, vv. 25–33.

6.66 The causes of suffering can be either conscious or unconscious, but the experience of suffering only occurs in something that is conscious. Therefore the problem lies with the state of being conscious. The cause is irrelevant.

6.68 'The force of prior actions' is a free translation of the single, often misunderstood term *karma*, on which see 1.2 note.

6.81 'The three worlds' are the three worlds or planes of existence of Buddhist cosmology, viz. the *kāmaloka*, the world of sensuous experience (which includes the human realm); the *rūpaloka*, the world of [subtle] form; and the *arūpaloka*, the world without [subtle] form. These realms correspond to levels of consciousness which can be attained in meditation. See 5.15 note.

6.84 Rivalry between monks for lay support is clearly the context for a number of the emotional difficulties discussed by Śāntideva.

6.91 These are just two of a standard set of eight vices, namely hunting, gambling, sleeping during the day, calumny, philandering, drinking, entertainment from song, dance, and instrumental music, and travelling for pleasure. In Sanskrit drama they are the causes of any tragedy or misfortune which befalls the main characters. The contrast drawn in this verse is between those things which are of real benefit and those which merely give pleasure. The social stigma of drinking and gambling is high, and they are all eight proscribed for the Buddhist monk or nun. Both lead to unclarity of mind, addiction, and are responsible for considerable material distress—as demonstrated by the devastating war of the epic Mahābhārata which began as a direct consequence of Yudhiṣṭhira losing his entire kingdom to his cousins through uncontrolled gambling.

6.94 This verse also occurs in the *Śikṣā Samuccaya* (Bendall and Rouse, 243).

6.95a This half verse also occurs in the *Śikṣā Samuccaya* (Bendall and Rouse, 243–4).

6.98 'Sense of urgency', *saṃvega*, is the sense of spiritual shock that involves both dissatisfaction with worldly matters and a conviction that one needs to pursue the spiritual path. It is therefore a positive motivating factor, without which the Buddhist may become complacent and lose spiritual drive. Praise can easily lead to such complacency.

6.101 On 'blessing', *adhiṣṭhāna*, see 5.18 note.

6.105 'One who has gone forth' is a literal translation of the term *pravrājaka*. This term, with cognate forms, is used to denote a person who has taken the lower ordination into the Buddhist monastic community, and has the status of a 'novice'. This can be taken as soon as the child is 'old enough to scare away crows', although the higher ordination, the *upasampadā*, can only be taken after the age of 20. The term also has a wider usage, not specifically Buddhist, to refer to any wanderer who has gone forth and rejected the restraints of society to pursue the spiritual life. That this is the intended sense in this verse can be inferred from the fact that novice monks cannot confer ordination, and therefore cannot be said to cause ordination through that function. The sense in which such a person could be a cause of another's going forth can only be inspirational, by their example. The most famous instance of this is the episode in the traditional biography of the historical Buddha, in which, as a young prince prior to his Enlightenment, he is inspired to leave home and pursue the spiritual quest by the sight of just such a wanderer.

6.112 Śāntideva quotes from the *Dharmasaṅgīti Sūtra* to this effect in the *Śikṣā Samuccaya* (Bendall and Rouse, 152).

On 'field [of merit]', see 2.24 note and 5.81 note.

6.113 'Transmission of the Buddha's qualities' translates *buddha-dharmāgama*. This expression is composed of three elements, of which the latter two are ambiguous: *dharma* can refer both to the Buddha's teaching and to the qualities of the Buddha (see 1.1 note), here referring to the quality of forbearance; and *āgama*, meaning 'acquisition, result', or more specifically 'that coming' from the Buddha, is in this sense widely used to denote the Buddhist scriptural tradition. The expression could therefore be read in two ways: 'the transmission (in active and passive senses) of the Buddha's teachings' or 'of the Buddha's qualities'. The author is discussing envy of fellow monks, who are collectively the institutional vehicle for the preservation and transmission of the Buddhist canon of scripture, as well as the basis for the development of Buddha-qualities such as, in this case, forbearance.

6.115 This verse also occurs in the *Śikṣā Samuccaya* (Bendall and Rouse, 155).

6.117 Śāntideva has in mind here the kind of offering made at the beginning of Ch. 2.

6.119 This verse occurs in the *Śikṣā Samuccaya* (Bendall and Rouse, 155). 'Those who befriend without pretext' are the Buddhas and Bodhisattvas. This becomes clearer in subsequent verses.

6.120–34 These verses occur in the *Śikṣā Samuccaya* (Bendall and Rouse, 154–5).

6.120 On the Avīci hell, see 4.21 note. Those who dismember their own bodies and descend into hell are the Bodhisattvas. In the Buddhist tradition there are many stories illustrating the extraordinary generosity of those on the path to Buddhahood. These are often cast as stories about former existences of the historical Buddha. A typical example is that in which the Bodhisattva feeds his own body to a starving tigress to prevent her from the unmotherly act of eating her own cubs. This story is told in the *The Sūtra of Golden Light* (see Emmerick 1990, ch. 18, pp. 92–106).

6.123 The image of the body engulfed by fire is often used to demonstrate the relative nature of sense pleasure. All monks would have been familiar with the 'Fire Sermon', the second discourse, according to tradition, delivered by the Buddha after his enlightenment, in which he likens all experience of the senses to being on fire. For this discourse, see Rhys Davids and Oldenberg 1982, 134–5.

6.124 The Great Compassion is an attribute of the Buddhas and Bodhisattvas, an inclusive compassion towards all beings, informed by the insight, central to the Mahāyāna perspective, that all beings lack any abiding essence, and that all phenomena are in essence the same.

6.125 As they are the lowest part of the body, placing the feet on, near, or towards someone's head is a strong sign of disrespect in Indian culture. Similarly, to place one's head at someone's feet is a sign of subservience to them. Śāntideva asks for this to be done as a sign of his servitude to the world.

CHAPTER 7

7.1 The intended comparison in this verse is with the movement of the body. According to traditional Indian physiology even physical movement results from the element of vital wind inside the body.

7.6 On Yama, see 2.42 note.

7.11 The image in vv. 11–12 is that of a live fish which has been trapped and is about to be cooked and eaten.

7.16 'The array of capacities' is that listed in v. 32 below. These constitute the positive powers or capacities of the mind which should be cultivated. Dedication and self-mastery are discussed in vv. 67–75 below. The practices of 'regarding oneself and others as equal and the exchange of self and others' are described in the next chapter, 8.90 ff.

7.18 We have not identified the source of this quotation.

7.20 Many popular stories illustrating the career of the Bodhisattva towards Buddhahood emphasize the gift of some part of the body as a measure of generosity. Cf. 6.120 note.

7.24 The greatest illness is to remain in cyclic existence. On the imagery of the Buddha as a doctor see 4.48 note. 'Conduct' translates *upacāra*. This term means both 'behaviour' and 'medical treatment'. The 'sweet conduct' is therefore the treatment offered by a doctor, but also the conduct of the doctor, i.e. the compassionate attention given by the Buddha to suffering beings, and the conduct he enjoined upon his patients, which is the Bodhisattva training.

7.26 'Understanding' translates *prajñā*.

7.27 'False projections' are the ultimately untrue constructions imposed upon experience in the non-Awakened mind and which prevent us from 'seeing the way things really are'.

7.29 The *śrāvakas*, literally 'hearers', are the disciples of the Buddha who follow what is deemed an inferior Buddhist path, or Hīnayāna. See General Introduction, p. xvi. Because their goal is only their own liberation, the path of the *śrāvakas* is in theory quicker than that of the Bodhisattva who has undertaken to liberate all beings.

7.31 From the earliest period the Buddhist tradition distinguished between *kāma-chanda*, desire for pleasure, and *dharma-chanda*, righteous desire. (See vv. 117 and 118 of the *Dhammapada*, in note to v. 40 below.) In this sense it acknowledges that desire motivates all action, but that just as there is good and bad action, there is also good and bad desire. Here Śāntideva refers to *dharma-chanda*, righteous desire, which constitutes the fundamental level of motivation for the spiritual aspirant, here the Bodhisattva.

The praises referred to are those of the Awakening Mind. See Ch. 1, especially v. 14 and note.

7.32 Here Śāntideva outlines the structure of the rest of his discussion of vigour.

7.37 The Dispensation, or *śāsana*, is another term for the Teaching of the Buddha.

7.40 It is not clear if Śāntideva had a specific verse or verses in mind, but the reader might compare this statement, and vv. 42 and 43 below, with vv. 117 and 118 of the *Dhammapada*: 'If a person performs an evil deed, let him not do it again and again. Let him not form a desire for it. Suffering is the accumulation of evil.' 'If a person performs a meritorious deed, let him do it again and again. Let him form a desire for it. Happiness is the accumulation of meritorious deeds.'

7.42 'Welcoming reception' here translates the term *argha*, which can mean both 'value, price' or 'worth', and 'the respectful reception given to an honoured guest'. Thus for one who does good, that person's desires are met by their own value (because they are skilful desires, they have a positive consequence), and the value which they command is also the reception that is offered an honoured guest, the honoured guest being righteous desire.

7.44 The imagery here is that of the *Sukhāvatīvyūha Sūtras*, two well-known Mahāyāna discourses, in which the devotees of the Buddha Amitābha are assured rebirth as a Bodhisattva in the heart of a lotus in the Sukhāvatī realm, where they are guaranteed to gain Awakening listening to the sound of the Buddha's voice teaching the Dharma. (See Müller 1969 for a translation of both from the Sanskrit, and Chang 1983 for an abridged translation of the longer *sūtra* from the Chinese translation.)

7.46 The *Vajradhvaja Sūtra* is not known to survive in Sanskrit, except for those passages quoted by Śāntideva in the *Śikṣā Samuccaya*. The method he refers to here is described in the words of the *sūtra* itself (see Bendall and Rouse, 255 ff.).

Here pride is meant in a positive sense.

7.49 'The secondary defilements' translates the term *upakleśa*. On some occasions this is used as a synonym of *kleśa*, defilement, but it is also understood to refer to a set of 'secondary defilements' which are enumerated variously by different traditions and in different contexts. The *Dharma-saṃgraha* (LXIX) lists 24 secondary defilements: anger, enmity, hypocrisy, contentiousness, envy, avarice, deceit, duplicity, pride, malice, shamelessness, recklessness, sloth, arrogance, infidelity, indolence, carelessness, forgetfulness, inattention, lack of awareness, wickedness, torpor, distraction, and discursive thought. They are secondary because they are derived from the defilements or *kleśas* proper, that is, greed, hatred, and delusion.

7.52 Garuḍa is a mythical fierce flesh-eating bird, the enemy of serpents. His name means 'devourer'.

7.56 Śāntideva begins in this verse a play upon the positive and negative senses of pride.

7.58 Śāntideva's play on words reaches the height of its ambiguity with this verse, in which he employs several terms which can be read either positively or negatively. 'Despised on all sides', *sarvataḥ paribhūtāḥ*, is synonymous with the expression *sadāparibhūta*, the name of a famous Bodhisattva figure in the *Lotus Sūtra* (ch. 20). The part of his story relevant to this verse concerns his Bodhisattva training, which consisted of telling other Buddhists that he did not despise them, since they had all been predicted to full Buddhahood by the Buddha. Partly because some of the recipients of this assurance did not seek that goal and others did not think it possible, and partly with a predictable human response to such treatment, these people became increasingly irritated with Sadāparibhūta, eventually expressing their irritation with fists, feet, and missiles. At this it appears that Sadāparibhūta would withdraw to a safe distance, wherefrom he would shout the reassurance that he still did not despise them! Because of this conduct of his, he was named Sadāparibhūta, itself taken as a pun, meaning 'Always despised' and 'Never despising'! 'Sustained by pride', *mānastabdhāḥ*, means either 'supported' or 'helped by pride', or 'full of', even 'puffed up with pride'. 'The mortified', here translating *tapasvinaḥ*, means either 'spiritual practitioners' or 'miserable, wretched people'. (On *tapas* see 5.16 note.) The overall effect of the verse is that one finds oneself reading it as a continuation of the account of those people with negative pride, only to find that those described in the next verse are those with positive pride.

7.65 The word used for elephant here, *karī*, is cognate with *karma*, the term translated as task, and literally means both one who acts and one who has a hand or trunk (the thing which acts), i.e. an elephant.

7.66 In this verse Śāntideva again chooses to use very strong, almost perverse language. Here one should have a 'thirst' for the next task. The term used is *tṛṣṇā*, an otherwise pejorative term, used ubiquitously in the sense of 'craving', and in that sense something to be expunged.

7.70 The vow referred to is the Bodhisattva vow to liberate all beings from cyclic existence.

This simile may be a reference to a story in the commentary on the *Telapatta-jātaka* (Cowell *et al.* 1981, Jātaka no. 96, pp. 232–3): a man is made to carry a pot brimming with oil through a crowd which is watching the local beauty queen dance and sing. Though tempted to look at her, he must concentrate his attention on carrying the pot because he is being followed by a guard who will chop his head off if he spills so much as a drop. Alternatively, the *Śikṣā Samuccaya* gives the simile of a servant carrying a pot brimming with oil over a slippery surface for an irascible king (Bendall and Rouse, 314).

7.74 'The teaching on vigilance' may refer to the fourth chapter of this work, entitled 'Vigilance regarding the Awakening Mind'; or it may be a reference to the Buddha's final words to his followers before his death, 'Strive with vigilance!'

CHAPTER 8

8.1 'Meditative concentration', *samādhi*, is a state of meditative absorption in an object, involving a high degree of concentration, albeit without any sense of force.

8.2 Although Śāntideva's advice to disregard distracting thoughts can be construed in a non-technical sense, the term used for distracting thought, *vitarka*, immediately places his comment in the context of the technical language of Buddhist meditation. *Vitarka* is defined differently by various Buddhist schools, but could be described as the relatively gross, sub-vocal conceptual activity of the mind, associated with the initial application of one's attention to a subject. It is present in normal, everyday mental activity, as well as in the first of the stages of meditative absorption (*dhyāna*), but drops away upon entry to the second. His advice therefore would have immediately been understood to mean that one should engage in tranquillity or calming meditation, with a view to experiencing the higher stages of meditative absorption.

8.3 The author deals with attachment in vv. 5–8. He discusses the feelings of a monk who has not come to terms with celibacy. A thirst for acquisitions, etc. would be directed towards the donations from lay supporters.

8.4 'Tranquillity' is the fruit of 'calming meditation', *śamatha-bhāvanā*, while 'insight' is the product of 'insight meditation', *vipaśyanā-bhāvanā*.

8.7 The idea of 'seeing things as they really are' is central to the Buddhist concept of Awakening, for which it has been used as a synonym since the earliest period.

8.25 This verse is missing in the canonical Tibetan translation.

8.27 All these places are recommended for meditation from the earliest period of the tradition.

8.30 Śāntideva questions when he will ever perform this meditative exercise, which was recommended by the Buddha himself. Reflection upon the decay of the human body was employed from the earliest period to counteract greed and lust. The whole process was facilitated by the practice of disposing of corpses in the open. There are frequent references in early Buddhist texts to charnel grounds, where corpses were left to the elements rather than being cremated. Such charnel grounds were used for various religious practices in Indian religions, especially where the practitioner was concerned to overcome some kind of conditioning, either social (the fear of pollution from corpses) or personal, as with greed.

8.35 The four men are the 'pall-bearers'. One should not wait for death, but renounce life as a householder and live as a renunciate in the forest immediately, before it is too late.

8.36 Metaphorically he died previously to the world when he renounced it and ceased to be part of society. Brahmanical Hindus who become renunciates go so far as to have their own funeral when they renounce society and not at the end of their life.

8.37 It is held in the Buddhist tradition that one's state of mind when dying has a significant influence on one's future birth. For a good rebirth it is therefore very important at the time of death to be able to practise the 'recollections'. There are six subjects of recollection: the Buddha, his teaching, the *Saṅgha*, moral conduct, liberality, and heavenly beings. See also 5.32 note.

8.39 'A state of single-pointed thought' translates *cittaikāgra*, a technical term for a characteristic of the second meditative absorption, *dhyāna*. On meditative absorption, see Introduction to Ch. 8.

8.41 Messengers and go-betweens are clearly people of lower status. The enamoured person is therefore degrading himself by treating with great respect those who should normally show respect to him, in order to have contact with the one he loves. Within the monastic community such activities are expressly forbidden.

8.59 The field is the mother's womb, the seed the father's sperm, and the nourishment the mother's blood. All are considered impure.

8.76 They have to give birth wherever the husband happens to do his work. Both the jungle and scrubland would be physically dangerous and isolated.

8.81 On 'momentary good fortune' see 4.16 note.

8.83 'Path', literally 'the way to go or act': the Buddhist path of conduct which leads to Awakening.

8.88 'King' translates *indra*, which is also the name given to the chief of all the gods in the realm of sensual experience, shared with human beings.

8.89 'Distracted thoughts' translates *vitarka*.

8.96 This verse is the first of the root verses of the *Śikṣā Samuccaya*.

8.97–109 The following verses also occur in the *Śikṣā Samuccaya* (Bendall and Rouse, 315–17): 97, 98, 100, 101a, 104, 107, 108, 109.

8.98 This verse refers to the theory of rebirth accepted by all schools of Buddhism. Although there is rebirth there is no permanent soul or individual which is reborn, so the person who dies is not the same person as the one who is born in the next life. The difficulty of reconciling the theory of 'no-self' with that of rebirth has been an ongoing doctrinal issue for the philosophical schools of Buddhism, on a par with the problem in Christianity of the good creator god creating evil. Different solutions were attempted by different schools. An early simile for the process is of a flame which lights another flame: the two are not the same, but part of a single continuum. In vv. 97–8, then, the question is: why perform acts of merit to ensure a good rebirth when that is not something the person performing the merit-making action experiences?

8.101 'The continuum of consciousnesses' translates *saṃtāna*, a term used to refer to the continuous succession of moments of consciousness which make up an individual's experience of consciousness. See 4.47 note and 9.9b–10 note. 'The combination of constituents' translates *samudāya*, another technical term. It literally means 'a co-arising' and refers to any combination of elements perceived as a unit, such as the body. Both the continuum of consciousnesses and the combination of constituents may be falsely identified as the locus of an enduring, unchanging Self.

8.104 This verse counters the sentiment that it is better to get on with life and ignore the misery in the world because knowledge of that misery will only make one more unhappy.

8.106 The story of Supuṣpacandra, echoing that of the *Khantivāda Jātaka* (see Cowell *et al.* 1981, vol. 3), is told in the 35th chapter of the *Samādhirāja Sūtra*. There, a holy monk, Supuṣpacandra, travels to a barbarous region against the warnings of his fellow monks, where he goes to the royal capital and begins to teach. He attracts the attention of an audience, including thousands of the king's children, ministers, and wives, who are all converted. King Śūradatta envies his beauty and is full of jealousy to find his wives lavishing attention and adulation upon the monk, and his sons showing the monk such respect, discarding all the finery the king had lavished on them. He commands his sons to kill the monk, but they refuse and try to dissuade their father from so heinous an act. But the king manages to find a particularly vile executioner who willingly chops the monk into bits, right there on the highway. The king goes about his usual business, until a week later when he chances upon the monk's dismembered remains, not even slightly discoloured, but still fresh and pure. At this the king is filled with remorse, for he now realizes that he had chopped up someone special. He laments his terrible crime, and bewails his impending descent to hell, to the accompaniment of the dirges sung by the gods, who have gathered round the site of the monk's execution. Fortunately, the king confesses his crime to the *Saṅgha* and takes refuge in the Buddhas before he dies, for, eventually, in a future birth, it is that wicked king Śūradatta who becomes the historical Buddha, Siddhartha Gautama, of our era. There is no English translation yet published of this chapter of the *Samādhirāja Sūtra*.

8.107 Like the Bodhisattva Kṣitigarbha (see 2.52 note), those whose most important objective is to end the suffering of others will even go down to the worst hell, Avīci (see 4.21 note), as happily as geese go down among lotuses. Preventing suffering is so important to them that even the worst place in the universe does not deter them. The Bodhisattva Avalokiteśvara is also described as entering the Avīci hell to save beings in the second chapter of the *Kāraṇḍavyūha Sūtra* (see 10.18 note).

8.109 The resulting reward, *vipāka-phala*, would be merit leading to advantages for oneself, such as advancement on the spiritual path, or more material benefit, such as rebirth in heaven.

8.111 According to ancient Indian physiology, the sperm of the father and the blood of the mother give rise to the individual who, in Buddhist terms, then mistakenly perceives the product as his self. To emphasize this aspect of human origin, as Śāntideva does, is to play heavily upon caste Hindu repulsion for 'polluting' bodily fluids.

8.116 On 'giving oneself as food', see 6.120 note.

8.118 On Avalokita, otherwise known as Avalokiteśvara, see 2.13 note. The *Lotus Sūtra*, ch. 24 (Sanskrit, see Kern 1884) or ch. 25 (Chinese, see Hurvitz 1976), and the *Gaṇḍavyūha Sūtra* (Cleary 1987, 153–5), both describe the wide-ranging perils from which one receives protection by calling upon the name of the Lord Avalokita.

8.123 On the Three Jewels, see 1.1 note. On the Avīci hell, see 4.21 note. The monastic code contains regulations forbidding the appropriation by individual monks of property donated for the benefit of the Three Jewels.

8.125 Literally, the author contrasts two states: that of a *piśāca*, a flesh-eating demon, with that of the king of the gods.

8.156 Possibly a reference to the *Tathāgataguhya Sūtra*, from which a number of verses are quoted earlier in this chapter, between v. 97 and v. 109.

8.162 Great Sage is a common epithet for the Buddha, but to read it as such here does not make sense given the vindictive intention of the passage as a whole. In his description of monastic life in India, I-tsing refers to the office of 'great sage', occupied by the monk responsible for instilling the monastic code of discipline in the monks under his jurisdiction (see Takakusu 1896, 119). We think that the 'great sage' of this verse refers to the holder of that disciplinary office.

8.178 The body will be lost in the ashes of the cremation fire.

8.185 In a broad sense this verse recapitulates previous material. One needs vigour, the subject of the previous chapter, in order to ward off sloth and torpor, which are in themselves standard hindrances to meditation. Also, as in the penultimate verse of the preceding chapter (see 7.74 note), the author emphasizes the need for vigilance, *apramāda*. His reference to following the learned anticipates the end of this chapter and the beginning of the next chapter, on Understanding.

8.186 The 'obscuring veil' refers either to the 'obscuration' caused by the defilements, or the 'obscuration' regarding what is cognized, caused by believing that objects of consciousness are real entities. The earlier meditations of this chapter counteract the former, while the latter is removed by understanding, the realization of emptiness, which is the topic of the next chapter.

CHAPTER 9

9.1 The 'collection of preparations' refers to the five perfections (generosity, ethical conduct, vigour, forbearance, and meditative absorption) which are expounded in the preceding chapters.

9.4 Śāntideva is setting the ground-rules for philosophical debate, which in the Indian context frequently proceeds by the use of analogy, as is well illustrated in this chapter. This pertains irrespective of what the combatants intend to prove, because two parties may accept a single statement but interpret its significance differently. This common agreement was a major tool in the Madhyamaka attempt to invalidate the statements about reality made by other schools of philosophy.

9.6 Much attention was devoted to the problems of epistemology in Indian philosophy, and most systems developed a hierarchy of 'valid means of knowledge'. Almost universally, 'scripture' (the exact body of scripture varying according to particular traditions) would stand as the highest or most authoritative means of knowledge, thus revealing the interrelationship of religion and philosophy in this milieu. 'Direct perception' would be the second most authoritative means of knowledge, followed by further means, such as inference and analogy. Śāntideva therefore states that, from his stance as a Prāsaṅgika Mādhyamika, all 'valid means of knowledge' are merely indicators of conventional truth. This is consistent with the Prāsaṅgika Mādhyamika attempt to reject all statements regarding reality made by other traditions and other schools of Buddhism, by showing that they involve internal inconsistencies—hence the importance of 'analogies accepted by both parties' (see v. 4 above).

An example of something which may be considered pure, though really impure, is the human body, on which see 8.47 ff. Another such false view is to regard something impermanent as permanent.

9.7a The Protector, i.e. the Buddha, taught in terms of really existent entities. For example, the injunction not to kill assumes the existence of something which can kill and something which can be killed. The author defends the apparent paradox of an injunction not to kill an entity, the existence of which he has just claimed is established only by conventional truth, on the basis that the conduct enjoined is that which is spiritually effective, i.e. leads to liberation.

9.7b–8 An opponent argues that, since the Buddha used the language of conventional truth, he *de facto* belied his claims about ultimate reality. In the next verse, Śāntideva defends the use of conventional language by drawing upon the distinction agreed upon at the beginning of the discussion: namely, that the spiritually advanced know more about the way things really are than ordinary people. Therefore the prerogative to use language of different kinds lies with them. The Buddha was not lying, but using 'skilful means' in adapting his teaching to his audience. There are different levels of conventional truth too: the Buddha is always right at whatever level he is talking.

9.8 On 'women as impure', see above, 9.6 note.

9.9a Argument with the Hīnayānist begins. All Buddhists accept that merit is gained by worshipping the Buddha. Whether one sees the causal process whereby this happens as real or illusory, the process itself is unaffected.

9.9b–10 The Hīnayānists put forward the view that there is no permanent, unchanging self but a continuum of states. The Mahāyānists accept this. However, the Hīnayānists are accused of regarding that continuum as real. Śāntideva argues that there is no more reason for regarding the continuum as real than the 'person'. An illusion can also continue for some time, but this does not make it real.

9.11a The Cittamātra (Mind-only) Buddhists come into the argument: they accept that external phenomena, such as individual people, are illusory, but claim that the conscious mind itself must exist or there would be no bad intention behind murder. All Buddhists agree that good or bad acts lead to good or bad consequences, and accept that it is the intention behind an act which leads to merit or evil. Here the Cittamātra is represented as taking good and evil as moral absolutes from which he can make an ontological argument, i.e. that consciousness really exists.

9.11b Śāntideva counters that good and evil are not moral absolutes, but are values arising within the realm of conventional truth as a result of the illusory projection on the part of consciousness. Both parties would agree with the response because both agree that illusion is the problem.

9.13a All Buddhists deny the existence of a single cause of everything. Just as magic spells are not the only cause of illusion, the mind cannot be the sole source of illusion either. Thus the Mādhyamika forestalls a possible claim by the Mind-only opponent that the mind is the source of all illusion.

9.13b–14a The Cittamātra argues that if everything is an illusion, then even the Buddha's Awakening is an illusion, in which case there is no point in pursuing the spiritual path leading to Awakening. In other words, the Cittamātra accuses the Mādhyamika of being inconsistent, and of effectively destroying the basis of the Path, namely, the Awakening of the Buddha.

9.14b–15a The Mādhyamika replies that the illusory perceptions of the un-Awakened continue until the causes are removed, and therefore they will see a Buddha in terms of conventional truth until such a point as they themselves are Awakened. The status of a Buddha is not determined by the illusions of the un-Awakened.

9.15b If a Buddha is somebody whose false perception has ceased, how, without consciousness, could he see the illusion of the un-Awakened, and offer them teaching?

9.17–18 This is a paraphrase of a passage from the *Ratnacūḍa Sūtra*, quoted in the *Śikṣā Samuccaya* (Bendall and Rouse, 235, lines 6–8), which states that the mind cannot see itself, just as a knife cannot cut itself and the tip of a finger cannot touch itself.

9.19a The Cittamātra likened the self-existent mind to a light-source illuminating itself. This argument was necessary because it was irrefutably established by the highest source of valid knowledge, scripture, that mind must have an object of which it is aware. The Mādhyamika accepts that a source of light can bring illumination to other objects but not that it can illuminate itself, because, by definition, a light-source is simply the function of illumination, and is not itself an object which can be hidden from itself by darkness.

9.21 The author replaces the term *citta*, which has been used up until this point for 'mind', with what is for him a more derogatory term, 'intellection', *buddhi*, which he relegated to the sphere of conventional truth in v. 2 above.

9.22 The daughter of a barren woman is a standard analogy for something which everyone would agree cannot exist.

9.23 The objection is to ask how the mind can experience something that is not present, as it does in the act of memory. 'The shrew's poison' is an analogy used to explain memory in philosophical argument. The shrew's bite is inferred, and in that way remembered, when the poison takes effect! A hibernating bear is bitten but does not realize it until he comes out of hibernation.

9.24a The cause referred to is the mind. It is the cause of perception. It perceives external phenomena, which are not in immediate contact with the mind, through the intermediaries of the senses and infers that it itself must exist to be able to see them. In this way it is self-aware.

9.25 This may be the Mādhyamika bringing the argument back to the main soteriological issue and is by tradition interpreted as such. However, it could be the Cittamātra conceding the point about the self-awareness of the mind, but reasserting the real issue, shared by both parties. Both agree that, whether or not the mind is the basis of the projection that what is perceived has ultimate reality, that projection is false and the cause of suffering.

9.27b The Cittamātra claims that there must be something real, i.e. the conscious mind, to act as a basis for the appearance of cyclic existence.

9.30 The Cittamātra concedes for the sake of argument that even the mind is like an illusion, but points out that you still have the problem of the defilements. He uses the analogy of an illusory woman created by a magician.

9.31 'Influence' translates *vāsanā*, lit. 'perfume', on which see 1.2 note. On 'the defilements and what is cognized', *kleśa-*, *jñeya-āvaraṇa*, see 9.46 note and 8.186. On 'emptiness', see General Introduction, p. xxii.

9.33 This verse can be understood as a part of the Mādhyamika's argument, as it is in the standard dGe lugs pa (pronounced Gelukpa) interpretation. The non-existence of an entity is the negation of the existence of that entity. One cannot negate what does not exist. Therefore there cannot be a non-existence of something which has never existed. The basis of non-existence is existence.

9.35 The vow of the Conqueror is to help all beings gain Enlightenment. Re 'the wishing-gem and the magical tree', see 3.19 note. On the 'vow' of the Conqueror, see Introduction to Ch. 10.

9.40 The truths referred to here are the Four Truths of the Nobles which form the backbone of non-Mahāyāna expositions of the Dharma. The four truths are that: there is suffering or unsatisfactory; suffering has an origin; suffering can cease; and there is a path that leads to the cessation of suffering. On the Four Truths see also 4.48 note. These are the subject of the first discourse of the historical Buddha after his Awakening. From a Madhyamaka perspective, even these truths should be understood to be empty.

The scriptures which expound the necessity of understanding emptiness are the *Prajñāpāramitā Sūtra*, or the 'Perfection of Wisdom Sūtras'. They form the scriptural authority for the Madhyamaka school. They are not accepted as scripture by non-Mahāyāna schools.

9.41 The Mahāyāna scriptures are not accepted as the word of the Buddha by the non-Mahāyāna schools, but Mahāyāna schools accept both non-Mahāyāna and Mahāyāna scriptures. Since there must be a time before which each person has accepted any Buddhist scripture, the Mādhyamika points out that the fact that there are people who do not accept the authority of a text does not affect its validity.

9.42 The criterion referred to here is that a text is established if both parties accept it. The Vedas are the earliest and most authoritative scriptures of Brahmanical Hindu orthodoxy. Their authority is rejected by all Buddhists.

9.43 'Scripture', here translating *āgama*, lit. 'the tradition', is the term given to the sections of the *sūtra-piṭaka*, the collection of the Buddha's discourses. These are accepted as canonical by both Mahāyāna and non-Mahāyāna schools.

9.44 The Buddhist monastic community has undergone schisms in the course of its history. These schisms have taken place as a result of disagreements over the interpretation of the monastic rules which define the institution of monkhood. The different ordination lineages resulting from such schisms do not accept each other's monastic code as valid. In this way the monkhood is imperfectly established.

Those *arhats*, enlightened ones according to the Hīnayāna, grasp onto entities, i.e. believe some things are ultimately real, and have not realized 'emptiness'. For this reason, according to the Prajñāpāramitā literature, they cannot be fully enlightened, so their Enlightenment is also imperfectly established.

9.45 'Undefiled action' refers to ethically neutral actions. Episodes in the later literature describe even *arhats*, the enlightened followers of the Hīnayāna, acting in a manner determined by actions prior to their Enlightenment (see Lamotte 1974). These offer extraordinary images of some of the Buddha's enlightened disciples, such as the high-caste Mahākāśyapa who could not rid himself of habitual snobbery, and who, despite his reputation for asceticism, could not help but jig to a tune because of previous lives spent as a monkey; Gavāmpati, who had been an ox in many previous lives, and who habitually regurgitated his food in order to chew the cud; and Madhuvasiṣṭha, another ex-monkey, who could not resist climbing on walls and in trees. There is even a story of a Pratyekabuddha who, having been a courtesan in past lives, still dressed 'like a coquette'—an enlightened transvestite!

9.46 The delusion that there are really existent entities is itself a form of subtle craving from the Mahāyānist perspective. This delusion is the *jñeyāvaraṇa*, 'the obscuration over what is cognized', mentioned in v. 31. This verse and the next refer to the seventh, eighth, and ninth of the twelve 'links', *nidānas*, in the chain of dependent origination, the *pratītya-samutpāda*, which describes the process of rebirth and suffering in cyclic existence (see 6.3). This description forms the second of the Four Noble Truths, on which see above, 9.40 note.

9.48 The meditative attainment of non-perception is a profound state of meditative absorption in which the processes of perception (*saṃjñā*) and feeling (*vedanā*) cease, but return within seven days, if the meditator has not died meanwhile!

9.49–51 Though these verses are in all the Sanskrit manuscripts and the Tibetan translation, the 10th-century commentator Prajñākaramati says they are interpolations, because they are out of sequence and disrespectful to Mahākāśyapa, one of the historical Buddha's chief disciples. They are not among the verses included in the Tun-huang recension.

9.49 Non-Mahāyāna criteria for accepting a text as canonical are: it is the word of the Buddha as handed down by an unbroken lineage of teachers and pupils; it is found in the Discourses; it is in accordance with the treatise on the rules of the Discipline; it does not contradict the spirit of the Teaching.

9.51 In ch. 4 of the *Saddharma-puṇḍarīka Sūtra* (the *Lotus Sūtra*), Mahākāśyapa ('Great Kāśyapa'), acting as spokesman for himself and three others, confesses to the Buddha that they had all held back from the superior Mahāyāna teaching because of complacency and lack of understanding.

9.52 This refers to the Bodhisattva remaining in cyclic existence even after Awakening. This accuses *arhats*, those Enlightened according to the Hīnayāna who do not remain to help others, of fear and attachment—presumably fear of the suffering in cyclic existence and attachment to their own comfort. However, in addition to the reading taken here, *saktitrāsāntanirmuktyā*, and translated as 'through freedom from the two extremes, attachment and fear', Prajñākaramati offers an alternative, *saktitrāsāt tu anirmuktyā*: 'On the contrary, by not being liberated from the fear of attachment, through delusion they remain in cyclic existence. Is this the fruit of emptiness?' This latter reading would require a different interpretation of the verse, as the sarcastic response of the opponent to v. 48.

9.54 On the obscurations see 8.186 note and v. 46 above. 'Omniscience' is a synonym for the Perfect Understanding of a Buddha.

9.57–9 These verses contain a standard 'insight', *vipaśyanā*, meditation, on which see Introduction to Ch. 8. Its purpose is to establish that no part of the psycho-physical organism can be identified as the 'Self'.

9.59 The six consciousnesses are consciousness of sight, sound, smell, taste, touch, and mental objects.

9.60 In the Sāṃkhya school of philosophy the Self is said to be pure consciousness. Śāntideva's choice of sound as the example in this verse rather than the more usual example of sight (as the 'first' of the senses) may have been made with reference to the early non-Buddhist identification of the universal essence, *brahman*, with sound.

9.61 According to Sāṃkhya, the Self is pure consciousness, not consciousness of anything in particular. The consciousness illuminates, as it were, any mental processes which take place. Those mental processes are not an aspect of the Self, but of the material body in which it resides.

9.64 'Goodness', 'passion', and 'darkness' are the universal constituents ('qualities' or 'strands') which make up everything that exists, according to Sāṃkhya philosophy. This argument therefore refutes the ultimate existence of such things as father or son on the opponent's own terms.

9.66 The idea that all people are one and the same is unacceptable to Sāṃkhya. According to them the different Selves are not part of one universal Self but many and separate, one reason being that, if this were not so, when one person died all would die.

9.67 This is an awkward point for the Sāṃkhya. For them, consciousness is what marks out the individual 'souls' from the gross matter of everything else, but it was difficult to explain what type of matter (which makes up the entire universe) constitutes the soul to make it so different. If difference is false, then how can a particular group of things be similar? The 'souls', for example, would not be marked off from the rest of matter by the shared distinction of being made of a particularly subtle or pure matter. Nor would they be similar to each other, rather than all one and the same, if there was nothing at all to distinguish them.

9.68–9 These two verses refute the Nyāya theory of the Self as permanent and changeless, experiencing through its mind.

9.71 The location of the consequence is at a future point.

9.72 'It is taught' means it is taught in Buddhist scripture. On 'the continuum of consciousnesses', see 4.47 note and 8.101 note.

9.75 The problem is that the advanced Bodhisattva knows that there are no beings in conventional terms but continues to practise compassion. The opponent points out the contradiction in this. Śāntideva replies that for pragmatic purposes the Bodhisattva continues to practise compassion as if beings really existed. The Bodhisattva needs beings towards whom he is compassionate in order to complete his Bodhisattva training. See Introduction to Ch. 8.

9.80 The Vaiśeṣikas held the view that the body is the whole which possesses all the parts.

9.84 We have accepted here the alternative reading provided by Prajñākaramati: *kaṣṭham*, 'post', rather than *kāyaḥ*, 'body'.

9.86 The directions are the cardinal points, the nadir, and the zenith, here used to analyse the atom into different parts.

9.88 Pleasure and pain cannot exist as independent realities unless they exist independently of other factors. It is axiomatic that something that really exists is permanent.

9.89 A sensation is by definition something experienced, so if not experienced it does not exist.

9.91 How else could sensations, a single category, be both painful and pleasurable—the same thing causing both pain and pleasure depending on the circumstances?

9.92 On meditative absorption, see Introduction to Ch. 8. The spiritually developed are nourished both literally, in so far as it was thought that experience of meditative absorption provided a subtle nourishment to the body, and metaphorically, in that meditation of the sort just described 'feeds' that understanding which makes an individual spiritually advanced.

9.95 If two things are touching, the point of contact is a part of the whole of each. If the two are wholly in contact they must be the same thing, so it is not contact.

9.97 Sensation requires the contact of the sense object (*viṣaya*), the sense organ (*indriya*), and consciousness (*vijñāna*). See 4.47 note.

9.102 The aggregates are the five categories, form, sensation, apperception, volitions, and consciousness, which exhaustively describe the psycho-physical organism called a human being.

9.104 Consciousness is understood by Buddhists to be consciousness of something. In that sense consciousness is conditioned by its objects, because they allow the arising of a moment of consciousness. Therefore, the object of which one is conscious must exist before one can have that particular consciousness. See 4.47 note.

9.105 What does not occur prior to or simultaneously with something must occur after it. An overlap is not considered because all things are momentary and the moments are discrete.

9.106 On the two truths, see above, v. 2.

9.118 This begins an argument against the Nyāya-Vaiśeṣika theory that God is the permanent cause of the world, creating everything (through his desire) under certain conditions such as time and the presence of accessory causes such as atoms (which are permanent).

9.121 Something eternal has no beginning and so cannot have been created.

9.123 If God is the cause of something and he is eternal, the effect of which he is the cause would also be eternal, i.e. the world and everything in it would be eternal, but things are seen to be impermanent.

9.126 Sāṃkhya is one of the six classical schools of orthodox Indian philosophy. There is also a debate with them in vv. 60 ff. above.

9.128 According to Sāṃkhya, everything in the universe is made up of the three constituents.

9.129 According to Sāṃkhya pleasure is part of the material world, while consciousness is separate, the function of the *puruṣa* or individual soul.

9.132 If the sensation of pleasure really exists it must be permanent and unchanging, so it would not be able to change from one state (here, grossness) to another (here, subtlety).

9.134 Sāṃkhya holds the view that everything which exists already existed in its cause, e.g. the pot exists in the clay. Otherwise, causation would be random: a pot could be formed from milk, and yoghurt from clay.

9.136 Even sages who accept this theory do not wear cotton seed instead of cloth.

9.137 Sāṃkhyas accept direct perception, *pratyakṣa*, as the highest of the *pramāṇas*, valid means of knowledge, after scripture. However, if they qualify it by saying that only the direct perception of the spiritually advanced is valid, direct perception *per se* ceases to be an authoritative means of knowledge, which would agree with the point of view held by the Madhyamaka.

9.146 Something non-existent cannot be affected in any way, nor become existent, since that would be a contradiction in terms. Yet only something which is not already existent could be said to come into existence. The Madhyamaka points out the inherent contradiction in all possibilities.

9.150 The banana tree forms, from an underground stem, a false trunk composed of leaf sheaths, so that if the sheaths are peeled away there is no remaining core or 'essence'.

9.161 On Māra, see 10.9 and 10.32.

9.162 On 'the opportune moment', see 1.4 note and 4.15–16.

9.164 Hell is here likened to a fire which must be entered time and time again as long as one remains in cyclic existence. Between lives in hell one may simply be so relieved to be out of the fire that one forgets that the horror will inevitably be repeated.

CHAPTER 10

10.1 The title *Bodhicaryāvatāra* means 'undertaking the way or conduct to Awakening', so the author is referring both to the title of the work he has composed and the practices which are described in that work.

10.4 Sukhāvatī is the name of a 'pure land', i.e. a perfect world created by the Buddha Amitābha. All those reborn in that world enjoy delightful and unceasing access to the Dharma and speedily attain Awakening. See 7.44 note. For a translation of the *Sukhāvatī-vyūha Sūtra*, see Cowell, Müller, and Takakusu 1969.

10.6 Sword-leaved forests and thickets of torturing thorns grow in hell, whereas the wish-fulfilling tree grows in heaven.

10.7 The *cakravāka* is a type of water-bird symbolic of faithful love in classical Sanskrit literature.

10.9 In biographies of the Buddha the terrible weapons with which Māra, the embodiment in Buddhism of delusion, attacks the Buddha immediately after his Awakening are turned into a rain of flowers. Kāma, the Indian god of love and spring, is armed with a bow, and arrows which are flowers.

10.11 On Yama, see 2.42 note. On Vajrapāṇi, see 2.53 note.

10.12 Kamalapāṇi, 'the one who holds a red lotus in his hand', is a synonym of Padmapāṇi, an epithet of Avalokiteśvara, the Bodhisattva of Compassion, who sometimes appears holding a lotus. See 2.13 note.

10.13 The 'prince in monk's robes' is a reference to the Bodhisattva Kṣitigarbha. See 2.52 note.

10.14 On Mañjughoṣa, see 2.13 note.

10.15 On Samantabhadra, see 2.13 note.

10.17 Hungry ghosts, or *pretas*, are one of the six types of living being in Buddhist cosmology. They experience constant, insatiable cravings for sustenance. See 4.5 note. Uttarakuru is the northernmost of the four continents of this world, a place of long-lasting contentment.

10.18 Avalokiteśvara (see 2.13 note) is also depicted in the third chapter of the *Kāraṇḍavyūha Sūtra* nourishing the hungry ghosts with streams of eight kinds of liquid flowing from each finger, toe, and pore of his skin. There is no English translation of this text yet published.

10.19 Māyādevī was the mother of the historical Buddha, Siddhārtha Gautama, who emerged from her side at birth, causing her no pain.

10.27 The inopportune births, so called because one cannot benefit therein from the Buddha's teachings, are eight in number. These are in hell, as an animal or hungry ghost, as a long-lived god, in a barbarian region, as one holding biased views, as one who is deficient in faculties, or at a time when there is no Dharma taught by a Buddha. The ability to recall former births is a sign of high spiritual attainment. It is one of the ten characteristic powers or knowledges of a Buddha.

10.28 Gaganagañja, 'Sky-treasure', is a Bodhisattva, so called because his generosity is like the sky, in that it is infinite and pure (see the quote from the *Gaganagañja Sūtra* in the *Śikṣā Samuccaya*, Bendall and Rouse, 247).

10.32 On Māra, see note to v. 9 above. Māra tried to trick the Buddha by sending his daughters as voluptuous women (representing lust) to seduce him; and an army of demons (representing fear) to terrify him; and tried to trick him into doubt by demanding that he present a witness to prove he really was enlightened.

10.36 'Circle' here translates *maṇḍala*, which is also the term used for diagrammatic descriptions in circular form of Buddhas and Bodhisattvas in their temples, and sometimes with their entourage, especially as an object for meditative concentration in Mahāyāna visualization meditations. Each Buddha and Bodhisattva has his or her characteristic colour and is usually depicted surrounded by a halo of radiant light.

10.39 In Sanskrit and Pali literature rain production is attributed to a sky god, so the expression 'the god rains' is a standard idiom.

10.40 On spells, see 4.27 note. 'The mutterers' refers to the priests and other religious or magical practitioners who recited religious or magical formulae.

10.44 'Those who enter the spiritual community' translates the term *pravrajitās*, a synonym for *pravrājaka*, on which see 6.105 note.

10.47 The wish is for beings to attain Awakening 'in a single, divine embodiment', for example in the Sukhāvatī realm (on which see 7.44 and note, and v. 4 and note above), rather than spend aeons perfecting the Bodhisattva training, during the course of which they would inevitably undergo great suffering and have to make great effort to achieve the perfect virtues of a Buddha.

10.50 Pratyekabuddhas, 'awakened on their own' or 'by a cause', are those who gain Awakening in a time or place where they have no access to the Buddha's teaching and do not bring others to Enlightenment. Śrāvakas, or 'hearers', are those who seek Enlightenment through the teachings of a Buddha. The term is used by the Mahāyāna for adherents of the so-called Hīnayāna tradition who are thought to seek an inferior goal: personal enlightenment, rather than the liberation of all, which is the goal of the Bodhisattva.

10.51 On Mañjughoṣa and Śāntideva's association with him, see General Introduction, p. xi, and 2.13 note. On the recollection of former births, see above, 10.27 note. The *pramuditā bhūmi*, or 'stage of delight', is the first of the ten stages of *bhūmis* attained by the Bodhisattva *en route* to Buddhahood. On the *bhūmis*, see 4.11 note and Introduction to Ch. 10.

10.53 Mañjunātha, 'gentle protector', is an aspect of Mañjuśrī, on whom see references in 10.51 note above.

10.56 The author here expresses the intention of suffering the consequences of the evil actions of others to save them from that suffering.

MORE ABOUT OXFORD WORLD'S CLASSICS

American Literature
British and Irish Literature
Children's Literature
Classics and Ancient Literature
Colonial Literature
Eastern Literature
European Literature
History
Medieval Literature
Oxford English Drama
Poetry
Philosophy
Politics
Religion
The Oxford Shakespeare